Handbook of
Food Preparation

EIGHTH EDITION

PUBLISHED BY THE AMERICAN HOME ECONOMICS ASSOCIATION
1555 KING STREET • ALEXANDRIA, VA 22314

Cover design and illustration by Loy Walton

Handbook of Food Preparation
Copyright 1946, 1950, 1954, 1959, 1964, 1971, 1975, 1980
The American Home Economics Association

Library of Congress Cataloging in Publication Data
American Home Economics Association.
Food and Nutrition Section. Terminology Committee.
Began publication with 1946 edition.

Bibliography: p.
1. Food.   2. Cookery.   I. Title.
TX355.A49   641.02   59-53013 rev.
ISBN 0-8461-1417-8

5M5/85PCP

TABLE OF CONTENTS

ACKNOWLEDGMENTS

The American Home Economics Association is indebted to many persons and organizations who over the years have assisted in the tremendous task of collecting the information contained in this Handbook. Among the organizations are the American Egg Board, American Dry Milk Institute, American Institute of Baking, Evaporated Milk Association, National Dairy Council, National Canners Association, National Live Stock and Meat Board, Western Beet Sugar Producers, the Agricultural Marketing Service and the Agricultural Research Service of the United States Department of Agriculture, the National Marine Fisheries Service of the National Oceanic and Atmospheric Administration, United States Department of Commerce, and the Food and Drug Administration of the United States Department of Health and Human Services.

Contributions and helpful criticisms have come from many Association members. Among these in particular are:

Eleanor Ahern	Eugenia Hatcher	Elizabeth Osman
Millicent Atkin	Marjorie M. Heseltine	Jeanne Paris
Mercedes Bates	Elizabeth Hester	Catherine J. Personius
Maura Bean	Marion Jacobson	Marion C. Pfund
Grace Bennett	Pearl Janssen	Martha Pittman
Ferne Bowman	Karen Johnson	Joan Rock
Frances Carlin	Barbara Kennedy	Helen Rose
Helen Carlisle	Rose Kerr	Jean Simpson
Ruth Chambers	Florance B. King	Susan Skidmore
Alice M. Child	Esther Latzke	Clara Gebhard Snyder
Monica Clark	Belle Lowe	Reba Staggs
Jessie A. Cline	Andrea Mackey	Gertrude L. Sunderlin
Lydia Cooley	Rowena Carpenter Mainland	Doris H. Tisdale
Sylvia Cover	Beth Bailey McLean	Frances O. Van Duyne
Marylee Duehring	Bernadine Meyer	Betty M. Watts
Esther Easton	Kathryn Bele Niles	Elizabeth Wood
Mary Fuqua	Isabel T. Noble	Frances G. Young
Gloria Hansen	Anna M. Olsen	

Chairmen of terminology committees, 1943-1970: Elsie H. Dawson, 1943-1954; Mary T. Swickard, 1954-1957; Gladys L. Gilpin, 1957-1960; Olive M. Batcher, 1960-1965, 1967-1970; Ruth Matthews, 1965-1967.

PREFACE TO
1980 REVISED EDITION

This Handbook, with its history of nearly 35 years, is dedicated to all those who find food buying and preparation a creative outlet, a necessity, or a misadventure upon occasion. With about 10,000 items in a supermarket to choose from and many new cookbooks, homemakers demonstrate much interest in preparing and serving food at home. These culinary ventures often spawn questions: What can I substitute for cake flour? How can I convert recipes to metric? How many cups of cooked macaroni will I get from a pound of raw macaroni? What's the difference between natural cheese and cheese food? What are the basic recipe proportions for a cake? How long can I keep hamburger in the freezer? How can I tell if the cantaloupe is ripe? This Handbook brings together a wealth of information compiled from a multitude of resources over the years.

New information has been added. This includes a section on how to protect and save nutrients and more about how to preserve food by canning, drying, and freezing. Other major revisions concern nutrition labeling, foreign cookery terms, and various new food products and kitchen equipment.

The Food and Nutrition Section of AHEA, and especially the Handbook Revision Committee, hopes this publication will answer many puzzling problems. My special thanks to the Handbook revision editor, Margaret McWilliams, California State University, Los Angeles; Ivy Celender, of General Mills, Inc., and former Food and Nutrition Section chairman; and E. Karla Vollmar, Missouri Cooperative Extension Service, and her committee members, who made valuable contributions.

MARY P. CLARKE
Chairman, Food and Nutrition Section,
1979-81

1980 Committee Members
Margaret McWilliams, chairman
E. Karla Vollmar, coordinator
Ruth E. Baldwin
Mary Clarke
Carla Dill
Mary Lou Gibbs
Carole Ann Harbers

Mary Jo Harbour
Zoe Ann Holmes
Carole Bielefeld Jarrett
Patricia Kendall
Elizabeth Lu Kissel
Mary Kramer
Claudine Kratzberg

Don Kropf
Jane Fay Quan
Lois Rhinesperger
Doris Robinson
Frances E. Volz
Lorelle Young

1

GENERAL FOOD INFORMATION

Construction of Recipes

The writing of recipes carries with it a double responsibility. First, each recipe must be accurate and complete in essentials and written so simply and clearly that it cannot be misunderstood. At the same time it is important to present the recipe in a way that appeals to users while keeping within space limits.

A recipe is made up of two major parts—the list of ingredients and the method of preparing the product. These should be as practical as possible. Readily available ingredients, level measurements, and a simple procedure are ideal components of a recipe and should be used whenever possible. However, when the quality of a dish depends upon special ingredients or an unusual procedure, the recipe should include this information also.

Following are some well-tried rules for editing and setting up recipes. These should be a useful guide in the writing of new recipes or in the editing of recipe material for publication. Guidelines for metric usage also are presented.

Ingredients

1. List all ingredients with measurements in the order used.

2. Do not abbreviate unless space is a problem.

3. Give ingredients in the easiest units of measure, as ¼ cup instead of 4 tablespoons. Use standard measurements.

4. Use weights instead of measures when it is helpful, as for uncooked meat, poultry, fish,

cheese, etc. Include weight or fluid measure for canned products.

5. Specify types of products needed, as *cake flour, all-purpose flour, dark corn syrup*.

6. For eggs, list *egg yolks* or *egg whites* or *eggs*, and include simple preparation, as *eggs, slightly beaten*. If special preparation is needed, as for meringue, explain in the method, detailing all necessary steps.

7. Safeguard a recipe by giving the exact names of products used. Or use descriptive names. (Many commercial firms will supply generic names for products upon request.)

Method

1. Use short sentences and clear, simple directions that anyone can follow easily.

2. Give word pictures, like *chill until syrupy,* or *beat until foamy throughout,* or *mixture thickens as it cools*. These are always helpful, especially with unfamiliar mixtures.

3. Without being wordy, use methods for combining or cooking ingredients that represent best accepted procedures. For example, specify the best way to sift dry ingredients together, or to thicken a sauce, or to fold in beaten egg white—these can be expressed in the same terms whenever they occur in recipes. This practice results in a workman-like consistency of phrasing, from recipe to recipe.

4. Give thought to the most efficient order of work to avoid using extra bowls, cups, measuring tools, extra beating, and so forth.

5. Specify sizes of baking pans or casseroles, as: *9-inch round layer pans, 1½ inches deep* or a *shallow 1-quart casserole.*

6. Try to give both general and specific tests or temperatures. Then the recipe provides a double check on important stages. For example: *Cook to 238°F or until a small amount of syrup forms a soft ball in cold water.*

7. For the yield, give the number and size of servings to expect or the total measure, as: *Makes 4 1-cup servings, or makes 1 quart.*

Accuracy

1. Read over the edited recipe. Does it say exactly what is meant? Is it simple, clear, and complete, yet as brief as it can be?

2. Recheck the ingredients, amounts, and method against the original recipe data. Recheck the order of ingredients as listed against the order used. Check for any omissions in temperatures, times, yields, and so forth.

3. With every typing of the recipe, read the new copy carefully against former copy.

4. With every printing of the recipe, check first proofs against original correct copy then proofread at each succeeding stage. And read proofs just for sense at least once.

Recipe Forms

The most-used forms for presenting recipes are given here. Each has advantages.

Standard form. This familiar form gives all ingredients first, then the method. The listed ingredients show just what is needed to make the recipe. In this form, when an ingredient is modified the exact measurement should be given. For example: *2 cups sifted flour,* not 2 cups flour, sifted; *2 cups diced cooked carrots,* not 2 cups carrots, diced and cooked; *2 cups packed brown sugar,* not 2 cups brown sugar, packed. But *1 cup heavy cream, whipped,* not 1 cup whipped cream. The method follows in paragraphs or steps. This form is especially good for recipes using many ingredients. Following is an example of the *standard form:*

Soft Gingerbread

1⅔ cups sifted cake flour
¼ cup sugar

1 teaspoon double-acting baking powder
¾ teaspoon soda
½ teaspoon salt
½ teaspoon cinnamon
½ teaspoon ginger
¼ teaspoon cloves
¼ cup shortening (at room temperature)
½ cup molasses
½ cup water
1 egg, unbeaten

1. Preheat oven to 350°F (moderate).

2. Sift dry ingredients together into mixing bowl. Add shortening. Combine molasses and water and pour three-fourths of this mixture into mixing bowl.

3. Beat 2 minutes at a low speed of electric mixer or 300 vigorous strokes by hand.

4. Add egg and remaining liquid, then beat 1 minute longer in mixer or 150 strokes by hand.

5. Pour batter into greased and lightly floured 9 x 9 x 2-inch pan.

6. Bake at 350°F 30 minutes, or until toothpick inserted in center comes out clean.

7. Serve hot with butter or lemon sauce.

Standard form in metric units. At the time of this writing, there is some controversy over the pending conversion of the United States to the metric system. The following recipe is a rather literal conversion, with minimal rounding of measures to provide the metric measurement. It is probable that the 250 milliliter (mL) cup will become the standard and that measuring spoons will be available to measure 1, 2, 5, 15, and 25 milliliters.

Soft Gingerbread

400 milliliters sifted cake flour
60 milliliters sugar
15 milliliters double-acting baking powder
12 milliliters soda
7 milliliters salt
7 milliliters cinnamon
7 milliliters ginger
5 milliliters cloves
60 milliliters shortening (at room temperature)
120 milliliters molasses
120 milliliters water
1 egg, unbeaten

1. Preheat oven to 175°C (moderate).

2. Sift dry ingredients together into mixing bowl. Add shortening. Combine molasses and water and pour three-fourths of this mixture into a mixing bowl.

3. Beat 2 minutes at a low speed of electric mixer or 300 vigorous strokes by hand.

4. Add egg and remaining liquid, then beat 1 minute longer in mixer or 150 strokes by hand.

5. Pour batter into greased and lightly floured 23 x 23 x 5-centimeter pan.

6. Bake at 175°C 30 minutes, or until toothpick inserted in center comes out clean.

7. Serve hot with butter or lemon sauce.

Action form. This recipe style combines narrative action with listed ingredients. Although this style is easy to follow, it takes more space and is difficult to arrange economically or attractively on paper. The ingredients are described in the same way as in the standard form. Following is an example of the *action form*.

Soft Gingerbread

Preheat oven to 350°F (moderate).
Measure and sift together into mixing bowl:
   1⅔ cups sifted cake flour
   ¼ cup sugar
   1 teaspoon double-acting baking powder
   ¾ teaspoon soda
   ½ teaspoon salt
   ½ teaspoon cinnamon
   ½ teaspoon ginger
   ¼ teaspoon cloves
Add ¼ cup shortening (at room temperature).
Mix together:
   ½ cup molasses
   ½ cup water
Pour three-fourths of this molasses-water mixture into dry ingredients.
Beat 2 minutes at a low speed of electric mixer or 300 vigorous strokes by hand.
Add remainder of liquid and 1 unbeaten egg.
Beat 1 minute in mixer or 150 strokes by hand.
Pour batter into greased and lightly floured 9 x 9 x 2-inch pan.
Bake at 350°F 30 minutes, or until toothpick inserted in center comes out clean. Serve hot.

Descriptive form. In this recipe form, each in-gredient is followed by the necessary modification. For example: *carrots, diced, cooked; cake flour, sifted; evaporated milk, whole or skim; brown sugar, packed; eggs, slightly beaten; process Cheddar cheese, if desired.* This enables the cook to see readily what ingredients are needed.

The amounts of the ingredients are given in a separate column. Each step in the procedure is a separate paragraph, which appears parallel to the ingredients involved. To save space, the procedure may be placed below the ingredients. This is the newest recipe form and is easy to follow. An example of the *descriptive form* (Hot Chicken Sandwich, page 4) illustrates this construction.

Narrative form. This form includes the amounts of ingredients with the method. It is especially suited to the short recipe, the spoken recipe, or the recipe of few ingredients where the method is more complex. It can be expanded for detail or condensed for offhand recipe ideas. Unless the recipe is short, this is the hardest form to follow, but it uses very little space. An example of the *narrative form* follows:

Baked Cod Fillets

Thaw one pound frozen cod fillets. Cut into serving portions. Arrange fillets in a well-greased baking dish. Brush with melted butter or margarine and sprinkle with salt and pepper. Pour ¾ cup milk over fish. Combine 2 tablespoons melted butter or margarine with one cup soft bread crumbs and sprinkle over fish. Bake at 400°F *or* 205°C about 40-45 minutes or until fish flakes easily when tested with a fork. Makes 3-4 servings.

Oven Temperature Terminology

Most recipe writers in giving oven temperatures state the degrees first and follow with the descriptive term, thus, 400°F *or* 205°C (hot) oven. The following listing shows the commonly accepted descriptive terms for each temperature range in degrees Fahrenheit:

250°F to 275°F	Very slow oven	(120°C to 135°C)
300°F to 325°F	Slow oven	(150°C to 165°C)
350°F to 375°F	Moderate oven	(175°C to 190°C)
400°F to 425°F	Hot oven	(205°C to 220°C)
450°F to 475°F	Very hot oven	(230°C to 245°C)
500°F to 525°F	Extremely hot oven	(260°C to 275°C)

Hot Chicken Sandwich

6 servings

Toast, whole-wheat, dry	6 slices	Preheat broiler.
Chicken, cooked, sliced	⅓ to ½ pound, as desired	Place toast slices on a shallow baking pan. Cover with slices of chicken.
Cream of chicken soup, condensed, canned	10½-ounce can	Combine soup and evaporated milk in saucepan.
Evaporated milk	⅓ cup	Heat to simmering.
Tomato slices	6 large or 12 small	Pour hot soup mixture over sandwiches. Arrange tomato slices on top of sandwiches.
Bacon slices, cut in thirds, partly cooked	4	Top with bacon slices and olives.
Olives, stuffed, sliced	6	Broil until sandwiches are hot and bacon is crisp.

High-Altitude Food Preparation

At altitudes above 3,000 feet (914 meters, m), preparation of food may require changes in time, temperature, or recipe. The reason: lower atmospheric pressure due to the thinner blanket of air above. At sea level the atmosphere presses on a square inch (6.5 square centimeters, cm²) of surface with a weight of 14.7 pounds (65.4 newtons, N), at 5,000 feet (1,524 m) with 12.3 pounds (54.7 N), and at 10,000 feet (3,048 m) with only 10.2 pounds (45.4 N)—a decrease of about ½ pound (2.2 N) per 1,000 feet (305 m). This decreased pressure affects food preparation in two ways:

• Water and other liquids evaporate faster and boil at lower temperatures.

• Leavening gases in breads and cakes expand more.

APPROXIMATE BOILING TEMPERATURES OF WATER AT VARIOUS ALTITUDES

Altitude	Boiling Point of Water	
Sea level	212.0°F	100.0°C
2,000 ft. (609 m)	208.4°F	98.4°C
5,000 ft. (1,524 m)	203.0°F	95.0°C
7,500 ft. (2,286 m)	198.4°F	92.4°C
10,000 ft. (3,048 m)	194.0°F	90.0°C

There are no definite rules to use when modifying a sea level recipe for use at high altitudes. However, some general guidelines are worth consideration.

Altitude Adjustments for Boiled, Cooked, and Fried Foods

At high altitudes water boils at a lower temperature than it does at sea level. Specifically, each 500 foot (152.4 m) increase in altitude causes a 1°F (−17°C) drop in the boiling point. The internal heat needed to cook foods consequently takes more time to develop because they are being cooked at a lower temperature. Foods such as vegetables, eggs, and braised or simmered meats require a longer cooking period at high altitudes than at sea level.

Sugar cookery. The higher the altitude, the lower the boiling point of liquids and the sooner evaporation begins. Therefore, the cooked-stage temperature for candies, syrups, and jellies should be decreased by the difference in the boiling water temperature at your altitude and that of sea level.

Puddings and cream pie fillings. At altitudes of 5,000 feet (1524 m) or higher, problems may be encountered in the use of cornstarch for thickening. Satisfactory products can be made, provided maximum gelatinization of starch is obtained. This cannot be obtained in a double boiler, but can be reached using direct heat.

Deep-fat frying. The lower boiling point of water in foods requires lowering the temperature of the fat to prevent food from overbrowning on the outside while being undercooked on the inside. The decrease varies according to the food fried, but a rough guide is to lower the frying temperature about 3°F (−16°C) for each increase of 1,000 feet (305 m) in elevation. Sea level temperatures for deep-fat frying are:

Chicken—350°F *or* 175°C

Doughnuts, fish, fritters, oysters, scallops, soft-shell crabs—350°F to 375°F *or* 175°C to 190°C

Cauliflower, croquettes, eggplant, onions—375°F *or* 190°C

French fried potatoes—385°F to 395°F *or* 195°C to 200°C

As an example, at 8,000 feet croquettes would be fried at 350°F *or* 175°C instead of temperatures given above.

Canning, Freezing, and Pressure Cooking

Fruits, tomatoes, and pickled vegetables may be canned in a boiling water bath. Because of the lower boiling point of water at high altitude, the processing time should be increased 1 minute for each 1,000 feet (305 m) above sea level if this time is 20 minutes or less. If the processing time in the recipe is more than 20 minutes, increase by 2 minutes per 1,000 feet (305 m).

Other vegetables, meats, and poultry (low-acid foods) should be heated at 240°F (115°C) for the appropriate time in order to destroy heat-resistant bacteria. A steam pressure canner must be used to obtain a temperature of 240°F (115°C). At sea level, 10 pounds (68.9 kilopascals, kPa) of steam pressure will produce this temperature, but at altitudes of 2,000 feet (609 m) and above, steam pressure must be increased to reach 240°F (115°C). The increase is ½ pound (3.45 kPa) each 1,000 feet (305 m) above sea level, as illustrated below. The table

also gives steam pressure adjustments for pressure cooking at 228°F (110°C) and 250°F (120°C). When canning in a steam pressure canner with a weighted, rather than dial gauge, the 15 lb. rather than 10 lb. weight should be used at altitudes between 2,000 and 10,000 feet (610 and 3,048 m).

An important step in preparing vegetables for freezing is heating or *blanching* before packing. It is generally recommended that food be blanched one minute longer at altitudes of 5,000 feet (1524 m) and above that at sea level to compensate for a lower blanching temperature.

Altitude Adjustments for Leavened and Baked Foods

Breads. At high altitudes the rising time of yeast leavened products such as breads is shortened. Since the development of a good flavor in bread partially depends on the length of the rising period, it is well to maintain that period. Punching the dough down twice gives time for the flavor to develop.

In addition, flours tend to be drier and thus able to absorb more liquid in high, dry climates. Therefore, less flour may be needed.

Cakes. Most cake recipes perfected for sea level need no modification up to an altitude of 3,000 feet (914 m). Above that, decreased atmospheric pressure may result in excessive rising, which stretches the cell structure of the cake, making the texture coarse, or breaks the cells, causing the cake to fall. This can usually be corrected by decreasing the amount of leavening. Also, increasing the baking temperature 15° to 25°F (−8° to −4°C) "sets" the batter before the cells formed by the leavening gas expand too much.

STEAM PRESSURES AT VARIOUS ALTITUDES AND TEMPERATURES

Altitude	Pressure Required for 228°F (109°C)	Pressure Required for 240°F (115.6°C)	Pressure Required for 250°F (121°C)
Sea level (0 m)	5 lb (34.5 kPa)	10 lb (68.9 kPa)	15 lb (103.4 kPa)
2,000 ft (609 m)	6 lb (41.4 kPa)	11 lb (75.8 kPa)	16 lb (110.3 kPa)
3,000 ft (914 m)	6.5 lb (44.8 kPa)	11.5 lb (79.3 kPa)	16.5 lb (113.8 kPa)
4,000 ft (1,219 m)	7 lb (48.3 kPa)	12 lb (82.7 kPa)	17 lb (117.2 kPa)
5,000 ft (1,524 m)	7.5 lb (51.7 kPa)	12.5 lb (86.2 kPa)	17.5 lb (120.7 kPa)
7,000 ft (2,134 m)	8.5 lb (58.6 kPa)	13.5 lb (93.1 kPa)	18.5 lb (127.6 kPa)
10,000 ft (3,048 m)	10 lb (68.9 kPa)	15 lb (103.4 kPa)	20 lb (137.9 kPa)

CAKE RECIPE ADJUSTMENT GUIDE FOR HIGH ALTITUDES

Adjustment for Customary Measurements	3,000 Feet	5,000 Feet	7,000 Feet
Reduce baking power For each teaspoon, decrease	1/8 tsp	1/8 to 1/4 tsp	1/4 tsp
Reduce sugar For each cup, decrease	0 to 1 Tbsp	0 to 2 Tbsp	1 to 3 Tbsp
Increase liquid For each cup, add	1 to 2 Tbsp	2 to 4 Tbsp	3 to 4 Tbsp
Adjustment for Metric Measurements	1,000 Meters	1,500 Meters	2,000 Meters
Reduce baking powder For each 5 mL, decrease	1.0 mL	1.0 to 1.25 mL	1.25 mL
Reduce sugar, For each 250 mL, decrease	15 to 30 mL	30 to 60 mL	45 to 60 mL
Increase liquid For each 250 mL, add	15 to 30 mL	30 to 60 mL	45 to 60 mL

Fast and excessive evaporation of water at high altitudes leads to a higher concentration of sugar, which weakens the cell structure. To counterbalance this problem, sugar is often decreased and liquid increased.

Only repeated experiments with each recipe can give the most successful proportions to use. The accompanying table is a helpful starting point. Try the smaller adjustment first—this may be all that is needed.

Fat, like sugar, weakens cell structure. Therefore, rich cakes made at high altitudes also may need less fat (1 to 2 tablespoons per cup/15 to 30 mL per 240mL) than when made at sea level. On the other hand, because eggs strengthen cell structure, the addition of an egg may help prevent a "too-rich" cake from falling.

Angel food and sponge cakes present special high altitude problems. The leavening gas for these cakes is largely air. It is important not to beat too much air into the eggs. They should be beaten only until they form a peak that falls over, not until they are stiff and dry. Overbeating causes too much expansion of air cells and leads to their collapse. Using less sugar, more flour, and a higher baking temperature also will help strengthen the cell structure of foam-type cakes.

The amount of leavening in cake mixes cannot be reduced. Therefore, adjustments for these products usually take the form of strengthening the cell walls of the cake by adding all-purpose flour, possibly an egg yolk, and liquid. Suggestions for high-altitude adjustments are provided on most cake mix boxes. Follow these suggestions.

Cookies. Although many sea-level cookie recipes yield acceptable results at high altitudes, they often can be improved by a slight increase in baking temperature, a slight decrease in baking powder or soda, fat, and sugar and/or a slight increase in liquid ingredients and flour. Many cookie recipes contain a higher proportion of sugar and fat than necessary, even at low altitudes.

Quick breads. Quick breads vary from muffin-like to cake-like in cell structure. Although the cell structure of biscuits and muffin-type quick breads is firm enough to withstand the increased internal pressure at high altitudes without adjustment, a bitter or alkaline flavor may result from inadequate neutralization of baking soda or powder. In such cases, a slight decrease in the baking soda or baking powder usually will improve results.

Quick breads with a cake-like texture are more delicately balanced and usually can be improved at high altitudes by following the adjustment recommendations given above for cakes.

Microwave Cooking Basics

Most microwave ovens operate at a frequency of 2450 megahertz (MHz). When microwaves are absorbed by food, the polar (charged) molecules attempt to align with the field, which changes 2450 million times per second. Heat is evolved rapidly within the food, primarily due to this molecular friction. Microwaves are nonionizing and do not cause chemical or molecular changes such as those induced by ionizing radiation.

There are no standards for cooking power of microwave ovens. Cooking power of most consumer ovens falls within a range of 500-650 watts. Ovens designed for both conventional and microwave cooking supply 300-400 watts cooking power. The higher the cooking power, the faster the cooking will be.

Estimated Cooking Power of a Microwave Oven

- Weigh 1000 g water in a beaker.
- Determine initial temperature (°C) of water.
- Heat water in microwave oven 2 minutes.
- Determine final temperature (°C) of water.
- Subtract initial temperature from final temperature to obtain $\Delta T°C$.
- Cooking power in watts (W) = $\Delta T°C \times 35$. (35 is a calculated factor that converts $\Delta T°C$ into watts of cooking power.)

Although some ovens are equipped with temperature sensing probes, most microwave heating is controlled by adjusting the time according to the cooking power, the mass and density of the food, and its starting temperature.

Estimated Cooking Time for an Oven of Different Power Level

Cooking time (min) for oven$_2$ =

$$\frac{\text{Cooking time (min) for oven}_1 \times \text{cooking power (W) for oven}_1}{\text{Cooking power (W) for oven}_2}$$

Power controls are not standardized for microwave ovens. The number of settings indicates the approximate fraction of the power that is reduced for each successive setting.

Cooking power may not be evenly distributed throughout the oven, but new features are minimizing this problem. Microwave ovens designed for cooking more than one food at a time are constructed intentionally so that different amounts of energy are directed into different areas of the oven.

Testing Distribution of Cooking Power

- Select test material, such as egg white, or cake or muffin batter.
- Place equal amount of test material in 9 to 12 identical containers.
- Space containers of test material evenly throughout oven.
- Turn oven on full power for two minutes.
- Areas where there is a greater concentration of power will be indicated by visible signs of cooking.

Note: Water (100 mL/container) can be used for this test, and differences in temperature of water from container to container can be determined after five minutes of heating. Hotter temperatures indicate a greater concentration of power.

Mass and Shape of Food

As the mass of food increases, the length of time required to heat or cook increases. The relationship approaches linearity but varies with each food. The major heating by microwaves occurs in the outer 2 cm of the mass. The center of large masses of food must be heated by conduction of heat from the hot portions during a standing period following microwave heating.

Techniques for Promoting Even Heating

- Subdivide food into uniform portions if possible.
- Stir food periodically during cooking if possible.
- Turn and invert large portions of food during cooking.
- Use a rack or trivet to hold foods out of drippings.
- Avoid irregular shapes and square corners. If

irregular shape is unavoidable, shield portions of food that are thin with a small piece of aluminum foil during cooking. Foil should not touch the side of the oven.

• Place the thicker or more dense portions of food toward the outside of the container.

• Arrange food in a doughnut shape whenever possible.

• Plan for standing time during which hot food continues to cook after the oven is turned off. This is particularly important for large masses of food. Covering with aluminum foil during this time prevents excessive loss of heat from the surface of the food.

• For foods requiring long cooking times, use reduced power for part of the cooking, or manually cycle the energy on and off at intervals. The off interval allows time for the temperature to equalize in the food.

Initial Temperature of Food

The lower the initial temperature of the food, the longer the time required to achieve the desired end temperature by microwave heating. Starting with frozen food increases this time even more, since additional energy is required to melt the ice (latent heat of fusion).

Density of Food

The more dense the food, the greater the amount of microwave energy required for heating. When units differing in density or thickness are heated simultaneously, the less dense or thinner portions should be placed near the center of the container, where less microwave energy will be received. For example, place peas in the center of a ring of mashed potatoes.

Water Content

Free water is the most polar food constituent and the most reactive to microwaves. The rapid conversion of water to steam, which occurs in microwave heating, necessitates the puncturing of food membranes or skins to prevent the food from exploding.

Ice absorbs less microwave energy than water. When frozen foods are heated, pockets of free water can form and become superheated, resulting in an explosive release of steam. Most of the defrost cycles on microwave ovens provide for energy pulsing on and off, allowing time

during the off cycle for equilibration of temperature in the food.

Microwaves and Food Systems

Meat, Poultry, Fish

Tender cuts of meat are more suitable for microwave cooking than less tender cuts. Ground beef patties, steaks, or chops can be cooked with high power. However, reducing cooking power, particularly after the meat is hot, is recommended for roasts. Reduced power for the entire cooking period is needed to slow the process sufficiently for tenderization of pot roasts. Several of the recommendations for promoting even heating are applicable to cooking meats by microwaves.

Roasts should not exceed 13 cm in diameter. Even with this limitation, 20 to 40 minutes of standing time may be needed for conduction of heat to the center of the meat after microwave cooking is stopped. From 5 to 15 minutes standing time is needed for fish or poultry, depending upon the size. The slower the cooking and the smaller the mass, the shorter the standing time required. Since the internal temperature of the meat will rise during standing, the following internal temperatures are suggested as a guide for terminating cooking:

> Rare beef 52°C (125°F)
> Medium beef 60°C (140°F)
> Well done beef 70°C (158°F)
> Lamb 70°C (158°F)
> Pork 68°C (155°F)
> Reheating fully cooked ham 55°C (131°F)
> Poultry ($>$ 1.5 kg) 77°C (170°F)

Use only thermometers designed for microwave ovens, or use conventional thermometer when the oven is turned off. If the meat does not achieve the desired internal temperature during the standing period, it can be sliced and cooked a few minutes longer without detrimental effects on eating quality.

An even coating of fat (about 0.5 cm thick) provides a means of basting a roast during microwave cooking. Fat, which collects in the bottom of the container during roasting, should be removed midway during cooking so that it will not shield the underside of the meat from microwaves.

Bone tends to cause uneven cooking by microwaves because of its reflective effect. Therefore, boneless cuts of meat are preferred for microwave cooking.

Since less evaporation occurs with microwave than with conventional heating, only about ¼ cup of liquid is required for moist heat cookery of less tender cuts of meat. The meat should be prepared for cooking by piercing with a long-tined fork. If a pot roast is large (more than 13 cm in diameter), cutting it into chunks will lessen the time required to heat it to a temperature sufficiently high to start solubilization of collagen.

Small portions of meat, poultry, or fish should be turned once during cooking. Place whole birds breast side down first and turn midway in the cooking process. The larger the mass, the more often it should be turned. For example, roasts weighing 2 kg or more should be turned about three times. The skin of whole poultry or poultry pieces should be pierced in several places prior to cooking.

Browning aids, such as a browning utensil or coatings, are recommended for meat patties, steaks, or chops or for chicken pieces. Coatings will be less crisp than with conventional cooking. Crisping can be achieved by placing the product under a conventional broiler after cooking by microwaves. For products that tend to become dry, such as pork chops, covering with a sauce is recommended.

Milk, Cheese, and Eggs

Milk tends to foam excessively when heated to the boiling point by microwaves. Therefore, a large container is required for heating milk alone or for casseroles and other foods containing large amounts of milk. Products containing cheese should be cooked at reduced power (or for a very short time) to prevent a rubbery texture.

With fast cooking of eggs or egg-milk combinations, the temperature span is reduced between optimum coagulation and overcoagulation. Slowing the cooking and giving it close attention are necessary. As a rule, egg foams and products composed largely of egg foam are less satisfactory when cooked by microwaves than when cooked conventionally.

Starch Pastes, Pasta, Rice

Since gelatinization of starch is enhanced by rapid heating, starch cookery is well suited to microwave heating. Periodic stirring is essential for lump-free starch-thickened sauces. The sauce should be brought to the boil to achieve maximum thickening, but boiling should not be continued due to the tendency for the swollen starch granules to rupture.

Rice and pasta require time to absorb moisture. They cook well by microwaves, but little time is saved by this method of cookery. Ten to 14 minutes at reduced power is required for cooking 225 g of pasta by microwaves after the water has been brought to a boil. Addition of a small amount of oil reduces the tendency to boil over. Reheating pasta and cereals, however, is fast and requires no additional water. Stirring at least once is advisable during reheating.

Sugar Solutions

Microwave cooking of sugar solutions minimizes the problems of scorching and of crystal build-up on the sides of the cooking container. With candy, the solution can be brought to a rapid boil, and boiling can be continued at a reduced level of microwave power. A large container is essential to prevent boiling over. Jams or preserves can be made in small batches by microwave heating. The power should be reduced after the mixture has reached the boiling point to minimize the possibility of overcooking.

Vegetables and Fruits

Vegetables and fruits are easily cooked by microwaves. The speed of cooking favors the retention of color and pleasing flavor. Overcooking may result in a rubbery texture. For vegetables which require short cooking by conventional methods, little time is saved by microwave heating. However, for long-cooking vegetables, such as whole potatoes, time may be reduced as much as 85 or 90 percent. Many vegetables can be cooked without added water, but for those with a high cellulose content, texture is improved by cooking with a small amount of water. Most vegetables and fruits should be covered, and salt should be added after cooking to prevent dehydration. Skins on whole vegetables serve as a cover and should be pierced to permit steam to escape and to minimize the possibility of explosions.

Baked Products

Cakes containing shortening, muffins, and

cornbread cook well by microwaves but do not form brown crusts. Leavening should be reduced by ⅓ for microwave cooking. For products prepared from mixes, the texture may be improved by allowing the batter to stand for 15 to 20 minutes before cooking. The surface of the products will appear slightly moist when cooking is complete. Allow 10 to 12 minutes standing time for layer cakes so that some continued cooking can occur. Lining the container with waxed paper will reduce the tendency for sogginess on the bottom of the cake. Biscuits, yeast bread, cookies other than bar cookies, and cakes without shortening are less satisfactory when cooked by microwaves than when baked conventionally.

Fats and Oils

Fat and oil heat rapidly when exposed to microwaves. However, during deep fat frying, microwaves are absorbed preferentially by the food, not the fat or oil. Also, the temperature of the fat decreases when cold food is added. Therefore, deep-fat frying in a microwave oven is not satisfactory.

Preparation of Meals by Microwaves

• Start with the long-cooking foods and those which hold heat well.

• Plan for continued cooking, particularly in large masses of food, after the microwave heating is stopped.

• If more than one food is cooked at one time, extend the length of time. Even with ovens designed for cooking meals, cooking time must be adjusted according to the amount of food cooked at one time.

• Use microwaves for partial cooking of some foods.

• Take advantage of the capabilities of microwaves for fast defrosting and for fast reheating of foods.

Adapting Conventional Recipes

• Compare recipes to those already proven successful for microwave cooking. Use these as a guide and modify the conventional recipe accordingly.

• Consider the major ingredients of the recipe

and their suitability for microwave cooking.

• Consider using small recipes at first; they are easier to convert to microwave cooking than large ones.

• Remember that casseroles and entrees will require only about ¼ to ⅓ as long for microwave as for conventional cooking. An interruption for testing doneness will not be detrimental to the finished quality of any product.

• Plan for the characteristics of microwave heating, such as less evaporation of liquid, greater expansion of leavened products, rapid evolution of steam, and continued heating after oven is turned off, particularly in dense foods. Utilize methods of slowing the cooking process to promote tenderizing of less tender meat and to prevent curdling of egg-milk products.

Choosing Utensils

• Choose utensils that are transparent to microwaves, such as glass, paper, dishwasher-safe plastics, china (without metal trim), earthenware, or straw. Do not use metal, aluminum foil, paper goods made from recycled paper, or Melamine ware. (Plastic containers may deform from heat if used for syrups or fats.)

• Use only thermometers designed for microwave ovens. Conventional thermometers can be used to test temperature of food when the oven is turned off.

• As covers use casserole lids, plastic film, paper plates, waxed paper, paper towels, or napkins. Choose porous materials, such as paper towels, if the surface of the food is dry.

• Slit boil-in-bag containers to permit steam to escape.

• Use round utensils instead of those with square corners. A heatproof glass can be used in the center of casseroles to achieve the ideal doughnut shape for microwave heating.

Reducing the Speed of Cooking

• Utilize oven controls for reducing power.

• Cycle energy on and off manually.

• Introduce an additional load, such as a container of water, to absorb part of the energy.

Enhancing Appearance of Food

The speed of microwave cooking and the tendency for food to give up heat to the surrounding atmosphere are not conducive to browning and crusting of the surfaces of food. Browning occurs if the food requires cooking for 20 minutes or more. Many foods are acceptable without a brown crust, and brown ingredients and sauces may be used to advantage on others.

Techniques for Enhancing The Appearance of Foods Cooked By Microwaves

Biscuits   Brown in browning utensil.
Top with toasted sesame seed, poppy seed, cinnamon and sugar, or dry onion mix.

Cakes   Sprinkle brown sugar and cinnamon in container before pouring batter, or sprinkle on top after cooking.
Use topping for upside-down cakes.
Chill baked cake, then ice.

Casseroles   Top with toasted bread crumbs, crushed chips, cereals, toasted nuts, grated cheese, chopped bacon.
Brown under broiler before or after cooking by microwaves.

Meat, poul- try, fish   Brush with brown sauce or gravy mix.
Sprinkle with paprika or dry onion soup.
Top, or coat, with toasted bread crumbs, nuts, or grated cheese.
Cover with sauce.
Glaze with brown sugar or other ingredients.
Brown on grill or broiler and complete cooking by microwaves.
Use browning utensil.

Muffins   Include bran as ingredient.

Pastry   Prepare with milk instead of water.
Add a few drops of food color.
Cook top crusts separately and place on cooked pie.

Slow-Cooker Cooking

The slow-cooker is especially helpful in cooking less tender cuts of meat, and cooks often wish to adapt favorite recipes for use in it. Instruction manuals may offer suggestions about techniques for using specific cookers. If not, the following steps will serve as a guide.

Adapting the Recipe

When adapting a recipe, first look for steps that may be omitted. For example, vegetables are not sautéed, meats are usually not browned (see exceptions under timing suggestions), and the product is not brought to a boil first. However, frozen vegetables and seafoods, especially those added near the end of cooking, may need to be partially or completely thawed before they are put in the cooker.

Cooks also seem to feel they can just "throw it all in the pot at once" but may be less than pleased with the overcooked pasta and rice that result from this.

Food Placement

Placement of foods in the cooker may determine the success or failure of any dish. Vegetables such as potatoes, carrots, and onions cook very slowly and should be kept small to medium in size and placed in the bottom of the pot. This also allows the meat juices to drip over the vegetables, enhancing their flavor. Unless the meat is very fatty, a rack usually is not necessary. If a sauce is used over meat or vegetables, it should be poured evenly over the food so that all parts are exposed for even cooking.

Most breads and cakes need a rack to prevent burning on the bottom while the top is not yet cooked. If a rack is not available, a ring of crumpled foil may serve the purpose.

Timing Factors

Proper timing for foods in the slow-cooker is

affected by many things, yet is crucial for best results.

• The temperature of the food when placed in the cooker will affect cooking time. Frozen foods take longer than refrigerated foods, which take longer than foods at room temperature. Fats on foods tend to increase the cooking temperatures and make the foods cook faster. However, if there is much fat present, the meat should be trimmed or browned or broiled to eliminate as much fat as possible. Fat occasionally causes an off-flavor to develop.

• Liquids speed heat transfer in the slow-cooker, but the amounts needed are much less than for standard cooking. There is almost always more liquid after cooking than before because the cooker lets little escape. For most recipes one cup may be sufficient, but a general rule of thumb is to use only one-half as much as in standard cooking. Additional amounts may be needed if cooking a pasta or rice product, which absorbs much liquid.

• Minerals, acids, and sugars also increase the cooking time in dried bean products and may affect other foods in hard-water areas. Sugars and acids such as tomatoes also affect dried beans and should be added only after the beans have softened.

• Some foods should be last additions to the slow-cooker. These include seafood and frozen vegetables as well as fresh mushrooms, which need one hour or less of cooking. Crushed or ground seasonings should be added near the end of cooking because they become diluted during the long cooking, while whole seasonings may withstand the long cooking and should be used in very small amounts (about one-half as much as usual). Rice and pasta may become gummy with long cooking and should be added only during the last hour unless directions specify earlier. Since sour cream and milk may curdle during long cooking, they need only a very short time; but condensed soups are satisfactory during the long cooking.

When adapting a recipe, the chart on this page may provide guidelines.

Food Labeling

Federal laws governing the labeling of food are enforced by the United States Department of

TIME GUIDE

IF RECIPE SAYS:	COOK IN CROCK-POT:
15 to 30 min.	1½ to 2½ hrs on High OR 4 to 8 hrs on Low*
35 to 45 min.	3 to 4 hrs on High OR 6 to 10 hrs on Low
50 min. to 3 hrs.	4 to 6 hrs on High OR 8 to 18 hrs on Low

HIGH: 300° • LOW: 190°

Most uncooked meat and vegetable combinations will require at least 8 hours on Low.

Agriculture (USDA) Federal Meat Inspection Act, Poultry Products Inspection Act, and by the Food and Drug Administration (FDA). The FDA, a division of the Department of Health and Human Services (HHS) is charged with the authority to assure the safety of the nation's food supply under the Food, Drug, and Cosmetic Act. These federal laws were originally passed in 1906, and although some revisions have been made since then, the basic concepts with respect to food labeling have remained unchanged for about 40 years. Significant advances in food technology during this time coupled with increasing demands for extensive and sophisticated information about food products, along with increasingly antiquated statutes, have led to a complex set of food labeling regulations.

Ingredient Labeling

Ingredient lists or total disclosure on food labels are required by FDA regulations to be in descending order of predominance by weight (e.g., canned peas: peas, water, sugar, salt). The law requires, with few exceptions (e.g., spices, flavors, colors), a label declaration of all ingredients in foods that are not standardized. Labels for all meat and poultry products, whether standardized or not, must list ingredients. Also, most ingredients must be listed on the label by the specific name of the ingredient. However, there are exceptions to this rule. Under the law, spices, flavorings, and colors may be declared in the ingredient statement without naming the specific ingredient used. Furthermore, generic or collective names can sometimes be used instead of the specific name.

Standard of Identity

Government regulations, called standards of identity, define the composition of many foods, state which optional ingredients may be used, and specify those ingredients which must be declared on the label. Examples of standardized foods are: most canned fruits and vegetables; milk; cheeses; ice cream; most breads; some food dressings; margarine; and certain seafoods. Required or mandatory ingredients in such standardized foods are exempt by law from label declaration.

Nutrition Labeling

Nutrition labeling information was seen on food labels in retail markets by 1973. The basic purpose of nutrition labeling is to provide accurate nutrition information about each food. Nutrition labeling, mainly a voluntary program, becomes mandatory (1) when a food manufacturer makes any kind of nutritional claim for the food product either on the label or in the advertising, (2) when the food is enriched or fortified with any essential nutrients.

Food labels providing nutrition information must use a standard format indicating serving size and servings per container. For each serving they must provide information on:

- number of calories

- amount of protein, carbohydrates, and fats—in grams

- amount of seven specified vitamins and minerals in percentage of U.S. RDA vitamins A and C, thiamin (vit. B_1), riboflavin (vit. B_2), niacin, calcium, and iron

Labels may list other vitamins and minerals as well as polyunsaturated and saturated fats, cholesterol, and sodium.

Low/Reduced Calories—Food Labeling

On September 21, 1978, the FDA established new rules on how low calorie and reduced calorie foods must be labeled. They apply to all foods introduced into interstate commerce on or after July 1, 1979.

The new rules require that a food labeled as *low calorie* must contain no more than 40 calories per serving. A food may be called *reduced calorie* only if its calorie content is at least one-third lower than a similar food for which it can substitute.

Other requirements of the new regulations are:

- Foods that claim to be lower in calories or reduced in calories must bear a complete nutrition label.

- All foods that claim to be reduced in calories must describe the comparison on which the claim is based (e.g., artificially sweetened peaches packed in water, 38 calories per ½-cup serving, 62% less than Brand X peaches in heavy syrup).

- Foods that are normally low in calories, such as celery, cannot use the term *low calorie* immediately before the name.

- For a food to be labeled *sugar free, sugarless,* or *no sugar,* it must also be labeled as either *low calorie* or *reduced calorie* and meet the requirements to use that labeling, or be accompanied by such statements as *not a reduced calorie food* or *not for weight control.*

- A food cannot be labeled as *diabetic* unless it is useful in the diet of diabetics.

Percentage Labeling

The FDA requires a declaration of the percentage of some "characterizing" ingredients as part of the name of some foods when the amount of the ingredients has information bearing on the consumer's acceptance of the food (e.g., if shrimp cocktail consists of 50% shrimp, the official name of the product is *Shrimp Cocktail—Contains 50% Shrimp*).

Other Information Required by Law

- common or usual name of food

- name and address of manufacturer, packer, or distributor

- listing of ingredients for most foods

- net weight declaration

The 1966 Fair Packaging and Labeling Act requires that any manufacturer or distributor of a consumer product must state, prominently and in a uniform location on the principal display panel of the label, the truthful net weight or volume contents of the package.

On consumer packages of one pound, one pint, or more, but less than four pounds or one gallon, the net weight or volume must be declared in a dual manner with the first expression in total ounces or fluid ounces, followed in parentheses by a declaration of the largest whole unit of weight or liquid measure and subdivisions thereof, e.g., 18 oz. (1 lb. 2 oz.).

Imitation and Substitute Foods

Under federal law, any food that imitates another food must be labeled *imitation*. Traditionally, FDA accepted the concept that substitute foods were inferior to the "real" foods and had to be labeled as imitations. In 1973 FDA reviewed its policy and decided to identify nutritionally inferior foods by requiring them to be called *imitation,* but allowed all other substitute foods to be sold without being called *imitation* if they bore a name that accurately described the food.

Fat and Oil Labeling

The regulations allow for some flexibility in the declaration of a fat or oil ingredient. For example, a vegetable oil may be declared as follows: *vegetable oil shortening (contains one or more of the following: soybean oil, palm oil, and/or corn oil).*

Food Additives

By the broadest definition, a food additive is any substance that becomes a part of the food product when added directly or indirectly. Today, some 2,800 substances are intentionally added to foods to produce a desired effect. As many as 10,000 other components find their way into various foods during processing, packaging, and storage.

The 1906 Food and Drugs Act and the more comprehensive Food, Drug, and Cosmetic Act of 1938 gave the government authority to remove adulterated and obviously poisonous foods from the market. The 1958 Food Additives Amendment, the Delaney Clause, and the 1960 Color Additives Amendment were laws specifically set up to regulate additives in foods. In these laws, legislation shifted the burden from the government to the manufacturer to prove that a food additive is safe. The FDA was also authorized to regulate additives only on the basis of safety.

The agency has no power to limit the number of additives approved, or to judge whether it is really needed.

Under the Food Additives Amendment, however, two major categories of additives are exempted from the testing and approval process. The first group of some 700 substances belongs to the "generally recognized as safe" (GRAS) list. The idea behind this was to free the FDA and the manufacturers from being required to prove the safety of substances already considered harmless because of past extensive use without known harmful effects. Also exempted from testing were the "prior sanctioned substances," those that had been approved before 1958 for use in food by either FDA or USDA. But the FDA since 1971 has been in the process of reviewing all items on the GRAS list.

An additive is intentionally incorporated into foods for one or more of these four purposes:

- to maintain or improve nutritional value
- to maintain freshness
- to help in processing or preparation
- to make food more appealing

The following Additives Index is a helpful guide to some substances commonly added to foods:

ADDITIVES INDEX

Key Definitions:

◇ *Maintain and Improve Nutritional Quality*

—Nutrients: enrich (replace vitamins and minerals lost in processing) or fortify (add nutrients that may be lacking in the diet).

○ *Maintain Product Quality*

—Preservatives (Antimicrobials): prevent food spoilage from bacteria, molds, fungi, and yeast; extend shelf life; or protect natural color or flavor.

—Antioxidants: delay/prevent rancidity or enzymatic browning.

☐ *Aid in Processing of Preparation*

—Emulsifiers: help to distribute evenly tiny particles of one liquid into another; improve homogeneity, consistency, stability, or texture.

—Stabilizers, Thickening Texturizers: impart

body; improve consistency or texture; stabilize emulsions; affect "mouthful" of food.

—Leavening Agents: affect cooking results— texture and volume.

—pH Control Agents: change/maintain acidity or alkalinity.

—Humectants: cause moisture retention.

—Maturing and Bleaching Agents, Dough Conditioners: accelerate the aging process; improve baking qualities.

—Anticaking Agents: prevent caking, lumping, or clustering of a finely powdered or crystalline substance.

△ Affect Appeal Characteristics

—Flavor Enhancers: supplement, magnify, or modify the original taste and/or aroma of food without imparting a characteristic flavor of their own.

—Flavors: heighten natural flavor; restore flavors lost in processing.

—Colors: give desired, appetizing, or characteristic color of food.

—Sweeteners: make the aroma or taste of food more agreeable or pleasurable.

(A)

Acetic	□ pH control
Acetone peroxide	□ mat-bleach-condit
Ammonium alginate	□ pH control
Annalto extract	△ color
Arabingalactan	□ stabilizer-textur.

(B)

Benzoic acid	○ preservative
Beta carotene	◇ nutrient △ color
BHA (butylated hydroxyanisole)	○ antioxidant
BHT (butylated hydroxytoluene)	○ antioxidant
Butyparaben	○ preservative

(C)

Calcium bromate	□ mat-bleach-condit
Calcium phosphate	□ leavening
Calcium propionate	○ preservative
Canthaxanthin	△ color
Carob bean gum	□ stabil-thick-tex
Cellulose	□ stabil-thick-tex

(D)

Dextrose	△ sweetener
Diglycerides	□ emulsifier
Disodium guanylate	△ flavor enhancer
Dried algae meal	△ color

(E)

| EDTA (ethylene-diaminetetra-acetic acid) | ○ antioxidant |

(F)

FD & C Colors
Blue No. 1	△ color
Red No. 2	△ color
Red No. 40	△ color
Yellow No. 5	△ color
Fructose	△ sweetener

(G)

Glycerine	□ humectant
Grape skin extract	△ color
Guar gum	□ stabil-thick-tex
Gum arabic	□ stabil-thick-tex

(H)

| Heptylparaben | ○ preservative |
| Hydrogen peroxide | □ mat-bleach-condit |

(I)

Invert sugar	△ sweetener
Iodine	◇ nutrient
Iron-ammonium citrate	□ anticaking
Iron oxide	△ color

(L)

Lactic acid	□ pH control
	○ preservative
Locust bean gum	□ stabil-thick-tex

(M)

Mannitol	△ sweetener
	□ anticaking
	□ stabil-thick-tex
Methylparaben	○ preservative
Modified food starch	□ stabil-thick-tex

(N)

| Niacinamide | ◇ nutrient |

(P)

Phosphoric acid	□ pH control
Polysorbates	□ emulsifiers
Potassium bromate	□ mat-bleach-condit
Potassium pro- pionate	○ preservative
Propylene glycol	□ stabil-thick-tex □ humectant

(R)

Riboflavin	◇ nutrient, △ color

(S)

Saffron	△ color
Silicon dioxide	□ anticaking
Sodium benzoate	○ preservative
Sodium citrate	□ pH control
Sodium nitrate	○ preservative
Sodium propionate	○ preservative
Sodium stearyl fumarate	□ mat-bleach-condit
Sorbitan mono- stearate	□ emulsifier

(T)

Tagetes (Aztec Marigold)	△ color
Tartaric acid	□ pH control
TBHQ (tertiary butyl hydro- quinone	○ antioxidant

Titanium dioxide	△ color
Tocopherols (vit. E)	◇ nutrient ○ antioxi- dant
Tragacanth gum	□ stabil-thick-tex

(U)

Ultramarine blue	△ color

(V)

Vanilla	◇ flavor
Vitamin A	◇ nutrient
Vitamin C	◇ nutrient ○ preservative ○ antioxidant

Key to abbreviations:

stabil-thick-tex = stabilizers-thickeners-
texturizers

leavening = leavening agents

pH control = pH control agents

mat-bleach-condit = maturing & bleaching
agents, dough condi-
tioners

anticaking = anticaking agents

Supplementary Aids to Food Preparation

SOLUBILITY OF SALT (Sodium Chloride)

Temperature of Solution		Percentage of Salt in Saturated Solution	Amount Dissolved by 100 Grams Water*
-20° C	-4° F	23.6 %	30.9 g
20° C	68° F	26.4 %	36.0 g
100° C	212° F	28.2 %	39.8 g

*The resulting solutions are saturated at the temperatures indicated.

BAKING TEMPERATURES AND TIMES

Type of Product	Oven Temperature*	Baking Time
Breads, etc.		
Biscuits	425° F to 450° F (220°C to 230°C)	10 to 15 min
Corn bread	400° F to 425° F (205°C to 220°C)	30 to 40 min
Cream puffs, popovers	375° F (190°C)	1 hr
Muffins	400° F to 425° F (205°C to 220°C)	20 to 25 min
Quick loaf breads	350° F to 375° F (175°C to 190°C)	1 to 1-1/4 hr
Yeast bread.	400° F (205°C)	30 to 40 min
Yeast rolls, plain	400° F to 425° F (205°C to 220°C)	15 to 25 min
sweet	375° F (190°C)	20 to 30 min
Cakes with fat		
Cup.	350° F to 375° F (175°C to 190°C)	15 to 25 min
Layer	350° F to 375° F (175°C to 190°C)	20 to 35 min
Loaf	350° F (175°C)	45 to 60 min
Cakes without fat		
Angel food and sponge	350° F to 375° F (175°C to 190°C)	30 to 45 min
Cookies		
Drop	350° F to 400° F (175°C to 205°C)	8 to 15 min
Rolled	375° F (190°C)	8 to 10 min
Egg, meat, milk, and cheese dishes		
Cheese soufflé, custards (baked in a pan of hot water)	350° F (175°C)	30 to 60 min
Macaroni and cheese	350° F (175°C)	25 to 30 min
Meat loaf	300° F (150°C)	1 to 1-1/2 hr
Meat pie.	400° F (205°C)	25 to 30 min
Rice pudding (raw rice)	300° F (150°C)	2 to 3 hr
Scalloped potatoes	350° F (175°C)	1 hr
Pastry		
One-crust pie (custard type), unbaked shell	400° F to 425° F (205°C to 220°C)	30 to 40 min
Meringue on cooked filling in prebaked shell	350° or (175°C) or 425° F (220°C)	12 to 15 min / 4 to 4-1/2 min
Shell only.	450° F (230°C)	10 to 12 min
Two-crust pies with uncooked filling	400° F to 425° F (205°C to 220°C)	45 to 55 min
Two-crust pies with cooked filling	425° F to 450° F (220°C to 230°C)	30 to 45 min

*When baking in ovenproof glassware, reduce temperature by 25°F or by 10°C. For example, when using a glass pie pan for pie shell, bake at 425°F (220°C) instead of 450°F (230°C) given in chart.

NOTE: For packaged mixes follow direction on package.

SUBSTITUTION OF INGREDIENTS

For:	Substitute:
1 tablespoon flour (used as thickener)	1/2 tablespoon cornstarch, potato starch, rice starch, or arrowroot starch, *or* 1 tablespoon quick-cooking tapioca
1 cup sifted all-purpose flour	1 cup unsifted all-purpose flour minus 2 tablespoons
1 cup sifted cake flour	7/8 cup sifted all-purpose flour, *or* 1 cup minus 2 tablespoons sifted all-purpose flour
1 cup sifted self-rising flour	1 cup sifted all-purpose flour plus 1-1/2 teaspoons baking powder and 1/2 teaspoon salt
1 cup dark corn syrup	3/4 cup light corn syrup and 1/4 cup light molasses
1 cup honey	1-1/4 cups sugar plus 1/4 cup liquid*
1 ounce semisweet chocolate	1/2 ounce baking chocolate plus 1 tablespoon sugar
1 cup corn syrup	1 cup sugar plus 1/4 cup liquid*
1 cup honey	1-1/4 cups sugar plus 1/4 cup liquid*
1 ounce chocolate	3 tablespoons cocoa plus 1 tablespoon fat
1 cup butter	1 cup margarine, *or* 7/8 to 1 cup hydrogenated fat plus 1/2 teaspoon salt, *or* 7/8 cup lard plus 1/2 teaspoon salt
1 cup coffee cream (20 percent)	3 tablespoons butter plus about 7/8 cup milk
1 cup heavy cream (40 percent)	1/3 cup butter plus about 3/4 cup milk
1 cup whole milk	1 cup reconstituted nonfat dry milk plus 2-1/2 teaspoons butter or margarine, *or* 1/2 cup evaporated milk plus 1/2 cup water, *or* 1/4 cup sifted dry whole milk powder plus 7/8 cup water
1 cup milk	3 tablespoons sifted regular nonfat dry milk plus 1 cup minus 1 tablespoon water, *or* 1/3 cup instant nonfat dry milk plus 1 cup minus 1 tablespoon water
1 cup buttermilk or sour milk	1 tablespoon vinegar or lemon juice plus enough sweet milk to make 1 cup (let stand 5 minutes), *or* 1-3/4 teaspoons cream of tartar plus 1 cup sweet milk
1 cup sour cream	1 cup plain yogurt *or* 7/8 cup sour milk plus 1/3 cup butter
1 cup buttermilk	1 cup plain yogurt
1 cup milk	1 cup buttermilk and omit 1 teaspoon baking powder, replacing with 1/2 teaspoon soda and 1 teaspoon shortening
1 cup butter	4/5 cup bacon fat, clarified; *or* 3/4 cup chicken fat, clarified; *or* 7/8 cup oil
1 teaspoon lemon juice	1/2 teaspoon vinegar
1 cup light brown sugar	1/2 cup dark brown sugar plus 1/2 cup granulated sugar

For:	Substitute:
1 teaspoon baking powder.	.1/4 teaspoon baking soda plus 5/8 teaspoon cream of tartar, *or* 1/4 teaspoon baking soda plus 1/2 cup fully soured milk or buttermilk, *or* 1/4 teaspoon baking soda plus 1/2 tablespoon vinegar or lemon juice used with sweet milk to make 1/2 cup, *or* 1/4 teaspoon baking soda plus 1/4 to 1/2 cup molasses
1 tablespoon active dry yeast.	.1 package active dry yeast, *or* 1 compressed yeast cake
1 whole egg	.2 egg yolks, *or* 3 tablespoons plus 1 teaspoon thawed frozen egg, *or* 2 tablespoons and 2 teaspoons dry whole egg powder plus an equal amount of water
1 egg yolk	.3-1/2 teaspoons thawed frozen egg yolk, *or* 2 tablespoons dry egg yolk plus 2 teaspoons water
1 egg white.	.2 tablespoons thawed frozen egg white, *or* 2 teaspoons dry egg white plus 2 tablespoons water

*Use whatever liquid is called for in the recipe.

NOTE: The amounts of corn syrup and honey are based on the way these products function in recipes and not on the sweetness equivalence with sugar.

TEMPERATURE CONVERSION TABLE

The numbers in the body of the table give in degrees F the temperature indicated in degrees C at the top and side.

To convert 178° C to Fahrenheit scale, find 17 in the column headed degrees C. Proceed in a horizontal line to the column headed 8 which shows 352° F as corresponding to 178° C.

To convert 352° F to Celsius (Centigrade) scale, find 352 in the Fahrenheit readings, then in the column headed degrees C, find the number which is on the same horizontal line, i.e., 17. Next, fill in the last number from the heading of the column in which 352 was found, i.e., 8, resulting in 178° C which is equivalent to 352° F.

Range: −29° C (−20° F) to 309° C (588° F)

Conversion Formulae: $T^{\circ} C = 5/9 (T^{\circ} F - 32)$
$T^{\circ} F = 9/5 T^{\circ} C + 32$

Degrees C	0	1	2	3	4	5	6	7	8	9
-2	-4° F	-6° F	-8° F	-9° F	-11° F	-13° F	-15° F	-17° F	-18° F	-20° F
-1	14° F	12° F	10° F	9° F	7° F	5° F	3° F	1° F	0° F	-2° F
-0	32° F	30° F	28° F	27° F	25° F	23° F	21° F	19° F	18° F	16° F
0	32° F	34° F	36° F	37° F	39° F	41° F	43° F	45° F	46° F	48° F
1	50° F	52° F	54° F	55° F	57° F	59° F	61° F	63° F	64° F	66° F
2	68° F	70° F	72° F	73° F	75° F	77° F	79° F	81° F	82° F	84° F
3	86° F	88° F	90° F	91° F	93° F	95° F	97° F	99° F	100° F	102° F
4	104° F	106° F	108° F	109° F	111° F	113° F	115° F	117° F	118° F	120° F
5	122° F	124° F	126° F	127° F	129° F	131° F	133° F	135° F	136° F	138° F
6	140° F	142° F	144° F	145° F	147° F	149° F	151° F	153° F	154° F	156° F
7	158° F	160° F	162° F	163° F	165° F	167° F	169° F	171° F	172° F	174° F
8	176° F	178° F	180° F	181° F	183° F	185° F	187° F	189° F	190° F	192° F
9	194° F	196° F	198° F	199° F	201° F	203° F	205° F	207° F	208° F	210° F

10	212° F	214° F	216° F	217° F	219° F	221° F	223° F	225° F	226° F	228° F
11	230° F	232° F	234° F	235° F	237° F	239° F	241° F	243° F	244° F	246° F
12	248° F	250° F	252° F	253° F	255° F	257° F	259° F	261° F	262° F	264° F
13	266° F	268° F	270° F	271° F	273° F	275° F	277° F	279° F	280° F	282° F
14	284° F	286° F	288° F	289° F	291° F	293° F	295° F	297° F	298° F	300° F
15	302° F	304° F	306° F	307° F	309° F	311° F	313° F	315° F	316° F	318° F
16	320° F	322° F	324° F	325° F	327° F	329° F	331° F	333° F	334° F	336° F
17	338° F	340° F	342° F	343° F	345° F	347° F	349° F	351° F	352° F	354° F
18	356° F	358° F	360° F	361° F	363° F	365° F	367° F	369° F	370° F	372° F
19	374° F	376° F	378° F	379° F	381° F	383° F	385° F	387° F	388° F	390° F
20	392° F	394° F	396° F	397° F	399° F	401° F	403° F	405° F	406° F	408° F
21	410° F	412° F	414° F	415° F	417° F	419° F	421° F	423° F	424° F	426° F
22	428° F	430° F	432° F	433° F	435° F	437° F	439° F	441° F	442° F	444° F
23	446° F	448° F	450° F	451° F	453° F	455° F	457° F	459° F	460° F	462° F
24	464° F	466° F	468° F	469° F	471° F	473° F	475° F	477° F	478° F	480° F
25	482° F	484° F	486° F	487° F	489° F	491° F	493° F	495° F	496° F	498° F
26	500° F	502° F	504° F	505° F	507° F	509° F	511° F	513° F	514° F	516° F
27	518° F	520° F	522° F	523° F	525° F	527° F	529° F	531° F	532° F	534° F
28	536° F	538° F	540° F	541° F	543° F	545° F	547° F	549° F	550° F	552° F
29	554° F	556° F	558° F	559° F	561° F	563° F	565° F	567° F	568° F	570° F
30	572° F	574° F	576° F	577° F	579° F	581° F	583° F	585° F	586° F	588° F

BASIC RECIPE PROPORTIONS

The following table shows proportions of ingredients to one another in certain basic recipes. The amounts of ingredients do not constitute full-size recipes and are not intended for family meal preparation.*

Product	Flour**	Liquid	Fat	Eggs	Sugar	Salt	Baking Powder†	Other Ingredients
Beverages								
Cocoa and chocolate		1 c milk (242 g)			2 tsp to 1 Tbsp (8.3 to 12.5 g)	Few grains		1 Tbsp cocoa (7 g) or 1/2 oz chocolate (14.2 g)
Coffee		3/4 c water (178 g)						1 to 2 Tbsp coffee (5.3 to 10.6 g)
Coffee, instant		3/4 c water (178 g)						1 to 2 tsp instant coffee (0.8 to 1.6 g)
Tea		3/4 c water (178 g)						1/2 to 1 tsp tea (0.75 to 1.5 g)
Breads								
Biscuits	1 c (115 g)	1/3 to 1/2 c milk (80.7 to 121 g)	2 to 4 Tbsp (23.6 to 47.2 g)			1/2 tsp (3 g)	1-1/4 or 2 tsp (4.5 or 5.8 g)	
Griddle cakes	1 c (115 g)	3/4 to 7/8 c milk (181.5 to 211.8 g)	1 Tbsp (11.8 g)	1/2 (25 g)	0 to 1 Tbsp (0 to 12.5 g)	1/2 tsp (3 g)	1-1/2 or 2 tsp (5.4 or 5.8 g)	
Muffins	1 c (115 g)	1/2 c milk (121 g)	2 to 3 Tbsp (23.6 to 35.4 g)	1/2 (25 g)	1 to 2 Tbsp (12.5 to 25 g)	1/2 tsp (3 g)	1-1/4 or 2 tsp (4.5 or 5.8 g)	
Popovers	1 c (115 g)	1 c milk (242 g)	1 to 2 Tbsp (11.8 to 23.6 g)	2 to 3 (50 to 150 g)		1/4 to 3/4 tsp (1.5 to 4.5 g)		
Waffles	1 c (115 g)	3/4 to 1 c milk (181.5 to 242 g)	1 to 3 Tbsp (11.8 to 35.4 g)	1 to 2 (50 to 100 g)		1/2 tsp (3 g)	1-1/4 or 2 tsp (4.5 or 5.8 g)	
Yeast bread	1 c (115 g)	1/3 c milk (80.7 g)	0 to 1 Tbsp (0 to 11.8 g)		1 tsp to 1 Tbsp (4.2 to 12.5 g)	1/4 tsp (1.5 g)		1/4 compressed yeast cake (12.8 g) or 1/4 small package active dry yeast (1.7 g)

Food								
Cakes and Pastry Cake with fat	1 c (cake or all-purpose (96 or 115 g)	1/4 to 1/2 c milk (60.5 to 121 g)	2 to 4 Tbsp (23.6 to 47 g)	1/2 to 1 (25 to 50 g)	1/2 to 3/4 c (100 to 150 g)	1/8 to 1/4 tsp (0.75 to 1.5 g)	1 or 2 tsp (3.6 or 5.8 g)	Flavoring
chiffon	1 c (cake) (96 g)	1/3 c water (79 g)	1/4 c (salad oil) (52.5 g)	3 (150 g)	2/3 c (134 g)	1/2 tsp (3 g)	1-1/4 or 1-1/2 tsp (4.5 or 4.4 g)	1/4 tsp cream of tartar (0.8 g) Flavoring
Cake without fat angel food	1 c (cake) (96 g)			1 to 1-1/2 c (whites) (246 to 369 g)	1-1/4 to 1-1/2 c (250 to 300 g)	1/2 tsp (3 g)		3/4 to 1-1/2 tsp cream of tartar (2.3 to 4.6 g) Flavoring
sponge	1 c (cake) (96 g)	0 to 3 Tbsp water (0 to 44.4 g)		5 to 6 (250 to 300 g)	1 c (200 g)	1/2 tsp (3 g)		0 to 3/4 tsp cream of tartar (0 to 2.3 g) Flavoring
Cream puffs	1 c (115 g)	1 c water (237 g)	1/2 c (144 g)	4 (200 g)		1/4 tsp (1.5 g)		
Doughnuts	1 c (115 g)	1/4 c milk (60.5 g)	1 to 1/2 tsp (3.9 to 5.9 g)	1/2 (25 g)	1/4 c (50 g)	1/4 tsp (1.5 g)	1 or 2 tsp (3.6 or 5.8 g)	Flavoring
Pastry	1 c (115 g)	2 Tbsp water (29.6 g)	4 to 5 Tbsp (47 to 58.8 g)			1/2 tsp (3 g)		
Egg dishes Custards		1 c milk (242 g)		1 to 1-2/3 (50 to 83.5 g)	1-1/2 to 3 Tbsp (18.8 to 37.5 g)	1/8 tsp (0.75 g)		Flavoring
Omelets		1 Tbsp milk (15.1 g)		1 (50 g)		1/8 tsp (0.75 g)		Seasonings
Soufflés (entree)	3 to 4 Tbsp (21.6 to 28.8 g)	1 c milk (242 g)	3 to 4 Tbsp (35.2 to 47 g)	3 (150 g)		1/4 to 1/2 tsp (1.5 to 3 g)		Seasonings

(continued on next page)

BASIC RECIPE PROPORTIONS (Continued)

Product	Flour**	Liquid	Fat	Eggs	Sugar	Salt	Baking Powder†	Other Ingredients
Puddings								
Cornstarch		1 c milk (242 g)		0 to 1 (0 to 50 g)	2 to 3 Tbsp (25 to 37.5 g)	1/8 tsp (0.75 g)		1 to 1-1/2 Tbsp cornstarch (8 to 12 g) Flavoring
Tapioca		1 c milk (242 g)		1/2 to 1 (25 to 50 g)	2 Tbsp (25 g)	1/8 tsp (0.75 g)		1-1/2 Tbsp quick-cooking tapioca (14.25 g) Flavoring
Rice (steamed)		1 c milk (242 g)			1 to 2 Tbsp (12.5 g)	1/8 tsp (0.75 g)		2 to 4 Tbsp raw rice (22.8 to 45.5 g) Flavoring
Rice (baked)		1 c milk (242 g)			1 Tbsp (12.5 g)	Few grains		1 Tbsp raw rice (11.4 g) Flavoring
Sauces								
White sauce thin	1 Tbsp (7.8 g)	1 c milk (242 g)	1 Tbsp (11.8 g)			1/4 tsp (1.5 g)		Pepper, if desired
medium	2 Tbsp (15.6 g)	1 c milk (242 g)	2 Tbsp (23.6 g)			1/4 tsp (1.5 g)		Pepper, if desired
thick	3 to 4 Tbsp (23.4 to 31.2 g)	1 c milk (242 g)	3 Tbsp (35.4 g)			1/4 tsp (1.5 g)		Pepper, if desired
Fruit sauce		1 c (fruit juice) (247 g)			2 to 4 Tbsp (25 to 50 g)	Few grains		3/4 to 1 Tbsp cornstarch (6 to 8 g) Fruit, if desired

*Weights are given for situations where ingredients are being weighed. Metric conversions can be done on the basis of 1 cup equals 236 milliliters and 1 teaspoon equals 5 milliliters.

** All-purpose flour unless cake flour is specified.

†Use the smaller amount with SAS-phosphate powder and the larger amount with tartrate powder.

TABLE OF EQUIVALENTS

Abbreviations and Symbols*

CAPACITY	TEMPERATURE
Bushel (bu)	Degrees Celsius (Centigrade) (°C)
Cubic Centimeter (cc)	Degrees Fahrenheit (°F)
Cup (c)	
Fluid Ounce (fl oz)	LENGTH
Gallon (gal)	Centimeter (cm)
Gill (gi)	Foot (ft)
Liter (l)	Inch (in)
Milliliter (mL)	Meter (m)
Pint (pt)	Millimeter (mm)
Quart (qt)	Millimicron (mμ)
Peck (pk)	
Tablespoon (Tbsp)	WEIGHT
Teaspoon (tsp)	Gram (g)
	Kilogram (kg)
TIME	Microgram (μg)
Hour (hr)	Milligram (mg)
Minute (min)	Ounce (oz)
Second (sec)	Pound (lb)

*Note that abbreviations are used in the singular form regardless of whether the item is singular or plural. For example, 20 g is the abbreviation for 20 grams.

Weight and Volume Equivalents

COMMON UNITS OF WEIGHT

1 gram	=	0.035 ounces
1 kilogram	=	2.21 pounds
1 ounce	=	28.35 grams
1 pound	=	453.59 grams

COMMON UNITS OF VOLUME

1 bushel	=	4 pecks
1 peck	=	8 quarts
1 gallon	=	4 quarts
1 quart	=	2 pints
	=	946.4 milliliters
1 pint	=	2 cups
1 cup	=	16 tablespoons
	=	2 gills
	=	8 fluid ounces
	=	236.6 milliliters
1 tablespoon	=	3 teaspoons
	=	1/2 fluid ounce
	=	14.8 milliliters
1 teaspoon	=	4.9 milliliters
1 liter	=	1000 milliliters
	=	1.06 quarts

Equivalents for One Unit and Fractions of a Unit

TABLESPOON			CUP			PINT		
1 Tbsp	=	3 tsp	1 c	=	16 Tbsp	1 pt	=	2 c
7/8 Tbsp	=	2-1/2 tsp	7/8 c	=	14 Tbsp	7/8 pt	=	1-3/4 c
3/4 Tbsp	=	2-1/4 tsp	3/4 c	=	12 Tbsp	3/4 pt	=	1-1/2 c
2/3 Tbsp	=	2 tsp	2/3 c	=	10-2/3 Tbsp	2/3 pt	=	1-1/3 c
5/8 Tbsp	=	1-7/8 tsp	5/8 c	=	10 Tbsp	5/8 pt	=	1-1/4 c
1/2 Tbsp	=	1-1/2 tsp	1/2 c	=	8 Tbsp	1/2 pt	=	1 c
3/8 Tbsp	=	1-1/8 tsp	3/8 c	=	6 Tbsp	3/8 pt	=	3/4 c
1/3 Tbsp	=	1 tsp	1/3 c	=	5-1/3 Tbsp	1/3 pt	=	2/3 c
1/4 Tbsp	=	3/4 tsp	1/4 c	=	4 Tbsp	1/4 pt	=	1/2 c
			1/8 c	=	2 Tbsp	1/8 pt	=	1/4 c
			1/16 c	=	1 Tbsp	1/16 pt	=	2 Tbsp

QUART			GALLON			POUND		
1 qt	=	2 pt	1 gal	=	4 qt	1 lb	=	16 oz
7/8 qt	=	3-1/2 c	7/8 gal	=	3-1/2 qt	7/8 lb	=	14 oz
3/4 qt	=	3 c	3/4 gal	=	3 qt	3/4 lb	=	12 oz
2/3 qt	=	2-2/3 c	2/3 gal	=	10-2/3 c	2/3 lb	=	10-2/3 oz
5/8 qt	=	2-1/2 c	5/8 gal	=	5 pt	5/8 lb	=	10 oz
1/2 qt	=	1 pt	1/2 gal	=	2 qt	1/2 lb	=	8 oz
3/8 qt	=	1-1/2 c	3/8 gal	=	3 pt	3/8 lb	=	6 oz
1/3 qt	=	1-1/3 c	1/3 gal	=	5-1/3 c	1/3 lb	=	5-1/3 oz
1/4 qt	=	1 c	1/4 gal	=	1 qt	1/4 lb	=	4 oz
1/8 qt	=	1/2 c	1/8 gal	=	1 pt	1/8 lb	=	2 oz
1/16 qt	=	1/4 c	1/16 gal	=	1 c	1/16 lb	=	1 oz

CONVERSION TO METRIC UNITS

Comparison of Avoirdupois and Metric Units of Weight

1 oz = 28.35 g (30 g)* 0.028 kg	1 g = 0.035 oz	1 lb = 0.454 kg	1 kg = 2.205 lb
2 oz = 56.70 g	2 g = 0.07 oz	2 lb = 0.91 kg	2 kg = 4.41 lb
3 oz = 85.05 g	3 g = 0.11 oz	3 lb = 1.36 kg	3 kg = 6.61 lb
4 oz = 113.40 g (125 g) 0.113 kg	4 g = 0.14 oz	4 lb = 1.81 kg	4 kg = 8.82 lb
5 oz = 141.75 g	5 g = 0.18 oz	5 lb = 2.27 kg	5 kg = 11.02 lb
6 oz = 170.10 g	6 g = 0.21 oz	6 lb = 2.72 kg	6 kg = 13.23 lb
7 oz = 198.45 g	7 g = 0.25 oz	7 lb = 3.18 kg	7 kg = 15.43 lb
8 oz = 226.80 g (250 g) 0.227 kg (0.25 kg)	8 g = 0.28 oz	8 lb = 3.63 kg	8 kg = 17.64 lb
9 oz = 255.15 g	9 g = 0.32 oz	9 lb = 4.08 kg	9 kg = 19.84 lb
10 oz = 283.50 g	10 g = 0.35 oz	10 lb = 4.54 kg	10 kg = 22.05 lb
11 oz = 311.85 g	11 g = 0.39 oz	11 lb = 4.99 kg	11 kg = 24.26 lb
12 oz = 340.20 g (375 g) 0.340 kg	12 g = 0.42 oz	12 lb = 5.44 kg	12 kg = 26.46 lb
13 oz = 368.55 g	13 g = 0.46 oz	13 lb = 5.90 kg	13 kg = 28.67 lb
14 oz = 396.90 g	14 g = 0.49 oz	14 lb = 6.35 kg	14 kg = 30.87 lb
15 oz = 425.25 g	15 g = 0.53 oz	15 lb = 6.81 kg	15 kg = 33.08 lb
16 oz = 453.59 g (500 g) 0.454 kg (0.5 kg)	16 g = 0.56 oz	16 lb = 7.26 kg	16 kg = 35.28 lb

*Figures in parentheses indicate common use.

Comparison of U.S. and Metric Units of Liquid Measure

1 fl oz = 29.573 mL	1 qt = 0.946L	1 gal = 3.785L	1 mL = 0.034 fl oz	1L = 1.057 qt	1L = 0.264 gal
2 fl oz = 59.15 mL	2 qt = 1.89L	2 gal = 7.57L	2 mL = 0.07 fl oz	2L = 2.11 qt	2L = 0.53 gal
3 fl oz = 88.72 mL	3 qt = 2.84L	3 gal = 11.36L	3 mL = 0.10 fl oz	3L = 3.17 qt	3L = 0.79 gal
4 fl oz = 118.30 mL	4 qt = 3.79L	4 gal = 15.14L	4 mL = 0.14 fl oz	4L = 4.23 qt	4L = 1.06 gal
5 fl oz = 147.87 mL	5 qt = 4.73L	5 gal = 18.93L	5 mL = 0.17 fl oz	5L = 5.28 qt	5L = 1.32 gal
6 fl oz = 177.44 mL	6 qt = 5.68L	6 gal = 22.71L	6 mL = 0.20 fl oz	6L = 6.34 qt	6L = 1.59 gal
7 fl oz = 207.02 mL	7 qt = 6.62L	7 gal = 26.50L	7 mL = 0.24 fl oz	7L = 7.40 qt	7L = 1.85 gal
8 fl oz = 236.59 mL	8 qt = 7.57L	8 gal = 30.28L	8 mL = 0.27 fl oz	8L = 8.45 qt	8L = 2.11 gal
9 fl oz = 266.16 mL	9 qt = 8.52L	9 gal = 34.07L	9 mL = 0.30 fl oz	9L = 9.51 qt	9L = 2.38 gal
10 fl oz = 295.73 mL	10 qt = 9.46L	10 gal = 37.85L	10 mL = 0.34 fl oz	10L = 10.57 qt	10L = 2.64 gal

TEMPERATURE OF FOOD FOR
CONTROL OF BACTERIA

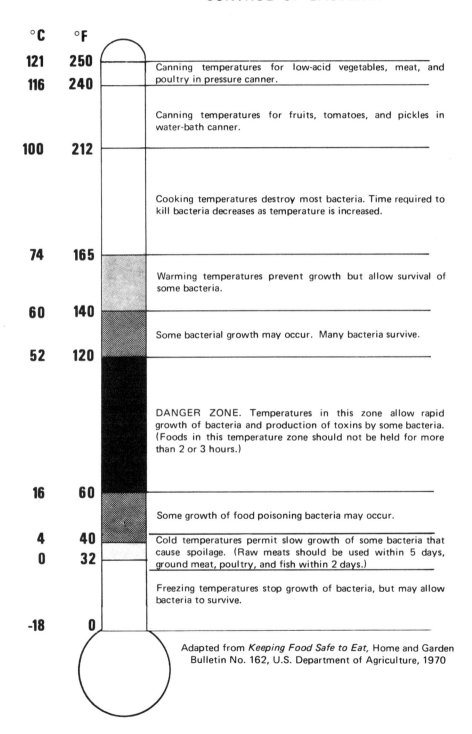

°C	°F	
121	250	Canning temperatures for low-acid vegetables, meat, and poultry in pressure canner.
116	240	
100	212	Canning temperatures for fruits, tomatoes, and pickles in water-bath canner.
		Cooking temperatures destroy most bacteria. Time required to kill bacteria decreases as temperature is increased.
74	165	
60	140	Warming temperatures prevent growth but allow survival of some bacteria.
52	120	Some bacterial growth may occur. Many bacteria survive.
		DANGER ZONE. Temperatures in this zone allow rapid growth of bacteria and production of toxins by some bacteria. (Foods in this temperature zone should not be held for more than 2 or 3 hours.)
16	60	
4	40	Some growth of food poisoning bacteria may occur.
0	32	Cold temperatures permit slow growth of some bacteria that cause spoilage. (Raw meats should be used within 5 days, ground meat, poultry, and fish within 2 days.)
-18	0	Freezing temperatures stop growth of bacteria, but may allow bacteria to survive.

Adapted from *Keeping Food Safe to Eat,* Home and Garden
Bulletin No. 162, U.S. Department of Agriculture, 1970

THICKENING AND GELLING AGENTS

Thickening Agent	Uses and Quantity Required	Precautions in Mixing	Effect of Temperature	Other Factors that Affect Thickening	Characteristics of the Gel
Agar	Salad and dessert jellies: 4 to 6 g (about 2 tsp) per pt of liquid	Soak in 3 to 6 times the weight of cold liquid, then dissolve by bringing to a boil	Gel forms on cooling to 40° C to 45° C (104° F to 113° F); softens at 80° C to 85° C (176° F to 185° F)	Gel strength not easily destroyed by heat or acid	Gel rigid, short, crumbly; transparent; may have weedy odor if sample not highly purified
Egg	Custard puddings and sauces: 2 to 3 medium eggs per pt of milk or 4 to 6 yolks	Blend well with sugar and milk. Coagulate by slow heating	Overcooking causes syneresis (weeping) and curdling	Sugar and dilution raise coagulation temperature; acid lowers it. Use of water instead of milk results in a flocculent precipitate rather than a gel	Baked custard forms firm, continuous clot. Stirred custard is soft, thickened but not set
Flour	Thin soup or sauce: 2 Tbsp (16 g) per pt of liquid. Medium sauces: 4 to 5 Tbsp per pt of liquid. Soufflés, molded pastes: 1/2 c per pt of liquid	Disperse in cold liquid or in fat or mix with sugar before adding hot liquid. Stir while cooking	Heat to 90° C (194° F) or above to obtain maximum thickening. Viscosity increases on cooling	Heating with acid causes thinning. High sugar concentrations retard gelatinization and reduce thickening power	Opaque paste

Waxy rice flour (mochiko, sweet rice flour)	Frozen sauces and gravies: to prevent curdling and liquid separation 4 to 5 Tbsp per pt of liquid. Also prevents gelation of thickened canned products	Same as flour, but waxy rice is less likely to lump	Maximum thickening at 70° C to 80° C (158° F to 176° F); little difference between hot and cold viscosity	Heating with acid and homogenization cause thinning	Does not gel. Forms short opaque paste
Gelatin	Molded desserts and salads: 7 to 12 g (about 1 Tbsp or 1 envelope) per pt of liquid according to grade	Soak in 3 to 6 times the weight of cold liquid, then dissolve by heating to 40° C (104° F) or by adding hot liquid, and then add sugar	Gel forms after a few hours' chilling. Softens at 26.5° C (80° F) and higher	Heating with acid causes reduction of gel strength. Raw pineapple prevents setting because of enzyme action	Gel firm but springy and quivery; transparent in appearance
Gum tragacanth	Salad dressings, sauces: 2 to 3 g per pt of liquid give thin paste; 6 to 8 g per pt give thick gel	Dissolve either in hot or cold water (dissolves much more rapidly in hot)	Little change in viscosity over a wide temperature range	Acid, alkali, or salt plus heat causes thinning	Gel thick and mucilaginous but not rigid even at high concentrations
Irish moss	Puddings, sauces: 4 to 6 g per pt of liquid give a thick paste; 15 to 25 g per pt of liquid give a stiff gel	Soak in cold water, then heat to 60° C (140° F) or above to dissolve	Gel melts at 27° C to 41° C (81° F to 106° F) depending on concentration	Acid plus heat causes thinning. Heat alone has no effect	Gel thick and mucilaginous; becomes rigid only at high concentrations; may have weedy odor if not highly purified

(continued on next page)

THICKENING AND GELLING AGENTS (Continued)

Thickening Agent	Uses and Quantity Required	Precautions in Mixing	Effect of Temperature	Other Factors That Affect Thickening	Characteristics of the Gel
Cornstarch and rice starch	1 Tbsp cornstarch or rice starch = 2 Tbsp flour	Same as flour	Same as flour	Same as flour	Pastes more translucent than flour paste
Potato starch and arrowroot starch	1 Tbsp potato or arrowroot starch = 2 Tbsp flour (See Effect of Temperature column). Suitable for starch-egg mixtures or fruit sauces where higher temperatures are not desired	Same as flour	Reaches maximum thickening at 70° C to 80° C (158° F to 176° F); higher temperature or further heating causes very marked thinning	Same as flour; thinning also brought about by excessive stirring	Pastes very transparent
Waxy cereal starches	Prevent gelation and syneresis of canned products during storage — may be used in combination with flour	Same as flour	Similar to waxy rice flour	Thinned by heating with acid	Waxy starches give somewhat ropy translucent pastes
Tapioca, pearl	About twice as much as quick-cooking tapioca	Soak several hours before cooking	Cook until tapioca is transparent	Same as quick-cooking tapioca	Same as quick-cooking tapioca

| **Tapioca, quick-cooking** | Puddings: 3 Tbsp per pt of liquid
Fruit pie fillings: 1-1/2 to 3 Tbsp for 8- or 9-inch pie
Soup: 1-1/2 to 3 Tbsp per qt of liquid | Mix in cold or hot liquid; no soaking necessary | Bring only to a boil. Mixture thickens as tapioca particles swell and become transparent. It continues to thicken while cooling | Stir while cooking. Over-stirring while cooling tends to disrupt tapioca particles, resulting in a sticky gelatinous mixture | Pastes transparent, non-homogeneous (particles remain distinct). Mixture thickens as it cools. Especially satisfactory for fruit pie fillings |

HYDROGEN ION CONCENTRATION AND pH OF SOME COMMON FOODS

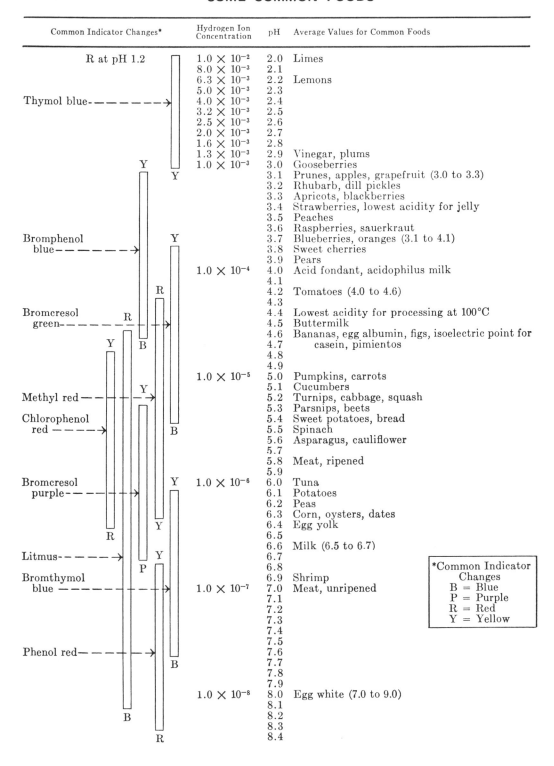

Common Indicator Changes*	Hydrogen Ion Concentration	pH	Average Values for Common Foods
R at pH 1.2	1.0×10^{-2}	2.0	Limes
	8.0×10^{-3}	2.1	
	6.3×10^{-3}	2.2	Lemons
	5.0×10^{-3}	2.3	
Thymol blue	4.0×10^{-3}	2.4	
	3.2×10^{-3}	2.5	
	2.5×10^{-3}	2.6	
	2.0×10^{-3}	2.7	
	1.6×10^{-3}	2.8	
	1.3×10^{-3}	2.9	Vinegar, plums
	1.0×10^{-3}	3.0	Gooseberries
		3.1	Prunes, apples, grapefruit (3.0 to 3.3)
		3.2	Rhubarb, dill pickles
		3.3	Apricots, blackberries
		3.4	Strawberries, lowest acidity for jelly
		3.5	Peaches
		3.6	Raspberries, sauerkraut
Bromphenol blue		3.7	Blueberries, oranges (3.1 to 4.1)
		3.8	Sweet cherries
		3.9	Pears
	1.0×10^{-4}	4.0	Acid fondant, acidophilus milk
		4.1	
		4.2	Tomatoes (4.0 to 4.6)
		4.3	
		4.4	Lowest acidity for processing at 100°C
Bromcresol green		4.5	Buttermilk
		4.6	Bananas, egg albumin, figs, isoelectric point for
		4.7	casein, pimientos
		4.8	
		4.9	
	1.0×10^{-5}	5.0	Pumpkins, carrots
		5.1	Cucumbers
Methyl red		5.2	Turnips, cabbage, squash
		5.3	Parsnips, beets
Chlorophenol red		5.4	Sweet potatoes, bread
		5.5	Spinach
		5.6	Asparagus, cauliflower
		5.7	
		5.8	Meat, ripened
		5.9	
Bromcresol purple	1.0×10^{-6}	6.0	Tuna
		6.1	Potatoes
		6.2	Peas
		6.3	Corn, oysters, dates
		6.4	Egg yolk
		6.5	
		6.6	Milk (6.5 to 6.7)
Litmus		6.7	
		6.8	
Bromthymol blue		6.9	Shrimp
	1.0×10^{-7}	7.0	Meat, unripened
		7.1	
		7.2	
		7.3	
		7.4	
		7.5	
Phenol red		7.6	
		7.7	
		7.8	
		7.9	
	1.0×10^{-8}	8.0	Egg white (7.0 to 9.0)
		8.1	
		8.2	
		8.3	
		8.4	

*Common Indicator Changes
B = Blue
P = Purple
R = Red
Y = Yellow

2

GLOSSARIES

Food Terms

Acid Hydrolysis Chemical reaction of starches, disaccharides, and proteins when heated with acid, producing a cleavage of molecules.

Acidulate To make slightly sour or acid by adding vinegar, lemon juice, or cream of tartar.

Aerated Water Bottled, carbonated water either occurring naturally or processed; artificially charged waters are marketed as soda water, club soda, carbonated water, or seltzer water.

Agglomerate To combine a clump of powdery grains usually for the purpose of preventing lumping when combined with liquid.

Analog Processed textured soy protein made to resemble closely a meat product.

Anthocyanins A group of pigments classified as flavonoids responsible for the red/blue colors found in certain vegetables and fruits. They are red in acid and blue-green in the presence of alkali.

Anthoxanthins A group of pigments classified as flavonoids that are colorless in acid but turn yellow in the presence of alkali.

Antioxidant A substance capable of chemically protecting other substances in foods against oxidation.

Ascorbic Acid (Vitamin C) Available in powder and tablet form, or in mixtures; may be used to prevent darkening of cut or peeled fruits such as apples, bananas, peaches.

Aseptic Canning A process in which food is heated rapidly to destroy food spoilage organisms, then transferred into sterile cans by procedures that prevent the re-entry of microorganisms into the cooked food during the filling and sealing operations.

Astringency A dry, puckery sensation produced in the mouth by certain foods; usually associated with unripe fruit.

Atmospheric Pressure Pressure of atmospheric layer of air which varies depending on altitude and weather conditions and determines boiling point.

Bain-marie Water bath or double boiler used to heat delicate sauces; also used to keep foods warm.

Bake To cook in an oven or oven-type appliance. Covered or uncovered containers may be used. When applied to meats in uncovered containers, method is generally called roasting.

Barbecue To roast slowly on a gridiron or spit, over coals, or under free flame or oven electric unit, usually basting with a highly seasoned sauce. Popularly applied to foods cooked in or served with barbecue sauce.

Baste To moisten meat or other foods while cooking to add flavor and to prevent drying of the surface. The liquid is usually melted fat, meat drippings, fruit juice, sauce, or water.

Batter A mixture of flour and liquid, usually combined with other ingredients, as in baked products. The mixture is of such consistency that it may be stirred with a spoon and is thin enough to pour or drop from a spoon.

Beat To make a mixture smooth by introducing air with a brisk, regular motion that lifts the mixture over and over, or with a rotary motion as with an egg beater or electric mixer.

Blanch (precook) To preheat in boiling water or steam. (1) Process used to inactivate enzymes and shrink some foods for canning, freezing, or drying. Vegetables are blanched in boiling water or steam, and fruits in boiling fruit juice, syrup, water, or steam. (2) Process used to aid in removal of skins from nuts, fruits, and some vegetables.

Bland Mild flavored, not stimulating to the taste; smooth, soft-textured.

Bleaching Agents Chemical agents added to freshly milled flour to provide quickly the baking characteristics that result normally after a period of aging.

Blend To mix thoroughly two or more ingredients.

Bloom In freshly laid eggs, the mucin layer that surrounds the shell, providing a barrier to certain aspects of deterioration. In chocolate, the surface color change caused by warm temperatures.

Boil To cook in water or a liquid consisting mostly of water in which bubbles rise continually and break on the surface. The boiling temperature of water at sea level is 212°F or 100°C. (*See boiling temperatures of water at other altitudes, page 4.*)

Botulism A type of food poisoning (often fatal) caused by toxins produced under anaerobic, low-acid conditions; due to inadequate heat processing.

Braise To cook meat or poultry slowly in a covered utensil in a small amount of liquid or in steam. (Meat may or may not be browned in a small amount of fat before braising.)

Bread To coat with crumbs of bread or other food; or to coat with crumbs, then with diluted slightly beaten egg or evaporated milk, and again with crumbs.

Brine A strong salt solution used in pickling, fermentation, and curing to inhibit growth of certain bacteria and provide flavor.

Broil To cook by direct heat.

Browning Reactions Darkening of some fruit when pared or cut due to oxidation of enzymes. Also specific protein and sugar reactions.

Cake Pan Utensil for baking cake. It may be round, square, or oblong with straight or slightly flared sides. Some have removable bottoms and some a tube in the center. Size is designated by dimensions (to nearest ¼ inch) of top inside.

Candied (1) Fruit, fruit peel, or ginger that is cooked in heavy syrup until plump and translucent, then drained and dried. The product is also known as crystallized fruit, fruit peel, or ginger. (2) Sweet potatoes or carrots, cooked in sugar or syrup. *To candy* a food is to cook it as described above.

Canner (Water bath) A large, covered cooking utensil with side handles and jar holder. Capacity is designated by the volume of water that the canner will hold. The water capacity must assure a 2- to 4-inch coverage above the tops of the jars.

Caramelize To heat sugar or foods containing sugar until a brown color and characteristic flavor develop.

Carotenoids A variety of yellow to red pigments found in fruit and vegetables that are relatively stable to cooking methods.

Casserole A covered utensil in which food may be baked and served. It may have one or two handles. Size is stated in liquid measurements.

Cellulose A polysaccharide found in cell walls of plants, fruit, and vegetables that provides structural rigidity; can be softened by cooking, but is not digested in the human alimentary tract.

Chicken Fryer A deep, covered fry pan or skillet. Lid may have basting rings.

Chlorophyll The green pigment found in vegetables that becomes olive-green when exposed to an acid cooking medium.

Chopped Cut into pieces with a knife or other sharp tool.

Coagulation The change from a fluid state to a thickened curd or clot due to denaturation of protein.

Colloidal Dispersion Combination of small particles and liquid in which the particles are too large to form a true solution and too small to form a coarse suspension; an example of a colloidal dispersion is gelatin and hot water.

Conserve A type of jam that is usually a blend of several fruits and also may contain nuts.

Continuous Phase The dispersion medium in a colloidal system; usually water in food emulsions.

Controlled Atmosphere Long-term storage technique in which temperature and humidity are rigidly controlled and air is replaced by carbon dioxide in order to retard produce respiration; particularly effective with apples.

Convection Oven Oven incorporating forced hot air drafts over foods during baking. May be portable appliance.

Cookie Sheet A flat, rectangular utensil which may be open on one, two, or three sides. Especially designed for baking cookies and biscuits.

Cream To soften a fat such as shortening or butter with a fork or other utensil, either before or while mixing with another food, usually sugar.

Creamed A term applied to foods that are either cooked in or served with a white sauce.

Curdle To effect a change from a smooth liquid to one in which clots float in a watery medium due to precipitation of protein by heat. Curdling may be observed in milk, cream soups and sauces, custards, and cheese dishes.

Cure To preserve beef or pork with a combination of salt or brine, sodium nitrate, seasonings, and sometimes smoking; cured meat develops a characteristic pink/red color as seen in corned beef, pastrami, ham, and hot dogs.

Custard Cups Small, bowl-shaped dishes for oven use. Each contains one serving.

Cut To divide food materials with a knife or scissors.

Cut In To distribute solid fat in dry ingredients by chopping with knives or pastry blender until finely divided.

Dash Less than ⅛ teaspoon of an ingredient, usually a spice.

Deboning A mechanical process in which meat is removed from bones efficiently; some powdered bone is also removed and the resulting meat is used in sausage products.

Dehydration A method of food preservation wherein most of the water from the food is removed, generally by heated air in a mechanical dryer. Foods may be dried in air, in superheated steam, in vacuum, or in inert gas, or by direct application of heat. Heat may be supplied by infra-red, dielectric, and microwave heating methods as well as conventional gas and electric methods. Mechanical driers include drum, vacuum shelf, conveyor belt, spray, rotary cabinet, kiln, tunnel, and tower driers.

Dehydro-Freezing A process for preservation of food which combines dehydration and freezing. Heated air is used to remove about half of the original moisture from the food before the product is frozen. Both weight and bulk in packaging are reduced in the process.

Denaturation The change that occurs in a protein molecule when exposed to conditions that cause it to change its shape while the chain remains intact, thus changing its characteristics. Heat applied to proteins, for example, causes coagulation to occur.

Dextrinization Process of heating dry starch during which the long starch molecule is broken up into smaller units in direct proportion to degree of heating; thickening ability of starch reduced in proportion to degree of dextrination reached.

Dice To cut into small cubes.

Dispersed Phase Element of an emulsion consisting of droplets which are suspended in the continuous phase; also called the discontinuous phase.

Double Boiler Utensil consisting of two saucepans which fit one over the other, allowing for boiling a small amount of water in the lower compartment to heat food placed in the upper compartment; provides gentle, controlled heat as upper compartment never reaches boiling temperature. Useful for heat-sensitive foods.

Double Fry Pan or Omelet Pan Consists of two shallow rectangular or semicircular pans attached by hinges, one acting as a cover for the other. Each pan is equipped with one handle.

Dough Mixture of flour and liquid, usually with other ingredients added. A dough is thick enough to knead or roll, as in making yeast bread and rolls, but is too stiff to stir or pour.

Dredge To cover or coat with flour or other fine substances such as bread crumbs or corn meal.

Drupe Fruit classification based on presence of single seed surrounded by flesh (cherries, apricots, peaches, plums).

Dry Measure Measuring tool with capacity of one cup, ½ cup, ⅓ cup, or ¼ cup (or 250 mL, 125 mL, and 50 mL). Capacity is based on the relation that one cup equals 16 level tablespoons.

Dutch Oven A deep cooking utensil with close-fitting cover. It is sometimes equipped with a trivet or rack, and may be with or without a bail or side handle. Capacity is stated in liquid measurement.

Egg Poacher An insert device with cutouts to hold shallow cups in a covered pan, or a covered pan with such an insert device.

Emulsification A process of breaking up large particles of liquids into smaller ones, which remain suspended in another liquid. Emulsification may be accomplished mechanically, as in the homogenization of ice cream mixtures; chemically with the use of acid and lecithin (from egg yolk) as in emulsification of oil for mayonnaise; or naturally, in body processes, as when bile salts emulsify fats during digestion.

Emulsify To make into an emulsion. When small drops of one liquid are finely dispersed (distributed) in another liquid, an emulsion is formed. The drops are held in suspension by an emulsifying agent, which surrounds each drop to form a coating.

Enzymatic Browning Discoloration found in cut fruit due to reaction of enzymes on exposure to oxygen.

Enzyme Protein substances that serve as organic catalysts in food effecting changes in color, texture, and flavor; inactivated by exposure to heat; activity retarded by refrigeration or freezing.

Fermentation Chemical changes effected by yeast accompanied by production of alcohol and carbon dioxide.

Fill Weight Weight of fruit or vegetable in can as opposed to total weight including liquid.

Flavonoid Group of pigments found in fruit and vegetables that include the anthocyanins, the anthoxanthins, and a group of related phenolic compounds.

Foam A type of colloidal dispersion in which bubbles of gas are surrounded by liquid; specific stability varies.

Fold To combine by using two motions, one which cuts vertically through the mixture, the other which turns over by sliding the implement across the bottom of the mixing bowl.

Food Additives Substances added to a food during its preparation. Sometimes a substance is added to increase the concentration of a substance that may be naturally present in the food, such as the vitamins. Substances are added to protect the food against spoilage, enhance its flavor, improve its nutritive value, or give it some new property. Additives include chemical preservatives, buffers and neutralizers, nutrients, nonnutrient sweeteners, coloring agents, stabilizers, emulsifiers, sequestrants. Some are generally recognized as safe; others are allowed for certain foods under certain conditions and in specified amounts. The Food and Drug Administration issues lists of permissible food additives.

Food Processor A multipurpose electric appliance equipped with four or more interchangeable blades capable of grating, slicing, mincing, chopping, and pureeing, as well as processing pastry and yeast dough.

Food Standards Specifications for certain foods including standards of (1) identity, in which the food is described, frequently with its composition, such as milk fat and moisture content of cheese; (2) quality, in which minimum specifications for such quality factors as tenderness, color, and freedom from defects are given; (3) fill of container; and (4) enriched products to guarantee uniformity of enrichment among brands. Most of these standards are regulated by the Food and Drug Administration, U.S. Department of Health and Human Services. Generally, the U.S. Department of Agriculture promulgates quality standards. *(For sources of information regarding food standards, see page 145.)*

Freeze-Drying A process of preservation wherein food is dried by sublimation (moisture does not go through a liquid stage during its removal). Moisture from fresh food is removed by first freezing and then drying the food under high vacuum conditions so that approximately 2 percent of the original water remains. The freeze-dried product may be stored without refrigeration and is much lighter in weight than the undried product. It is essentially unchanged in volume, and rehydration, therefore, is more rapid and more nearly complete than it is with conventionally dried foods.

Freezing A method of preserving food by chilling it very rapidly at a low temperature (usually −10°F *or* 24°C or below) and maintaining it at a temperature below 0°F *or* −18°C. Freezing is accomplished by direct immersion in a refrigerating medium, such as brine; by indirect contact with a refrigerant, such as conduction through metal plates; or by a blast of cold air. In flash-freezing, food is frozen at very low temperatures in a medium such as liquid nitrogen.

French Fryer An uncovered cooking utensil with a perforated, meshed, or sieve-like insert basket with one handle. Foods are cooked in hot oil.

Fricassee To cook by braising. Usually applied to fowl, rabbit, or veal cut into pieces.

Fry To cook in fat. Applied especially to (1) cooking in a small amount of fat, also called sauté or pan-fry; (2) cooking in a deep layer of fat, also called deep-fat frying.

Fry Pan or Skillet A shallow, covered or uncovered pan with one handle. Size is stated by the top diameter in inches.

Gel A liquid in solid colloidal system that lacks the ability to flow; can be formed by gelatin, pectin, starch, soured milk, and egg.

Gelatinization The absorption of liquid by starch granules accompanied by swelling of the granules and thickening proportional to starch/liquid ratio. Process can proceed while cold, but heat is required to complete the physical change.

Glacé To coat with a thin sugar syrup cooked to the crack stage. When used for pies and certain types of bread, the mixture may contain thickening, but is not cooked to such a concentrated form; or it may be uncooked.

GRAS List List of food additives which were "generally recognized as safe" to use at the time of implementation of the Food Additive Amendment in 1958. The safety of items on this list currently is being tested under the direction of the Food and Drug Administration.

Griddle A very shallow, uncovered, smooth, heavy utensil (occasionally with pouring lip) equipped with one or two handles. Size is stated by top outside dimension.

Grill To cook by direct heat. Also a utensil or appliance used for such cooking.

Grind To reduce to particles by cutting or crushing.

Homogenize To break up into small particles of the same size. Homogenized milk has been passed through an apparatus to break the fat into such small globules that it will not rise to the top as cream. In homogenized shortening, air has been distributed evenly through the fat particles.

Hydrogenation A process in which hydrogen is combined chemically with an unsaturated compound, such as oil, to form solid or semi-solid fat.

Hydrolysis The process of splitting molecules into simpler components effected by acid and heat or by enzymes.

Hydroponics The process of growing plants in nutrient solutions rather than in soil.

Ingredient Labeling System that requires food processors to list on the label ingredients (in descending order of weight) included in all manufactured items not covered by standards of identity.

International Unit (IU) Measure of vitamin content, particularly in milk.

Inversion Chemical change that sucrose undergoes either when heated with acid or combined with the enzyme invertase in which the molecule is split into its components glucose and fructose.

Irradiation A process in which food is exposed to radiation. *(See Radiation.)*

Isoelectric Point Point at which a protein molecule has neither a net positive nor negative charge. Solubility of proteins is rapidly reduced as the pH of the isoelectric point is approached; for example, when the curdling phenomenon in milk is observed.

Jam A sweet preserve in which fruit and sugar are cooked together until a thick paste is formed and fruit becomes a homogeneous mass.

Jelly A gelled clear product that may be either sweet when made from fruit juice or savory when made from meat stock.

Jelly Roll Pan Baking sheet with a rim around the four sides, measuring about 11 x 15 x 1 inches.

Julienne Meat, fruit, or vegetables cut into slivers resembling matchsticks. Also a soup with thin strips of vegetables.

Kettle A covered or uncovered cooking utensil with a vail handle. Capacity is stated in liquid measurement.

Knead To manipulate with a pressing motion accompanied by folding and stretching.

Lactic Acid Bacteria Group of microorganisms which converts lactose to lactic acid; responsible for the souring of milk.

Leavening Agent Air, steam, or a microbiological or chemical agent capable of producing carbon dioxide when activated.

Legumes Seeds formed in pods such as peas and beans; the plant has the ability to fix nitrogen in the soil. Good sources of protein.

Lipases Enzymes capable of splitting fats into simpler components.

Liquid Measure Measuring tool with a capacity of one quart or less and equipped with a pouring lip for liquids. Capacities and subdivisions include quarts, pints, fluid ounces, or cups. Subdivisions are based on the relation that ½ pint equals 1 cup, 236.6 milliliters, or 8 fluid ounces.

Loaf Pan A deep, narrow rectangular pan with slightly slanted sides for oven use.

Lukewarm Approximately 95°F *or* 35°C; tepid. Lukewarm liquids or foods sprinkled on the wrist will not feel warm.

Marinate To let food stand in a marinade which is a liquid, usually an oil-acid mixture such as French dressing.

Mask To cover completely. Usually applied to the use of mayonnaise or other thick sauce, but may also be applied to a flavor used as a mask or camouflage flavor.

Measuring Cups Standard cups designed to measure dry or liquid ingredients. The standard cup equals 8 fluid ounces, or 236.6 milliliters (mL). Sets of measuring cups intended for measuring dry or solid ingredients include ¼-, ⅓-, ½-, and 1-cup sizes, or 250 mL, 125 mL, and 50 mL. The standard cup for measuring liquids may be a 1-cup, 1-pint, or 1-quart, or a 1-liter, 500-mL, or 250-mL size with subdivisions marked on the side of the cup. The weight of a cupful of a specific ingredient depends on its density.

Measuring Spoons A set of individual measures that include the following: 1 tablespoon, 1 teaspoon, ½ teaspoon, ¼ teaspoon (or 25 mL, 10 mL, 5 mL, 2 mL, and 1 mL). Capacity of a measurer is determined by the amount of material it contains after it is leveled with the straight edge of a knife or spatula. The standard teaspoon equals 4.93 milliliters.

Microwave Oven Appliance utilizing microwaves for generating heat within the food. A magnatron tube changes electricity into microwaves at 2450 megahertz. Intermittent rapid interruption of microwave production yields various cooking speeds from defrost through fast. Some models incorporate programmed memory circuits to accommodate a series of commands, and/or utilize pressure-sensitive panels for receiving instructions by the user. Greater efficiency of microwave cooking reduces energy demand.

Mince To cut or chop into very small pieces.

Mix To combine ingredients in any way that effects a distribution.

Monosodium Glutamate A chemical which is added to food to enhance flavor. Its effect on flavor depends on the kinds and amounts of other flavor factors in the food.

Muffin or Cupcake Pan A tray-like utensil consisting of a number of suspended individual cups which are almost straight-sided, and which are an integral part of the pan.

Nutrition Labeling Extensive nutritional information provided on labels of products making a nutritional claim or specifying nutrients added to the product.

Open Roasting and Baking Pan A large rectangular pan especially designed for roasting meats and poultry, and for baking.

Organic Foods Foods claimed to be grown without chemical fertilizers or pesticides. As there is no legal definition of this term, it is impossible to verify where used.

Osmotic Pressure Force that operates when fruit is simmered, directing the passage of water in or out of the cell, depending upon the surrounding liquid. Also occurs when fruits are sugared and allowed to stand or when a dressing has been held on a green salad for many minutes.

Pan-Broil To cook uncovered on a hot surface, usually in a fry pan. Fat is poured off as it accumulates.

Pan-Fry To cook in a small amount of fat. *(See Fry and Sauté.)*

Panning Method of cooking vegetables in their own juices in tightly covered pan. A small amount of fat is used to moisten pan before juices escape.

Parboil To boil until partially cooked. Usually cooking is completed by another method.

Pare To cut off the outside covering.

Pasteurize To preserve food by heating and holding at a specific temperature for a specific length of time sufficient to destroy certain microorganisms and arrest fermentation. Applied to liquids such as milk and fruit juices. Temperatures used vary with foods but commonly range from 140° to 180°F (60° to 83°C).

Peel To strip off the outside covering.

Pickle Method of preserving food employing salt or brine and vinegar.

Pie Pans or Plates Round, open utensils with flared sides, especially designed for baking pies.

Poach To cook in a hot liquid using precautions to retain shape. The temperature used varies with the food.

Pome Fruit classification based on central core and presence of seeds; group includes apples, pears, and quinces.

Pot Roast A chunky piece of meat cooked by braising. *(See Braise.)*

Preserves A fruit spread in which fruit and a high concentration of sugar are cooked together until mixture thickens, but fruit is kept intact.

Pressure Cooker An airtight container for cooking food at a high temperature under steam pressure. It is equipped with a gauge for measuring and indicating the pressure on a graduated dial or with some other device. Pressure cookers are used in canning low-acid foods, for cooking less tender cuts of meat and poultry, and for cooking some vegetables.

Proteolytic Enzymes Enzymes capable of splitting proteins into simpler components. Examples are papain and bromelin.

Radiation The combined processes of emission, transmission, and absorption of radiant energy. Radiation is a method of food preservation in which small doses of ionizing radiation are applied to foods in order to prolong the shelf life of perishable foods, such as fresh seafood. Large dosages of radiations (2 to 5 million rads) destroy microbial growth and sterilize the food. For food preservation applications, alpha and beta particles and gamma rays are radiations available. Quality of the finished product, as well as economic factors, have limited the commercial application of radiation as a means of food preservation.

Rancidity State of spoilage unique to fats in which the flavor and odor deteriorate due either to hydrolysis or oxidation.

Reconstitute To restore concentrated foods such as dry milk or frozen orange juice to their normal state by adding water.

Rehydration To soak, cook, or use other procedures with dehydrated foods to restore water lost during drying.

Render to free fat from animal tissue by heating at low temperatures.

Retrogradation Tendency for gelatinized starch mixtures to form crystalline areas during storage (staling of baked products and starch pastes).

Roast To cook uncovered in hot air. Meat is usually roasted in oven or over coals, ceramic briquettes, gas flame, or electric coils. The term also applies to foods such as corn or potatoes cooked in hot ashes, under coals, or on heated stones or metal.

Roaster A covered pan, with or without a rack. Especially designed for cooking meats and poultry. Length and width are measured overall outside the pan, including handles.

Rotisserie An appliance designed to roast meat or poultry by dry heat on a turning spit.

Salmonellosis Food poisoning resulting from ingestion of salmonellae in improperly cooked or refrigerated pork, poultry, and eggs.

Saucepan A covered or uncovered cooking utensil with one handle. Capacity is stated in liquid measurement.

Sauce Pot A covered or uncovered cooking utensil equipped with two side handles. Capacity is stated in liquid measurement.

Sauté To brown or cook in a small amount of fat. *(See Fry.)*

Scald (1) To heat milk to just below the boiling point, when tiny bubbles form at edge. (2) To dip certain foods in boiling water. *(See Blanch.)*

Scallop To bake food (usually cut in pieces) with a sauce or other liquid. The food and sauce may be mixed together or arranged in alternate layers in a baking dish, with or without a topping of crumbs.

Sear To brown the surface of meat by a short application of intense heat.

Simmer To cook in a liquid just below the boiling point, at temperatures of 185°F to 210°F (85°C to 99°C). Bubbles form slowly and collapse below the surface.

Slow-Cooker Electric appliance which slow-cooks food at either of two low wattage settings, requiring approximately 4 to 12 hours. Process develops seasoning flavors. Due to slow heating, caution is recommended for certain foods prone to bacterial growth at warm temperatures.

Smoke Point Specific point for each fat at which it begins to smoke and emit irritating vapors when heated.

Sol A fluid colloidal systal in which the continuous phase is liquid.

Solution A uniform liquid blend containing a solvent (liquid) and a solute (such as salt) dissolved in the liquid.

Sorbic Acid An antimycotic agent used in foods such as cheese to retard mold growth.

Specific Gravity The weight of a definite volume of a substance in relation to the weight of an equal volume of water. (At 4°C, 1 mL water weighs one gram.)

Specific Heat Heat or thermal capacity of a substance in relation to that of water.

Spring Form Pan A round baking pan with removable sides to facilitate serving.

Standard of Identity Body of manufactured foods whose composition is rigidly specified by the Food and Drug Administration.

Staphylococcal Poisoning Gastrointestinal upsets caused by ingesting toxin produced by staphylococcal organisms in improperly stored or prepared cooked meat, poultry, milk, cream, and cheese dishes.

Steam To cook in steam with or without pressure. The steam may be applied directly to the food, as in a steamer or pressure cooker.

Steam Cooker A covered saucepan or sauce pot having one or more perforated insert pans equipped with a handle or handles.

Steep To allow a substance to stand in liquid below the boiling point for the purpose of extracting flavor, color, or other qualities.

Sterilize To destroy microorganisms. Foods are most often sterilized at high temperature with steam, hot air, or boiling liquid.

Stew To simmer food in a small amount of liquid.

Stir To mix food materials with a circular motion for the purpose of blending or securing uniform consistency.

Stir Fry Cooking method using tossing motions when cooking over high heat, particularly in oriental cuisines when a small amount of fat is used.

Sublimation Processing occurring in freeze-drying in which substance is caused to pass from the solid state (ice) to vapor; process reduces moisture content of the food.

Supersaturated Solution A solution that contains more solute than an unheated liquid could hold at a given temperature; unstable and prone to crystallization.

Surface Active Agents Emulsifying agents that can be added to unstable emulsions to increase stability.

Suspension Combination of powder and liquid that remains combined only so long as agitation is continued. Solid will settle to bottom when undisturbed. Example: starch in cold water.

Syneresis Drainage of liquid from a gel system when cut or disturbed.

Synergists Compounds that enhance the effect on foods far more collectively than each compound could do separately.

Texture Properties of food, including roughness, smoothness, graininess, creaminess, etc.

Textured Vegetable Protein Fabricated meats and meat extenders processed from soy beans providing excellent nutritive qualities and the potential for economy when sufficient volume can be utilized.

Toast To brown by means of dry heat.

Toxins Products of microbiological organisms that have harmful, possibly fatal, effects when ingested.

Tuber Enlarged, fleshy portions of root systems growing underground that can reproduce when the "eyes" are planted.

Unit Pricing System of marking grocery items with price per ounce or pound so that relative costs can be compared quickly.

Universal Product Code Grocery marketing system in which merchandise marked with code in the parallel lines on label is passed over an electronic scanner to facilitate checkout and reduce labor.

Utensils for Baking and Top-of-Range Cooking Inside dimensions (to nearest ¼ inch) of baking utensils are used to designate size. Most utensils are measured from the top inside for length, width, or diameter. In general, capacities are stated in liquid measurements when level-full.

Viscosity A property of fluids that determines whether they flow readily or resist flow. A pure liquid at a given temperature and pressure has a definite viscosity, which usually increases with a decrease in temperature. Sugar syrups, for example, thicken as their temperatures decrease.

Warm A temperature of 105° to 115°F (40° to 46°C) for liquid or food.

Whip To beat rapidly to incorporate air and increase volume. Generally applied to cream, eggs, and gelatin dishes.

International Culinary and Menu Terms

Aebleskiver Danish apple filled pancake fried in special pan; finished product is about two inches in diameter and shaped like a ball.

À la carte Method of ordering from a menu in which each dish is ordered separately and priced separately.

À la king Style of presentation in which food is mixed with a seasoned cream sauce.

À la lyonnaise In the style of Lyon, cooked with onions.

Albedo White inner portion lying under peeling of citrus fruit; source of commercial pectin.

Albóndiga (Spanish) meatball.

Al dente Literally "to the tooth," used in directions for cooking pasta to the slightly underdone stage preferred by Italians.

Almond paste Finely ground blanched almonds used as basis for marzipan candy, in pastry fillings, macaroons, and other desserts.

Anise Licorice-flavored seed used to flavor Italian sausage, the liqueurs anisette and pernod, and a number of baked goods, such as German springerle cookies and anisbrod.

Antipasto (Italian) assorted relishes.

Apéritif (French) mild alcoholic beverage drunk before the meal to stimulate appetite; popular types include vermouth, pale dry sherries, Dubonnet, and Campari.

Arrowroot Starch used for thickening puddings and sauces; prepared from a tropical root.

Aspic Jelly made of beef, veal, chicken, or fish stock that gels naturally because of dissolved gelatin; a cold dish coated with or molded with flavored stock.

Au gratin Sprinkled with crumbs and/or cheese and baked until browned.

Au jus Served with natural juice or gravy.

Baba French yeast cake usually flavored with rum, fruit, or fruit juice.

Baba au rhum Baba soaked in heavy, sweet rum syrup.

Bagel Jewish bread shaped like a doughnut that is boiled then baked; usually served toasted, split, and spread with choice of toppings, such as cream cheese and lox.

Baklava Middle-Eastern multilayered honey-glazed pastry made with filo sheets and a variety of nut fillings.

Bannock (Scotch) round unleavened bread made of barley or wheat flour, oatmeal, and usually cooked on a hot griddle.

Bar-le-duc (French) type of preserve made of berries; frequently made of currants.

Béchamel (French) basic white sauce usually made with milk and sometimes with stock.

Beignet (French) variety of fritters fried in deep fat.

Benedictine One of the oldest French liqueurs developed by the monks in the abbey of Fécamp in Normandy in the 16th century; flavored with aromatic herbs.

Beurre (French) butter.

Bisque (French) thick rich creamy soup made from fish or game.

Blanquette (French) stew of veal, lamb, chicken, sweetbreads, or any white meat, served in a creamy sauce and garnished with onions and mushrooms.

Bleu or au bleu (French) method of quickly cooking fish while still alive to guarantee maximum flavor and freshness; results in curled tail and bluish skin color.

Blini (Russian, Polish) small buckwheat crepe usually served with caviar or sour cream.

Blintz (Jewish) thin crepe with fruit or cheese filling, rolled and sautéed in butter.

Bombe (French) rich elaborate dessert made of ices, whipped cream, custard, and/or fruit frozen in a melon mold.

Borscht (Russian, Polish) thick soup made with a beet base, which may contain other vegetables, meat, and a topping of sour cream.

Bouillabaisse (French) thick hearty soup made from an assortment of fish; originally made in the Mediterranean region of France.

Bouillon (French) broth or clear soup made from various meats, fish, or poultry.

Bouquet garni (French) combination of herbs, usually thyme, bay leaf, and parsley, tied together and used as flavoring.

Bratwurst Mild German sausage, usually light gray in color.

Braunschweiger German smoked liver sausage.

Brie Soft French cheese served at room temperature so that it spreads.

Brioche Rich classic French yeast dough, usually shaped with a topknot.

Brochette (French) skewer.

Bulgur Cracked wheat originating in the Middle East; available as fine, medium, or coarse.

Buñuelos Spanish or Mexican fried doughnut.

Café au lait Beverage composed of equal parts of strong coffee and heated milk poured simultaneously into the cup; served at breakfast in Europe.

Café noir (French) black coffee.

Camembert Soft French cheese usually served at room temperature.

Canapé Toasted, buttered bread spread or topped with appetizers, flavored spreads, etc.

Canneloni (Italian) pasta dish made of squares of dough with meat or cheese fillings, rolled and baked in a sauce; crepes sometimes used instead of pasta.

Cannoli (Italian) cream-filled tubular pastry.

Capers Pickled buds of a Mediterranean shrub used as seasoning.

Capon Castrated male chicken, usually less than 10 months old and weighing from 4 to 8 pounds.

Cappuccino (Italian) After-dinner coffee made from hot milk and espresso coffee, flavored with cinnamon and/or brandy.

Carob Evergreen tree native to Mediterranean countries that produces a sweet pod that is processed to prepare a substance resembling chocolate in flavor; also called St. John's bread.

Cassoulet (French) stew made from dried beans, assorted meats, and sausages.

Caviar True black caviar is the eggs, or roe, of the sturgeon imported from Russia and Iran; red caviar is the roe of salmon.

Challah Braided Jewish Sabbath bread.

Chantilly (French) containing whipped cream.

Chapati Flat bread made from whole wheat baked on a griddle; from India.

Charlotte Refrigerator dessert made with gelatin and whipped cream poured into a mold lined with ladyfingers.

Chartreuse (French) herb-flavored liqueur; also any combination of chopped foods in a mold.

Châteaubriand Thick piece of filet mignon, usually prepared for two and served with bearnaise sauce.

Chestnut Sweet edible nut.

Chick pea Legume also called garbanzo beans, cecis.

Chiffonade (French) vegetables cut into shreds.

Chile con carne Red beans, tomatoes, meat, and chile pepper seasoning; stew characteristic of south-western United States.

Chile rellenos Omelet-type mixture containing green chile peppers stuffed with mild cheese.

Chitterlings (also chittlins) Well-cleaned small intestines of hogs cut in pieces and boiled, then fried and seasoned.

Chives Thin, tubular member of the leek and onion family.

Chorizo Hot Spanish or Mexican sausages.

Chowder Rich soups containing fish or shellfish; sometimes vegetables.

Churros Spanish or Mexican fried doughnuts.

Chutney Spicy-sweet relish originating in India, now popular in England.

Cider Fermented or unfermented apple juice.

Cilantro Pungent herb; also known as Chinese parsley or coriander leaves.

Cognac Brandy produced in the Cognac region of France.

Compote Stewed fruit, often based on dried fruit.

Coq au vin (French) chicken cooked in red wine sauce.

Coupe (French) ice cream dessert, usually served in a tall stemmed glass, similar to a sundae.

Court bouillon (French) well-seasoned stock in which fish or vegetables are poached.

Crème de cassis (French) liqueur flavored with black currants.

Crécy (French) containing carrots or carrot puree.

Crêpes (French) very thin pancakes.

Croissant Sweet crescent shaped roll or pastry.

Croutons Small cubes of toasted bread used to garnish soup or salad.

Curaçao (Dutch) orange-flavored liqueur.

Curry Blend of many spices; originating in India.

Demitasse Small cup of strong black after-dinner coffee.

Du jour "Of the day" used as soup du jour (soup specialty available that day).

Éclair (French) oblong shaped puffed pastry filled with pudding, whipped cream, fish, etc.

En brochette Broiled and served on a skewer.

Enchilada (Mexican) tortilla rolled around meat or cheese filling and covered with sauce.

En gelée In jelly.

En papillote Baked in an oiled paper bag.

Entrée In America the main course; in France the dish served before the main course.

Escargots (French) edible snails.

Espresso (Italian) strong black coffee.

Falafel (Israeli, Middle Eastern) croquettes made from mashed chick peas fried in deep fat.

Feijoada (Brazilian) soup/stew of beans, meat, and rice.

Fettucine (Italian) narrow, flat noodles.

Fettucine ala Romana (Italian) egg noodles served with melted butter and grated cheese.

File Powdered sassafras leaves used in Creole cooking, especially as a flavoring in gumbo.

Filet mignon Steak from the beef fillet.

Fillet Strip of boneless lean meat, fish, or poultry.

Filo (Middle Eastern) paper-thin pastry sheets.

Fines herbs (French) mixture of parsley, tarragon, chives, chervil, and sometimes thyme.

Flambé Served after flaming with brandy or other high proof liqueur.

Flan Baked custard with caramel sauce (also called crème caramel); also open-faced pastry tart with fruit toppings.

Florentine Served in the manner of Florence with spinach or a spinach base.

Foie gras (French) specially fattened goose livers ground to a fine smooth paste and seasoned.

Fondue Bourguignon Small pieces of meat deep fried at the table by each diner.

Fondue Suisse Melted cheese, white wine, and kirsch into which cubes of dry French bread are swirled.

Foo yung Chinese omelet with bean sprouts, meat, fish, etc.

Frittata (Italian) omelet with flavorful filling or topping.

Fritter Batter-dipped foods fried in deep hot fat or sautéed.

Fromage (French) cheese.

Garbanzo (Spanish) chick pea.

Gateau (French) cake.

Gazpacho (Spanish) chilled soup/salad of Spanish origin, also popular in Mexico; composed of finely chopped raw tomatoes, cucumbers, and other vegetables in spiced tomato juice.

Gefilte fish German/Jewish stuffed or chopped fish (also gefullete).

Genoise (French) rich light sponge cake; often used as a base for more elaborate desserts.

Gherkin Small cucumber used in making pickles.

Giblets Poultry liver, heart, gizzard, neck often used in stuffings.

Ginger root Spicy tropical root used for flavoring in many cuisines; available fresh, dried and powdered, candied, pickled, etc.

Ginseng Thick root of plant highly prized in the Orient for its stimulating, refreshing qualities; plant originated in Korea.

Gnocchi (Italian) small, tender dumplings made of potatoes, flour, or semolina.

Goulash (Hungarian) beef stew liberally seasoned with paprika.

Grand Marnier Orange-flavored liqueur with a cognac base; produced in France.

Grècque or a la grècque (French) in the Greek manner made with olive oil and/or rice and served cold; a dish of Greek origin.

Grenadine Sweet reddish syrup made from pomegranate juice used to color and flavor desserts and alcoholic beverages.

Gruyère Swiss cheese made from cow's milk; has smaller holes than regular Swiss and also sharper flavor; one of the cheeses used in classic Swiss fondue.

Guacamole (Mexican) smooth paste of avocado, tomato, onion, and green chiles used as an appetizer and salad dressing.

Gumbo Thick soup/stew characteristic of Creole cooking in Louisiana; also means okra.

Hassenpfeffer (German) spicy rabbit stew.

Hollandaise Thick rich sauce made of egg yolks, butter, and lemon juice.

Hops Dried flowers of a plant used to flavor beer and ale.

Horehound An old-fashioned herb used to flavor candy, cough drops, and beverages.

Hors d'oeuvres Attractive small appetizers.

Huevos (Spanish) eggs.

Imbottite (Italian) stuffed.

Imu Underground oven used for baking pigs, taro, etc.; originated with the Polynesians.

Italian meringue Type of meringue in which a hot syrup is beaten into the egg white foam.

Jardinière or a la jardinière (French) in the garden style; applied to meat and poultry dishes, served with fresh-cooked vegetables that are often diced.

Kahlua (Mexican) coffee-flavored liqueur.

Kasha Russian buckwheat groats; also used in other East European cuisines as a staple.

Kebob or kebab (Middle Eastern) skewered pieces of meat and vegetables roasted over the flames.

Kim chee (Korean) spicy pickled vegetables based on fermented cabbage.

Kippers Split, dried, salted, smoked herring; popular English breakfast food.

Kir (French) apéritif made from white wine and crème de cassis.

Kirsch Colorless brandy made from cherries.

Kuchen (German) cake or coffee cake.

Kolachi or Kolachy (Middle European) yeast bun filled with cheese or preserved fruit.

Kona Fine coffee named after area in Hawaii.

Kugelhopf (German) yeast-raised dough usually baked in a Turk's head mold.

Ladyfinger Fingerlike piece of sponge cake, often used to line molded refrigerator dessert.

Larding Threading narrow strips of fat through uncooked meat with a special implement called a larding needle; process provides juiciness and some tenderness to dry, tough cuts.

Lasagne (Italian) broad noodles layered with meat, cheese, and sauce.

Limpa (Swedish) rye bread flavored with orange rind.

Luau Hawaiian feast.

Lucia buns (Swedish) sweet rolls served on St. Lucia Day, December 13.

Macaroon Small dry pastry or cookie made of egg white, sugar, and flavoring.

Macedoine Mixture of evenly cut fruits or vegetables of different types and colors.

Manicotti (Italian) large tubular noodles stuffed with cheese, meat, or vegetables and served with sauce.

Marinade Seasoned liquid in which food is placed in order either to tenderize or to flavor it (or both).

Marrons (French) chestnuts.

Marrow Fatty soft center in animal bones used in continental dishes for flavor.

Marzipan Confection made of almond paste shaped and colored realistically to resemble fruit, flowers, etc.

Matzos (Jewish) thin flat pieces of unleavened bread eaten during Passover.

Menudo (Mexican) soup/stew made of tripe and green chiles.

Minestrone (Italian) thick vegetable soup.

Mocha type of Arabian coffee; also coffee flavored.

Moussaka (Middle Eastern) layers of eggplant alternated with chopped lamb or beef.

Mousse (French) light delicate dish usually made with gelatin with sweet or savory fillings, depending on the use—sweet for dessert, etc.

Mousseline sauce Made by combining whipped cream with Hollandaise sauce.

Neapolitan ice cream Ice cream prepared in three flavors arranged horizontally in brick form (vanilla, chocolate, and strawberry the usual flavor combinations).

Nesselrode Dessert or sauce made of candied fruit and chestnuts.

Newberg sauce Creamy sauce made of egg yolks, sherry, cream, and either lobster or shrimp.

Nicoise In the style of Nice, meaning use of tomatoes, onions, garlic, and olive oil; salad nicoise contains these ingredients plus anchovies and capers.

Nougat Chewy candy made of honey or sugar syrup and almonds.

Paella (Spanish) classic rice dish combined with various meats, sausage, fish, poultry, and vegetables seasoned and colored with saffron; originated in Barcelona, Valencia.

Panettone (Italian) wine-flavored yeast bread filled with candied fruit, raisins, and nuts.

Panocha Brown sugar fudge.

Pareve (Jewish) in the kosher cuisine, foods that are neither meat nor dairy such as fruits, vegetables, and eggs, and may therefore be eaten with either meat or dairy foods.

Parfait Layered dessert consisting of ice cream, syrups, and sauces, served in tall glass container; also frozen whipped cream mixture.

Parmesan One of the great Italian cheeses used both in cooking and as a topping; a very hard cheese that must be grated.

Pasta All forms of macaroni products.

Pâtè Ground, seasoned meat or meats served with or without pastry covering.

Petits fours Small fancy iced cakes.

Pilaf/pilau (Middle Eastern) browned rice, barley, or cracked wheat variously seasoned.

Pirozhki (Russian) small meat-filled pastries used as appetizers.

Pita Flat bread with a pocket inside that may be stuffed with meat and/or salad.

Plantain Large, starchy tropical banana that becomes edible only when cooked.

Poi (Hawaii and South Pacific) starchy, bland paste made from fermented taro root.

Polenta (Italian) corn meal porridge.

Praline Flat brown sugar candy with pecans.

Purée Cooked, sieved fruit or vegetables.

Quatre-épices (French) mixture of more than four spices and herbs pounded together.

Quiche Lorraine Unsweetened custard and bacon tart often served as a first course.

Ragoût (French) highly seasoned stew made with meat, poultry, or fish, and sometimes vegetables.

Ravioli (Italian) filled pasta dough that is boiled and served with a sauce.

Rennet Substance derived from stomach of calves that contains rennin, the enzyme that coagulates milk; used in cheese industry.

Ricotta (Italian) unripened soft white cheese similar to dry cottage cheese.

Rigatoni Large fluted tubes of Italian pasta, often stuffed and covered with sauce.

Rijsttafel (Indonesian) literally "rice table"; Dutch-Indonesian dinner of rice and an assortment of spicy foods.

Risotto (Italian) wide variety of rice dishes.

Roquefort (French) Blue-veined, pungent cheese; authentic roquefort comes only from a certain area in France and bears the trademark of a small red outline of a sheep on the label.

Roux (French) mixture of butter and flour used to thicken soups, sauces, and gravies.

Saffron Species of crocus whose stamens are used to color and flavor foods; gives a brilliant yellow color to food.

Sashimi (Japanese) raw fish served with dipping sauces, usually an appetizer.

Sauerbraten (German) pot roast of beef that has been marinated several days in spicy vinegar sauce.

Savarin (French) spongelike yeast cake soaked with liqueur, such as rum or kirsch syrup.

Scallions Green onions.

Scampi Delicate shellfish found in the Adriatic, seafood that resembles shrimp; prevalent use of the term on the menu for any shrimp dish is misleading.

Semolina Fine wheat meal used in macaroni products.

Seviche (Spanish) raw pickled fish appetizer served in Spain and Latin America.

Shallot Small, mild member of onion family with delicate, distinctive flavor.

Smorgasbord (Scandinavian) literally "sandwich table"; large assortment of hors d'oeuvres, cold salads, meats, desserts, etc.

Smorrebrod (Danish) open-face sandwiches, tastefully arranged and garnished.

Spumoni (Italian) rich ice cream containing candied fruit and nuts.

Stollen (German) pastry or yeast coffee cake containing dried and candied fruit and nuts; associated with Christmas.

Strudel (Austrian) thin leaves of flaky pastry filled with fruit or cheese based on a stretched dough; characteristic of central Europe.

Subgum In Chinese cuisine, meaning mixture of vegetables.

Suet Firm fat found in the region surrounding the kidneys of cattle; used widely in English and Continental cuisines.

Sukiyaki (Japanese) sautéed beef and vegetables; usually cooked at the table.

Sushi (Japanese) appetizer composed of vinegared rice and raw fish.

Tàble d'hôte (French) in restaurants, a fixed price for all the courses of a meal; opposite of a la carte.

Taco (Mexican) crisp fried tortilla folded around ground meat, lettuce, and cheese filling.

Tahina (Middle Eastern) oily paste prepared by grinding sesame seeds.

Tamale (Mexican) ground corn paste shell wrapped around meat filling.

Tamarind Tart tropical fruit.

Tempura (Japanese) batter dipped, deep-fried food of any type.

Teriyaki (Japanese) soy sauce marinade used to flavor meat and fish.

Tofu Soy bean curd used in oriental cooking.

Tortilla (Mexican) thin unleavened corn cake/bread; in Spain an omelet.

Tostada (Mexican) layered salad composed of tortilla, refried beans, shredded lettuce, ground meat, and grated cheese.

Tripe Stomach of cattle; used in French and other international cuisines.

Truffle Edible fungus that grows underground; highly prized for flavor and used also as garnish.

Vermicelli (Italian) very narrow type of spaghetti.

Vichyssoise (French) cream soup made with leeks and potatoes; usually served cold.

Vinaigrette (French) marinade or salad dressing of oil, vinegar, pepper, and herbs.

Vol-au-vent (French) flaky or puff pastry made into shells.

Weiner schnitzel (Austrian) Vienna style breaded, sauteed veal cutlet.

3

DAIRY PRODUCTS

All dairy products should be made from pasteurized milk and meet local ordinances and state standards as well as federal specifications.

Butter

Butter is made from sweet or sour cream and contains not less than 80 percent milk fat. A lactic acid culture may be added to the cream for a short "ripening" period before the cream is churned to develop desirable aroma and flavors. The addition of coloring* and salt is optional. Butter is packaged in 1-pound, ½-pound, and ¼-pound prints for retail stores and frequently in individual pats for restaurant and institutional use.

Butter that has been officially graded by the U.S. Department of Agriculture for sale on the retail market bears a shield on the package with a letter grade that indicates the quality of the butter at the time of grading. Occasionally the equivalent numerical flavor score of butter is shown under the grade shield. Grades for butter depend on quality factors of flavor, body, texture, color, and salt. The U.S. grade and score relationships are: AA or 93 score, A or 92 score, B or 90 score, and C or 89 score.

A variation is *whipped butter* which, as the name implies, has been stirred or whipped to incorporate air or some inert gas and thereby increase the volume and make the butter easier to spread. Much of the whipped butter sold in this country is unsalted. It is usually sold in 8- and 12-ounce paper containers.

Storage and Use

● To store butter, leave it in its original package and keep it in the food compartment of the refrigerator or in the freezer.

● Place partially used portions of butter in a covered dish, refrigerate, and use up within a few days.

● If butter is to be stored for several months, overwrap it in moisture-vaporproof packaging material and store in the freezer.

● In most recipes that call for butter, other fats may be substituted. Follow this rule: For each cup of butter allow 1 cup margarine or ⅞ to 1 cup hydrogenated fat or lard plus ½ teaspoon salt.

● To measure unwhipped butter, press it firmly into individual measuring cups or spoons and level with the straight edge of a spatula. Or measure butter according to these equivalents: 1 pound = 2 cups = 4 sticks = 32 tablespoons.

Cheese

Cheese comes in many forms and in a wide variety of flavors and textures.† Each one is best when used for its own particular purposes.

---

*The coloring which may be used in butter is annatto, a colorant derived from a plant source.

† Federal standards for minimum milk fat content of total cheese composition differ for different types of cheese. For information on nutrient content, see *Composition of Foods,* Agriculture Handbook No. 8, obtainable from the Superintendent of Documents, Washington, D.C.

Natural Cheese

Natural cheese is made from cow's, sheep's, or goat's milk or cream and is usually cured or aged for a specific period to develop flavor. It is prepared by coagulating milk and separating the curd or solid portion from the whey or watery portion. Natural cheese may be classified by texture or consistency and the degree or kind of ripening. Classifications include:

Very hard cheeses—Parmesan and Romano, bacteria-ripened

Hard cheeses—Cheddar and Swiss, bacteria ripened

Semisoft to hard cheeses—Edam, Colby, and Gouda, bacteria-ripened

Semisoft cheeses—Blue and Roquefort, mold-ripened; Brick and Muenster, bacteria-ripened

Soft cheeses—Brie, Camembert, mold-ripened; Limburger, bacteria-ripened; cottage cheese, cream cheese, farmer's, baker's, and Neufchâtel, unripened

The most common cheese in the United States is Cheddar, which is sold both colored and uncolored (yellow or white). Cheddar cheese is classed for grading according to: fresh or current make, medium cured, and cured or aged. The grades for Cheddar cheese of all ages are based on specifications for flavor, odor, body, texture, finish, appearance, and color with additional specifications applicable to cheese of different ages. The quality rating of cheese is seldom given in the retail market. Swiss cheese is rated for eye formation as well as for flavor, body, and texture.

Cheese Blends

These fall into four classifications:

Process cheese is pasteurized cheese made by blending one or more lots of cheese into a homogeneous mass with the aid of heat, water, and up to 3 percent of an emulsifier such as sodium citrate or disodium phosphate.

Cheese food is a product made from a mixture of one or more varieties of cheese with added milk solids, salt, and up to 3 percent of an emul-

sifier all of which are comminuted and mixed with the aid of heat. The moisture content of a pasteurized cheese food is somewhat higher than that permitted for process cheese; the milk fat content is lower.

Cheese spreads are similar to cheese foods except that a stabilizer is used, moisture content is somewhat higher, and milk fat content is lower. Spreads may be flavored with pimiento, olives, pickles, onion, or other added ingredients.

Coldpack cheese or club cheese is a blend of one or more varieties of natural cheeses prepared without heat and with no emulsifier. Spices or smoke flavoring may be added. Softer in texture than natural cheese, coldpack cheese spreads readily.

Storage and Use

• All cheese keeps best when refrigerated.

• Cottage cheese should be used within a few days after purchase.

• Uncreamed cottage cheese may be frozen in waxed cartons or freezer containers and will keep well for about a month.

• Creamed cottage cheese may freeze satisfactorily but tends to separate when defrosted.

• For full flavor and best texture, most cheeses should be served at room temperature, that is, 20 to 60 minutes after removal from the refrigerator. The exceptions are soft, unripened cheeses such as cottage or cream cheese which should be served chilled unless being used as an ingredient in omelets, casseroles, and other hot dishes.

• Cooking temperatures for cheese should be low to prevent stringiness and toughness. High temperatures cause cheese to become leathery.

• Cheese to be used in casseroles, sauces, or other cooked dishes will melt evenly and quickly if grated or cut into small pieces.

• Cheese that is thoroughly chilled grates or shreds more easily than cheese at room temperature.

Cream

Cream is the fat portion of milk that rises to the surface when milk is allowed to stand. Cream may be separated from milk by centrifugal force.

Fresh, Sweet Cream

Almost all fresh cream on the retail market has been pasteurized. The way in which fresh cream is used depends on the milk fat content.

Light cream is coffee or table cream. It usually has 20 percent milk fat but may contain 18 to 30 percent. Light cream is sometimes homogenized.

Light whipping cream contains 30 to 36 percent milk fat and whips up satisfactorily but does not freeze successfully. This is the form of whipping cream most commonly available.

Homogenized cream is light cream that has been mechanically treated to reduce the size of the fat globules.

Half-and-half is a mixture of milk and cream with 10 to 12 percent milk fat. Half-and-half is usually homogenized.

Heavy cream is heavy whipping cream that contains 36 to 40 percent milk fat.

Pressurized whipped cream is a mixture of cream, sugar, stabilizers, emulsifiers, and a gas-forming substance such as nitrous oxide, packed in aerosol cans under pressure. When the mixture is released through a nozzle, the gas infiltrates the cream and the resulting product is similar to beater-whipped cream. State regulations specify kind of cream and minimum fat content.

Cultured Cream

This is sweet cream that has been ripened (or soured) by the addition of a lactic acid culture and is popularly known as sour cream.

Dairy sour cream must comply with state requirements for minimum milk fat content of light cream (usually 18 to 20 percent). Sour cream is also on the market as salad cream or sour cream dressing.

Half-and-half sour cream consists of a mixture of milk and cream to which a culture has been added. The milk fat content is usually 10 to 12 percent.

Storage and Use

● Cream—whether sweet or sour—should be kept refrigerated at about 40°F until used. Either kind may be stored in its original container.

● Dairy sour cream does not freeze satisfactorily although some prepared dishes made with sour cream can be frozen successfully.

● In cooking, sour cream may be heated at a low temperature with gentle stirring but should not be boiled. Overstirring may cause the cream to thin and curdle.

● Recipes for sour cream sauces or gravies usually call for the cream to be added to other ingredients such as flour or a condensed soup that help prevent separation or curdling. In some recipes, the sour cream is folded into the cooked mixture at serving time.

Milk

Milk generally refers to cow's milk although goat's milk is available in some localities.

Fresh Sweet Milks

Fluid whole milk contains 87 percent water, at least 3.25 percent milk fat (sometimes called butterfat) and at least 8.25 percent nonfat milk solids.

Raw milk is milk in its natural state without treatment other than cooling. Very little, if any, raw milk is on the retail market.

Pasteurized milk is raw milk that has been subjected to temperatures no lower than 145°F for not less than 30 minutes or 161°F for not less than 15 seconds and then promptly cooled to 40°F or lower. (Other high temperatures for short times may also be used.) The U.S. Public Health Service has described standards for Certified and Grade A pasteurized milk. Many cities and states have regulations limiting the permissible bacterial count and milk fat content.

Homogenized milk is pasteurized milk that has been mechanically treated to reduce the size of the milk fat globules. This stabilizes the emulsion; the fat does not rise to form top cream.

Vitamin D milk is whole or skim milk in which the vitamin D content has been increased by a method and to an amount satisfactory to health and nutrition authorities. Content is usually a minimum of 400 IUs per quart.

Fortified or multivitamin milk is sold in some localities. It contains vitamins A and D and usually added amounts of riboflavin, thiamine, and niacin. Some fortified milk also contains iodine.

Skim milk is milk from which most of the fat has been removed. Skim milk usually contains less than 0.5 percent fat. Federal law requires fortification with 2,000 IUs of vitamin A per quart; vitamin D fortification is optional.

Low-fat milk is distinguished from skim milk by the amount of fat that has been removed. According to federal standards, the fat content of low-fat milk may range from 0.5 percent to 2 percent. Retail markets most frequently carry low-fat milk that has 0.5 percent, 1 percent, or 2 percent fat. Federal law requires fortification with 2,000 IUs of vitamin A per quart; vitamin D fortification is optional.

Acidophilus milk (nonfermented) is prepared by the addition of a lactobacillus acidophilus concentrated culture to low-fat milk that has been pasteurized, homogenized, and chilled.

Chocolate milk is whole milk to which sugar and chocolate have been added. If cocoa is substituted for chocolate, the milk is designated as chocolate-flavored. Milk fat for both chocolate and chocolate-flavored milk must be at least 3.25 percent.

Chocolate drink is made from skim milk or milk that contains less milk fat than the legal minimum for pasteurized milk. Flavoring ingredients are the same as those in chocolate milk. If cocoa is substituted for chocolate, the milk is designated as chocolate-flavored drink. Other flavors such as strawberry, coffee, or maple may be used for flavored milks or drinks.

Concentrated milk is fresh, whole milk that has been pasteurized, homogenized, and concentrated by the removal of two-thirds of the water.

Cultured and Soured Milks

Buttermilk is the thick, smooth product that remains when fat is removed from milk or cream, sweet or sour, in the process of churning. It contains at least 8.25 percent milk solids other than fat.

Cultured buttermilk is the soured product obtained by treating pasteurized skim or part skim milk by means of a suitable culture of lactic acid bacteria. It contains at least 8.25 percent milk solids other than fat. This form of buttermilk is generally available on the retail market.

Cultured milk is milk to which a suitable lactic acid culture has been added in the same manner as for cultured buttermilk. The milk fat content is not less than the legal minimum for pasteurized milk.

Sour milk is milk soured naturally or artificially by the action of lactic acid bacteria or artificially by the addition of vinegar or lemon juice.

Clabber is milk that has soured to the stage at which a firm curd has been formed but not to the point of separation of the whey.

Yogurt is a creamy textured product made by fermenting whole or partly skimmed milk with a bacterial culture. Nonfat milk solids and fruits or flavorings may be added.

Canned Milks

Evaporated milk is whole cow's milk from which about 60 percent of the water has been removed under vacuum at temperatures below boiling. It is homogenized to distribute the fat globules uniformly in the milk, and then sealed in cans and sterilized; or the homogenized milk may be sterilized and aseptically canned. According to federal standards, evaporated milk must contain at least 7.5 percent milk fat and not less than 25.5 percent total milk solids. The composition of evaporated milk mixed with an equal volume of water is slightly above the average for fresh milk. Evaporated milk may be fortified with vitamin D. The method used and the amount added must be satisfactory to health and nutrition authorities.

Sweetened condensed milk is the product resulting from the evaporation of about half the water from whole milk and the addition of refined cane and/or corn sugar in amounts sufficient for preservation, usually about 44 percent. According to federal standards, sweetened condensed milk contains at least 8.5 percent milk fat and not less than 28 percent total milk solids. Before the milk is canned, it is first heated and then cooled.

Dry Milks

Dry whole milk (dry milk solids) is the product resulting from removal of water from whole milk. It contains not less than 26 percent milk fat and not more than 4 percent moisture. U.S. grades of dry whole milk are Premium, Extra, and Standard.

Nonfat dry milk is the product resulting from the removal of fat and water from milk. It contains lactose, proteins, minerals, and water-soluble vitamins in the same relative proportions as fresh milk. Nonfat dry milk contains not over 5 percent moisture and 1.5 percent fat by weight. Most nonfat dry milk packaged for consumers is instant nonfat dry milk. This form is processed so as to yield a product consisting of rather coarse, creamy-white, free-flowing particles that dissolve readily in water. Nonfat dry milk is graded Extra and Standard. Both grades of non-fat dry milk are marketed in the instant form.

Storage and Use

• Fresh, sweet milk—like cream—may be stored in its original container and should be refrigerated at 40°F until used.

• Unopened cans of evaporated or sweetened condensed milk may be stored at room temperature.

• In many recipes—as, for example, creamed soups and sauces—evaporated milk may be substituted for other milks. Sweetened condensed milk, however, is not a satisfactory substitute because of the high sugar content that affects flavor and texture.

• Unopened packages or envelopes of dry milk may be stored at room temperature. Once dry milk has been reconstituted, however, it should be refrigerated immediately.

• To measure dry milk, pour from package or spoon lightly into individual measuring cup, heaping to the brim. Level with straight edge of spatula or knife. Shaking the cup to level the powder tends to pack it down and give an inaccurate measure.

• In recipes, dry milk may be added either to dry or liquid ingredients unless the recipe specifically calls for reconstitution.

• Yogurt in recipes should be folded in with the other ingredients and not beaten as beating breaks the texture. If the recipe ingredients include flour or cornstarch, the yogurt may be stabilized if it is first blended with the flour or cornstarch.

• For best flavor, milk for drinking should be served icy cold from the refrigerator.

• Use of acidophilus milk in cooking will destroy the culture.

Frozen Dairy Products

Ice Cream

Ice cream is made from a pasteurized mixture of milk, cream, sugar, stabilizers, flavorings, and sometimes eggs. Coloring may also be added. As the mixture is frozen, it is whipped to approximately 80 to 100 percent of its original volume. The finished product usually weighs about 4.5 pounds per gallon. Most state laws require that ice cream contain not less than 1.6 pounds of food solids per gallon. The milk fat content ranges from 8 to 14 percent, usually 10 to 12 percent for plain ice cream, although some special ice creams may be as high as 20 percent. Federal standards require that plain ice cream contain at least 10 percent milk fat and 20 percent total milk solids by weight. Ice cream with chocolate, nuts, or fruits must contain at least 8 percent milk fat and 16 percent total milk solids.

Ice Milk

Ice milk is a product made in the same manner and with the same ingredients as ice cream but in different proportions. It may be either soft- or hard-frozen. The milk fat content ranges from 2 to about 7 percent, and the total milk solids must be at least 11 percent according to the federal standard. Most states specify both minimum and maximum percentages of milk fat permitted. The size of container in which ice milk can be retailed may also be restricted.

Sherbet

Sherbet is a frozen product made of a pasteurized mixture of sugar; milk solids; stabilizer; food acid; flavorings such as fruit, fruit juices, or extract; and water. Federal standards specify that the milk fat content of sherbet be 1 to 2 percent and the total milk solids content be 2 to 5 percent.

Frozen Yogurt

Frozen yogurt is prepared by adding suitable stabilizers, sweeteners, fruits, and juices to cultured yogurt before freezing. It is whipped to about 60 percent over original volume.

Storage and Use

• Ice creams, ice milks, and sherbets should be stored in tightly closed cartons at 0°F or lower. For long storage the cartons should be wrapped with freezer wrap.

• Ice creams, ice milks, and sherbets that have softened or partly melted and then are refrozen lose volume and become coarse in texture.

• For easy serving, frozen dairy products should be removed from freezer to refrigerator 10 to 20 minutes before serving time.

Whipping Properties

Cream

Whipped cream has a foam that is thick, smooth, and glossy. The cream increases two to three times in volume, depending on the type of beater used and on other factors here listed:

• Cream whips best when cream, bowl, and beater are well chilled to at least 50°F (10°C).

• The more fat in the cream, the more stable the foam when cream is whipped. Fat content should be 20 to 40 percent.

• Cream that has been chilled for 48 hours whips more readily than chilled fresh cream. The two-day aging increases foam volume and stability.

• The addition of 4 to 6 percent nonfat dry milk to fresh cream before it is aged increases stability and smoothness of the foam.

• Pasteurization decreases foam volume and stability slightly.

• Homogenization decreases foam volume and stability considerably.

• Whipped cream should be kept chilled at 50°F (10°C) or below until used. It is likely to show considerable drainage within an hour.

• Whipped cream freezes well, particularly in individual serving portions.

Evaporated Milk

Whipped evaporated milk has a foam that is smooth, thick, and glossy but less stable than the foam of whipped cream unless the milk has been made acid or supplemented with gelatin. Evaporated cream when whipped, increases two to three times in volume, depending on type of beater used. Other factors that affect the whipping properties include the following:

• *Undiluted* evaporated milk will whip if it is first chilled to about 32°F or lower until fine ice crystals form.

• Acid increases the stability of the foam. To increase acidity, allow 2 tablespoons lemon juice or vinegar for each cup of undiluted milk; whip the milk and then fold in the juice.

• The addition of gelatin also stabilizes evaporated milk foam. For a whipped topping, soften ½ teaspoon unflavored gelatin in 2 teaspoons cold water and dissolve in 1 cup scalded evaporated milk. Chill thoroughly (to 32°F) and whip. Sprinkle with ¼ cup confectioner's sugar and whip only until blended.

• Whipped evaporated milk should be kept chilled until served. Topping will hold its foam from 45 minutes to an hour if refrigerated.

Nonfat Dry Milk

The foaming ability of commercial samples of nonfat dry milk varies widely. In general, when whipped as directed, nonfat dry milk about triples in volume. The foam is smooth and fine and remains stable for several hours. Directions are as follows:

• Use ⅓ cup cold water to ½ cup nonfat dry milk. Chill and whip until mixture is thick enough to stand in soft peaks. Add 1 tablespoon lemon juice and continue to whip until stiff peaks will form. Then beat in 2 to 4 tablespoons sugar.

• Whipped nonfat dry milk should be refrigerated and kept chilled until served.

Sour Cream

Sour cream can be whipped. Although it does not attain a high overrun, whipping does lighten the body. It is best to whip sour cream at a temperature above refrigerator temperature.

Note: For imitation dairy products, see **Miscellaneous Foods,** page 110.

4

MEAT

Meat is defined as the edible portion of mammals, chiefly cattle, swine, and sheep. It consists of lean tissue, fatty tissue, and bone. About 75 percent of the lean is water, 20 percent protein, and the remaining 5 percent fat, carbohydrate, and minerals. Muscle proteins include myosin, tropomyosin, and actin, and myoglobin (the pigment protein). Fatty tissue contains not only fat but water and the proteins of collagen and elastin. Fatty tissue is not soluble in water, but it may liquefy with heat.

Meat may be marketed fresh, frozen, freeze-dried, canned, cured, cured and smoked, or dried. Many meat items are available in both raw and cooked forms. The cooked meats require only reheating before they are served.

Types of Meat

Beef

The beef found on the retail market comes from steers, heifers, and cows (cattle over 12 months of age). Steers are males castrated at a very young age; heifers are females that have never borne a calf; cows are females that have had offspring. It also includes meat from bullocks, which are bulls under 24 months of age.

Veal, though not usually thought of as a form of beef, is actually the pale-colored meat from immature cattle, under 3 months of age. Veal contains little fat but a high water content.

Calf is meat from cattle slaughtered at about 3 to 8 months of age. Calf meat has mild flavor,

a large amount of connective tissue, and a darker color than veal.

Baby beef is a term sometimes used for meat from fed steers or heifers slaughtered when under 15 months of age.

Lamb

Usually this meat comes from sheep under 1 year of age. About 90 percent of the meat of sheep is marked as lamb.

Spring lamb refers to meat from young lambs slaughtered between March 1 and October 1.

Yearling mutton usually includes meat from sheep between 1 and 2 years of age, but the age at which lamb becomes yearling mutton is somewhat indefinite.

Mutton is meat from sheep older than 2 years.

Pork

This meat is usually from young swine of either sex under 1 year of age. The swine classifications used on the wholesale market are: *barrows* (young males); *gilts* (young females); *sows* (females that have borne young); *boars* (mature uncastrated males); *stags* (mature castrated males). Whereas most beef, lamb, and veal cuts are sold fresh, much pork is available cured or cured and smoked as well as fresh. Ham and bacon are both pork products. *(See Cured, Smoked, and Dried Meats.)*

Sausage

Seasoned chopped meat may be sold in bulk or as stuffed links with casing of natural or synthetic materials. Trimmings and some of the less popular meat cuts—such as head, jowls, liver, tongue, heart—from pork, beef, and veal may be used in the processing of sausage. More than 200 varieties of sausage are marketed in the United States.

Fresh sausage includes fresh cooked and/or smoked varieties which differ also in texture, seasonings, and meat content. Pork sausages and bratwurst and uncooked sausage meat must be cooked thoroughly before they are eaten.

Cooked sausages are heat processed in manufacturing. Some varieties, such as frankfurters, may require reheating while many are eaten cold without further cooking or heating.

Fermented sausages, usually of European origin, may be named for the town in which they originated. The fermented forms of sausage include semidry and dry or hard varieties which are often smoked and require no further heating. Examples are salami and cervelat. Semidry sausages do not keep so long as fully dry sausages which may be safely refrigerated for a considerable length of time.

Cured, Smoked, and Dried Meats

Curing and drying are among the oldest methods of preserving meats. Salt, sugar, nitrites, and nitrates may all be used in the curing process. Salt acts as the preservative; sugar improves flavor and texture. Today, nitrites are the primary curing ingredient used in meat products. Nitrites develop the characteristic red-pink color of the lean parts of meat, impart a typical cured flavor, and inhibit the development of toxin by Clostridium botulinum, which causes botulism. In the dry-cure method, the curing agents are rubbed over the meat surface. Most meats, however, are cured by injection of a sweet pickle curing solution. Hams and other cured meats are often smoked for added flavor.

Corned beef is a piece of boneless brisket or round that has been cured with a cold brine by a pumping process or diffusion.

Dried beef is meat from the round that has been cured, lightly smoked, and dried.

Bacon is the cured side or belly of pork. It is sold either sliced or in a slab.

Canadian bacon is cured and smoked boneless pork loin, usually from heavy hogs.

Hams are the hind legs of pork that are cured and sometimes smoked. There are cooked and uncooked varieties. Cook-before-eating hams have been heated to an internal temperature of 137°F (58°C). They require thorough cooking before they are eaten and should be cooked to an internal temperature of 160°F (72°C) before they are served. This variety may also be called uncooked, smoked, or regular. *Fully cooked hams* have been processed to an internal temperature of at least 148°F (65°C). To be served hot they should be heated to 140°F (60°C). Heating also improves the flavor. *Country-style hams* have been heavily cured and require soaking or simmering before they are baked. These hams may be cooked in liquid.

Variety Meats

These are the highly nutritious meats obtained from beef, pork, lamb, and veal. They include liver; heart; kidney; tongue; beef tripe (stomach tissue); brains; and beef, lamb, and veal sweetbreads (thymus).

Grades

Beef, veal, pork, lamb, and mutton carcasses may be graded with government grades by the U.S. Department of Agriculture or with a meat packer's brand by the packer. Grading is voluntary.

Federal meat grading and stamping are performed in accordance with standard specifications based on three principal grade factors: conformation, finish, and quality. The grade name enclosed in a shield is imprinted approximately every half inch along the carcass. Designations are as follows:

For beef the U.S. grades are: Prime, Choice, Good, Standard, Commercial, Utility, Cutter, and Canner. The last three are seldom, if ever, offered in retail stores.

Beef carcasses may also be yield graded on the predicted percentage of edible meat. Yield grades range from one to five, with one representing the highest yield, and five representing the lowest.

For **pork** the U.S. grades are: No. 1, No. 2, No. 3, No. 4, and utility. These grades are based on proportions of lean and fat and are used by some states and by some buyers and sellers of hogs or pork carcasses. At present, no federally graded pork is available to consumers.

For **veal, calf, lamb, and yearling mutton** the U.S. grades are: Prime, Choice, Good, Standard (no standard grade for lamb or yearling mutton), Utility, and Cull. There is no Prime Mutton. Class and grade are identified in the grade mark as U.S. Choice Veal.

Inspection

All meat and meat products moving in interstate commerce must be subjected to federal inspection. The round purple stamp "U.S. Inspd and P'S'D" (United States Inspected and Passed) imprinted on each primal (wholesale) cut is used to indicate that the meat is from animals judged wholesome by a government meat inspector and that the plant and processing have met sanitary regulations.

Meat produced and sold within a state must be inspected by state or federal inspectors. If the meat is state inspected, the standards must equal federal requirements.

Storage and Use

● Refrigerate fresh meat uncovered or loosely covered and use within a few days. Temperatures should be as low as possible without actually freezing the meat.

● Store cured meats in their original wrappers in refrigerator and use within a week or two.

● Refrigerate canned hams in unopened cans until ready to use unless label indicates otherwise.

● To keep cooked meats, wrap or place in covered dish and store in the refrigerator.

● For freezer storage beyond 1 or 2 weeks, wrap and seal meats tightly in moisture-vaporproof materials and store at 0°F (−18°C) or lower. Prepackaged meats should be either rewrapped or overwrapped in special freezer paper.

● To thaw frozen meat, keep it wrapped and let stand in the refrigerator. Thawing time will depend on size and thickness of the cut. To hasten the thawing of chops, steaks, cutlets, or other small cuts, seal in waterproof wrapping or watertight container and keep the meat immersed in cold water until defrosted. When using this method, allow an hour thawing time per pound of meat.

Cooking Methods

The length of time required to cook a given cut of meat by any method depends on the composition of the meat, size, weight, and shape of the cut. Timetables offer guides as to approximate time required for meat cuts to reach the desired internal temperature. The cooking times suggested are based on tests that were made with meat taken directly from the refrigerator.

Braising

Dredge meat in seasoned flour. Or omit flour, if desired, and season after browning. Brown meat on all sides in hot fat. Add small amount of liquid (¼ to ½ cup for pot roast). Cover tightly and simmer on top of range or in a 325°F (165°C) (slow) oven. Cooking times for the various cuts of meat are given below:

chops and cutlets (½ to 1 in) . . . . ½ to 1 hr
flank steak, lamb breast, lamb shank,
    boneless cured pork shoulder . 1½ to 2½ hr
lamb, pork, or veal cubes . . . . 1½ to 2 hr
chuck and round steak (1 to 1½ in),
    shortribs, lamb and veal shoulder
    roasts . . . . 2 to 2½ hr
beef cubes (1½ in) . . . . 1½ to 2½ hr
beef roasts and shanks (3 to 5 lb) .2½ to 3½ hr

Cooking in Liquid

Brown meat or not as desired. Season meat and place in deep kettle. Add liquid to cover the meat. Then cover tightly, turn heat low, and simmer (do not boil) until meat is tender.

For stews, roll pieces of meat in flour before browning in hot fat. Corned and smoked meats are not browned before they are cooked in liquid. Cooking times are as follows:

cubed meat for stew (1 to 2 in) . . 1½ to 2½ hr
smoked pork shoulder butt (2 to 3 lb) ..1½ to 2 hr
corn beef brisket (3 lb) . . . . .3 to 4 hr
beef shanks (4 lb). . . . . .3 to 4 hr
beef tongue (fresh or smoked, 3
    to 4 lb) . . . . .3 to 4 hr
smoked picnic shoulder (country
    style, 7 to 8 lb) . . . . .3 to 4 hr

MAXIMUM STORAGE TIME RECOMMENDATION FOR
FRESH, COOKED, PROCESSED MEAT, AND MEAT COMBINATIONS*

Variety	Stored in Refrigerator at 36° to 40°F (2 to 4°C)	Stored in Freezer at 0°F (18°C) or lower
Beef (fresh)	2 to 4 days	6 to 12 months
Veal (fresh)	2 to 4 days	6 to 9 months
Pork (fresh)	2 to 4 days	3 to 6 months
Lamb (fresh)	2 to 4 days	6 to 9 months
Ground beef, veal, and lamb	1 to 2 days	3 to 4 months
Ground pork	1 to 2 days	1 to 3 months
Variety meats	1 to 2 days	3 to 4 months
Luncheon meats	1 week	not recommended
Sausage, fresh pork	1 week	60 days
Sausage, smoked	3 to 7 days	
Sausage, dry and semi-dry (unsliced)	2 to 3 weeks	
Frankfurters	4 to 5 days	1 month
Bacon	5 to 7 days	1 month
Smoked ham, whole	1 week	60 days
Ham slices	3 to 4 days	60 days
Beef, corned	1 week	2 weeks
Leftover cooked meat	4 to 5 days	2 to 3 months
Frozen Combination Foods		
Meat pies (cooked)	—	3 months
Swiss steak (cooked)	—	3 months
Stews (cooked)	—	3 to 4 months
Prepared meat dinners	—	2 to 6 months

*The range in time reflects recommendations for maximum storage time from several authorities. For top quality, fresh meats should be used in 2 or 3 days, ground meat and variety meats should be used in 24 hours.

Broiling

Bacon, steaks, kabobs, patties, ham slices, chops, liver, and kidneys, are suitable for broiling. Trim the outer edge of fat from the meat to within ½ inch to reduce spattering. Slash the remaining fat at intervals to prevent curling. Place meat on rack of broiler pan 2 to 5 inches from heat. (Very thick steaks or chops should be placed farther from the heat and cooked more slowly than thin ones. Otherwise, the outside may char before the inside cooks.) Broil about half the time indicated in timetable. Season. Turn meat and broil for remainder of time. (Be sure broiled veal or fresh pork are thoroughly cooked.)

Large steaks take longer to reach a given stage of doneness than small steaks of the same thickness. Since tastes differ, time will depend in part on degrees of doneness desired. Very thick steaks or chops to be well done may be warmed or partially cooked in a 350°F (175°C) oven and then browned under the broiler. Broiling times are as follows:

bacon .... 4 to 5 min
ground meat patties .... 8 to 15 min
steaks (1 inch thick) .... 10 to 25 min

pork chops (¾ to 1 in thick) . . . . . 20 to 25 min
lamb chops (¾ to 1 in thick) . . . . 12 to 18 min
Canadian bacon . . . . 8 to 10 min
liver (½ in thick) . . . .   12 min
cured ham slices . . . . 12 to 20 min
kabobs . . . .   20 min

To test for doneness, cut a small slit in the lean part of the meat and note the color and texture. Or press the meat lightly with a fork. Very rare meat is soft and pulpy; medium rare is slightly resistant; and well-done meat is quite firm.

Pan-Broiling

Bacon, pork sausage, pork chops, or other fatty meats may be pan-broiled. Place meat in a heavy frying pan. Do not add fat or water. Do not cover. Cook slowly, turning occasionally. Pour off fat as it accumulates. Brown meat on all sides. Season and serve at once.

Pan-Frying

If desired, dredge meat in seasoned flour or crumbs for thorough browning. Flour or crumbs, however, are optional and may be omitted. Melt a small amount of fat in a heavy frying pan. Cook meat slowly, uncovered, over medium heat, turning occasionally until meat is tender. Use times given in broiling guide, pages 57-58.

Roasting

Season if desired. Place roast fat side up on a rack in an uncovered pan. Rib bones in some roasts serve as a rack. Insert meat thermometer. Add no water, no cover. Roast at 325°F (165°C) (slow oven) to the doneness desired. No basting is necessary. Plan to finish cooking 20 to 30 minutes before serving time so that the meat can "rest" and then be carved more easily. *(See timetable below.)*

TIMETABLE FOR ROASTING MEAT AT 325° F (165° C)*

Cut of Meat	Ready-to-Cook Weight	Time Required for Center of Meat to Reach a Given Temperature	
Beef rib roasts	4 to 6 lb	2 to 2-1/2 hrs	140° F (60° C) (rare)
		2-1/2 to 3-1/2 hrs	160° F (70° C) (medium)
		2-3/4 to 4 hrs	170° F (75° C) (well done)
Veal roasts	3 to 5 lb	2 to 3 hrs	170° F (75° C) (well done)
Lamb roasts	3 to 5 lb	2 to 3 hrs	150° F (65° C) (medium)
		2-1/4 to 3-1/4 hrs	180° F (82° C) (well done)
Pork loin roasts	4 to 6 lb	2-1/4 to 3-1/2 hrs	170° F (75° C) (well done)
		3-1/2 to 4 hrs	185° F (85° C) (well done)
Spareribs	3 lb	1-1/2 hrs	
Stuffed pork chops		3/4 to 1 hr	
Cook-before-eating smoked half ham (bone in)	5 to 7 lb	2 to 2-1/2 hrs	160° F (70° C)
Fully cooked smoked half ham (bone in)		1-1/2 to 2 hrs	140° F (60° C)
Smoked pork arm picnic shoulder	6 lb	3-1/2 hrs	170° F (70° C)

*Cooking time is based on meat taken directly from the refrigerator.

NOTE that oven temperature for roasting meat is 325° F (165° C); other temperatures given in chart are internal temperatures as registered on a meat thermometer.

A meat thermometer inserted in the center of the roast is the most accurate test for doneness. Insert the thermometer into the raw meat so that the bulb reaches the thickest part of the lean meat, and does not rest in fat or on bone. When the thermometer registers the desired internal temperature, push the thermometer into the meat a little farther. If temperature drops, continue cooking to correct temperature.

INTERNAL TEMPERATURES FOR PREPARING MEAT AND POULTRY

Meat	Temperature	
	C°	F°
Poultry	88	190
Lamb—well	82	180
Cured pork, fresh pork, veal, beef—well, lamb—medium	75	170
Beef—medium, lamb—rare	70	160
Beef—rare	60	140
Cooked ham	55	130

Cooking Frozen Meats

Defrost in original wrapper and cook according to directions for meat that has not been frozen. Or unwrap the meat and cook from the frozen state, allowing one-half to one-third more time than that required for unfrozen meats.

Cooking Variety Meats

All variety meats may be simmered or braised. Some, such as calves' liver and lamb or veal kidneys, may be broiled. Regardless of the method, variety meats are usually cooked to the well-done stage.

Heart. Prepare the meat by removing large blood vessels and by washing the heart in warm water. Simmer in salted water until tender—3 to 4 hours for beef heart, 2½ to 3 hours for lamb, pork, or veal heart. Or stuff the heart with a savory dressing and braise until tender.

Kidneys. To prepare kidneys, wash in cold water and remove the outer membrane. Cut pork or lamb kidneys in half lengthwise and beef and veal kidneys into pieces. Remove inner fat and tubes. Beef kidney is less tender than pork, lamb, and veal and should be cooked in liquid or braised. The other kidneys are tender enough to be broiled.

Or cook the split kidneys in liquid (usually water), cover pan tightly, and simmer kidneys until tender, about 1 hour. Beef kidneys require 1 to 1½ hours and veal kidneys ¾ to 1 hour.

Liver. Pan-fry or braise according to directions for other meats. Or to broil, dip slices in melted butter or margarine. Do not preheat broiler but place slices on a cold grid, turn broiler on, and cook the slices about three minutes on each side or until the liver loses color.

Sweetbreads and brains. These are usually simmered and then broiled or fried. To prepare sweetbreads and brains, wash them in cold water. For simmering, use enough fresh water to cover, add 1 teaspoon of salt and 1 tablespoon of vinegar or lemon juice for each quart of water. Simmer for 20 minutes. Drain. Remove any membrane. Then dip the meat in melted butter or margarine and broil for 10 to 15 minutes. Or—after simmering and removing membrane—coat with crumbs or flour and pan-fry about 20 minutes until tender and lightly browned.

Tongue. This is a delicacy that may be pickled, smoked, or cured or cooked fresh. To prepare fresh tongue for cooking, scrub thoroughly. Simmer in salted water until tender—about 2 hours for a 1½-pound tongue. (Some recipes call for the addition of bay leaf and peppercorns to the cooking water.) Remove the skin and cut away the roots before slicing tongue to serve. Tongue may be served hot or cold or reheated, whole or sliced, in a spicy sauce.

Note: For textured vegetable protein products made to resemble meats, see **Miscellaneous Foods,** page 112.

IDENTIFICATION OF MEAT CUTS

Location and bone of retail cuts of meat are often clues to the identification.

Location	Beef	Veal	Lamb	Pork
Breast	brisket short ribs short plate	breast foreshank riblets	breast riblets brisket	spareribs bacon salt pork

Shoulder
(chuck)
	arm steaks
	arm roasts
	blade steaks
	blade roasts
		arm steaks
		arm roasts
		blade steaks
		blade roasts
		neck
		shoulder
			arm and
			  blade chops
			shoulder roasts
			shoulder
			  boneless
				picnic
				  shoulder
				arm steaks
				Boston shoulder roast
				hocks
				Boston shoulder blade
				  steaks
				  roast

Rib (hotel)
rack
	steaks and
	  roasts
		chops and
		  roasts
		crown roast
			chops and
			  roasts
			crown roast
				blade chops and
				  roasts
				Canadian-
				  style bacon

loin	steaks and
	  roasts
	T-bone
	porterhouse
	filet mignon
	top loin
		chops and
		  roasts
			chops and
			  roasts
				chops and
				  roasts
				tenderloin

Sirloin
(hip)
	sirloin steak
	  (pin bone,
	  flat bone,
	  wedge bone)
	top sirloin steak
		steaks and
		  roasts
			chops and
			  roasts
				chops and
				  roasts

Leg, ham,
round
	round steak and
	  roasts
	rump
	round tip
	top (inside)
	  round
	bottom (outside)
	  round
		leg (round)
		  steaks and
		  roasts
		rump
		cutlets
			leg steaks
			  (chops) and
			  roasts
				leg (ham)
				  steaks and
				  roasts
				(fresh and
				  smoked)

5

FISH AND SHELLFISH

Nutritive Value of Fish

Fish is one of our most delicious and nutritious foods. An excellent source of high-quality proteins, minerals, and vitamins so necessary for good nutrition, it should play an important role in meal planning. Fish is included in the "Daily Food Guide" along with meat, poultry, and cheese, which provide high-quality protein essential for growth and repair of body tissue. The protein in fish contains little or no connective tissue, and therefore is very easily digested and assimilated by the body. This fact makes it especially valuable in diets for children, older people, and convalescents.

Vitamin Content

Fishery products contain useful amounts of the B complex vitamins, which include thiamine, riboflavin, niacin, vitamin B_6, vitamin B_{12}, and pantothenic acid. These are the vitamins valuable in maintaining the health of nerve tissues and for the normal operations of the energy-yielding processes of the body.

Mineral Content

Minerals are essential for certain functions of the body, particularly the maintenance of sound teeth and bones. Fish is a good source of calcium, iron, potassium, phosphorus, copper, iodine, manganese, cobalt, and other trace minerals. The flesh of both saltwater and freshwater fish is quite low in sodium content, making it particularly adaptable for low-sodium diets.

Fat Content

Of interest to weight-watchers is the fact that fish is high in protein but low in calories. The fat content of the different species varies widely; it may be less than 1 percent for fish of the cod family or as much as 20 to 25 percent for salmon or mackerel. When fish is cooked by means other than frying, and served without the addition of rich sauces, it tends to be calorie-shy.

Market Forms of Fresh and Frozen Fish

There are over 200 commercial species of fish and shellfish marketed in the United States today. When you are looking for variety, fishery products give you more choice than any other food group. You can buy fish fresh, frozen, canned, dried, salted, smoked, and in many convenience forms as well.

Fresh and frozen fish are marketed in various forms or cuts. Knowing these forms and their special uses is important in buying fish. The following are the best known market forms:

Whole or round are fish as they come from the water. Before cooking, the fish must be scaled and eviscerated and usually the head, tail, and fins are removed. The fish may then be cooked whole, filleted, or cut into steaks or chunks.

Dressed or pan-dressed are fish with scales and entrails removed, and usually the head, tail, and fins removed. The fish may then be cooked whole, filleted, or cut into steaks or chunks. The smaller size fish are called *pan-dressed* and are ready to cook as purchased.

Fillets are the sides of the fish cut lengthwise away from the backbone. They are ready to cook as purchased.

> Single fillets are cut from one side of a fish; the type most generally available on the market, they may or may not be skinless.

> Butterfly fillets are two sides of the fish cut lengthwise away from the backbone and held together by the uncut flesh and skin of the belly.

Steaks are cross-section slices from large dressed fish cut ⅝ to 1 inch thick. A cross section of the backbone is the only bone in a steak. They are ready to cook as purchased.

Chunks are cross sections of large dressed fish. A cross section of the backbone is the only bone in a chunk. They are ready to cook as purchased.

Raw breaded fish portions are cut from frozen fish blocks, coated with a batter, breaded, packaged, and frozen. Weighing more than 1½ ounces, they are at least ⅜ inch thick and must contain not less than 75 percent fish. They are ready to cook as purchased.

Fried fish portions are cut from frozen fish blocks, coated with a batter, breaded, partially cooked, packaged, and frozen. Weighing more than 1½ ounces, they are at least ⅜ inch thick and must contain not less than 65 percent fish. They are ready to heat and serve as purchased.

Fried fish sticks are cut from frozen fish blocks, coated with a batter, breaded, partially cooked, packaged, and frozen. Weighing up to 1½ ounces and at least ⅜ inch thick, they must contain not less than 60 percent fish. They are ready to heat and serve as purchased.

How Much To Buy

The amount of fish to buy per serving varies with the recipe to be used, the size of the serving, and the amount of bone in the fish. Count about 3 ounces of cooked, boneless fish as a serving—a little less for small children and a little more for adolescent boys and men.

The following list can help you decide how much fish to buy per serving:

Whole	¾ pound
Dressed or pan-dressed	½ pound
Fillets or steaks	⅓ pound
Portions	⅓ pound
Sticks	¼ pound
Canned	⅙ pound

Fish may be purchased fresh, frozen, and canned.

Fresh Fish

Fresh, whole, or dressed fish have the following characteristics:

• Flesh is firm, not separating from the bones; indicates fish are fresh and have been handled carefully.

• Odor is fresh and mild. A fish just taken from the water has practically no "fish" odor. The fishy odor becomes more pronounced with passage of time, but it should not be disagreeably strong when the fish are bought.

• Eyes are bright, clear, and full. The eyes of fresh fish are bright and transparent and often protrude; as the fish becomes stale, the eyes become cloudy, often turn pink, and become sunken.

• Gills are red and free from slime. The color gradually fades with age to a light pink, then gray, and finally brownish or greenish.

• Skin is shiny, with color unfaded. When first taken from the water, most fish have an iridescent appearance. Each species has its characteristic markings and colors, which fade and become less pronounced as the fish loses freshness.

Fresh fillets, steaks, and chunks have the following characteristics:

• Flesh is fresh-cut in appearance. It should be firm in texture without traces of browning or drying around the edges.

• Odor is fresh and mild.

• Wrapping of fillets, steaks, or chunks should be of moisture-vaporproof material, with little or no air space between the fish and the wrapping.

Frozen Fish

Fishery products that are sold in the frozen form are usually packed during seasons of abundance and held in cold storage until ready for distribution. Thus, the consumer is given the opportunity to select different species of fish throughout the year. High-quality frozen fish that are properly processed, packaged, and held at 0°F *or* −18°C or below will remain in good condition for relatively long periods of time. Frozen fish may be purchased by the pound in any of the following market forms: whole dressed, steaks, fillets, chunks, portions, and sticks.

Frozen fish of good quality have the following characteristics:

• Flesh   Should be solidly frozen when bought. The flesh should have no discoloration or freezer burn. Virtually all deterioration in quality is prevented when fish are properly held in the frozen state. Frozen fish that have been thawed and then refrozen are poorer in quality.

Odor   Frozen fish should have little or no odor. A strong fish odor means poor quality.

• Wrapping   Most frozen fish fillets, steaks, chunks, portions, and sticks are wrapped either individually or in packages of various weights. The wrapping should be of moisture-vaporproof material. There should be little or no air space between the fish and the wrapping.

Canned Fish

Canned fish includes salmon, tuna, Maine sardines, and mackerel, the ones most commonly sold.

Salmon, canned on the Pacific coast, is usually sold by the name of the species. These differ in color, texture, and flavor. The higher priced varieties are deeper red in color and have a higher oil content than the less costly kinds. Salmon are graded in descending order as red or sockeye; chinook or king; medium red, coho, or silver salmon; pink salmon; and chum or keta.

Tuna canned in the United States is produced from six species of tuna. Albacore, a lighter meat than the others, is the only tuna to be labeled white-meat tuna. The other species, yellowfin, blackfin, bluefin, and skipjack, are labeled light-meat tuna. Fancy or solid pack tuna usually contains three or four large pieces packed in oil or water. Chunk, flaked, and grated-style packs contain mechanically sized pieces packed in oil or water.

Maine sardines are small immature sea herring

that are packed in oil, mustard, or tomato sauce. They are canned in Maine.

Mackerel, processed in California, is Jack or Pacific mackerel, packed in brine or tomato sauce.

Cured fish are either salted or smoked and include salt herring, salmon, and salmon eggs, smoked chubs, sablefish, sturgeon, and whitefish. Lox is a mildly cured salmon.

Storing and Thawing Fish

Fresh fishery products should be placed in the refrigerator, in their original wrapper, immediately after they are received. A storage temperature of 35° to 40°F (04°C) is needed to maintain the quality of the products. Do not hold fresh fish in the refrigerator longer than a day or two before cooking.

Frozen fishery products should be placed in the freezer in their original moisture-vaporproof wrapper immediately after purchase unless the fish is to be thawed for cooking. A storage temperature of 0°F *or* −18°C or lower is needed to maintain the quality of frozen products. At a temperature above 0°F *or* −18°C chemical changes cause the fish to lose color, flavor, texture, and nutritive value. Do not hold raw frozen fishery products in the freezer longer than 6 months.

In thawing fish take into consideration the following:

• Schedule thawing so that the fish will be cooked soon after it is thawed. Do not hold thawed fish longer than a day before cooking.

• Place the individual packages in the refrigerator to thaw. Allow 24 hours for thawing a 1-pound package.

• If quicker thawing is necessary, place the individual packages in cold water to thaw. Allow 1 hour or longer for thawing a 1-pound package.

• Do not thaw fish at room temperature or in warm water.

• Do not refreeze.

• Fish portions and sticks should not be thawed before cooking.

(*Continued on page 66*)

TIMETABLE FOR COOKING FISH

Method of Cooking	Market Form	Amount for 6	Cooking Temperature	Approximate Cooking Time (minutes)
Baking	Dressed	3 pounds	350° F or 175° C	45 to 60
	Pan-dressed	3 pounds	350° F	25 to 30
	Fillets or steaks	2 pounds	350° F	20 to 25
	Frozen fried fish portions	12 portions (2½ to 3 ounces each)	400° F or 205° C	15 to 20
	Frozen fried fish sticks	24 sticks (¾ to 1¼ ounces each)	400° F	15 to 20
Broiling	Pan-dressed	3 pounds		10 to 16 (turning once)
	Fillets or steaks	2 pounds		10 to 15
	Frozen fried fish portions	12 portions (2½ to 3 ounces each)		10 to 15
	Frozen fried fish sticks	24 sticks (¾ to 1¼ ounces each)		10 to 15
Charcoal Broiling	Pan-dressed	3 pounds	Moderate	10 to 16 (turning once)
	Fillets or steaks	2 pounds	Moderate	10 to 16 (turning once)
	Frozen fried fish portions	12 portions (2½ to 3 ounces each)	Moderate	8 to 10 (turning once)
	Frozen fried fish sticks	24 sticks (¾ to 1¼ ounces each)	Moderate	8 to 10 (turning once)
Deep-Fat Frying	Pan-dressed	3 pounds	350° F	3 to 5
	Fillets or steaks	2 pounds	350° F	3 to 5
	Frozen raw breaded fish portions	12 portions (2½ to 3 ounces each)	350° F	3 to 5

Method		Amount	Temperature	Time (minutes)
Oven-Frying	Pan-dressed	3 pounds	500° F or 260° C	15 to 20
	Fillets or steaks	2 pounds	500° F	10 to 15
Pan-Frying	Pan-dressed	3 pounds	Moderate	8 to 10 (turning once)
	Fillets or steaks	2 pounds	Moderate	8 to 10 (turning once)
	Frozen raw breaded or frozen fried fish portions	12 portions (2½ to 3 ounces each)	Moderate	8 to 10 (turning once)
	Frozen fried fish sticks	24 sticks (¾ to 1¼ ounces each)	Moderate	8 to 10 (turning once)
Poaching	Fillets or steaks	2 pounds	Simmer	5 to 10
Steaming	Fillets or steaks	1½ pounds	Boil	5 to 10

TIMETABLE FOR BAKING OR BROILING SHELLFISH

Type of Fish or Seafood	Approximate Weight or Number for 6	Baking		Broiling
		Temperature	Time	
Clams				
Live	36 clams	450°F or 230°C	10 to 15 min	4 to 5 min
Shucked	2 lbs	350°F or 175°C	8 to 10 min	4 to 5 min
Crabs				
King	4 lbs	350°F	8 to 10 min	—
Lobsters				
Live	6 lbs	400°F or 205°C	20 to 25 min	12 to 15 min
Oysters				
Live	36 oysters	450°F	10 to 15 min	4 to 5 min
Shucked	2 lbs	350°F	8 to 10 min	4 to 5 min
Scallops				
Shucked	2 lbs	350°F	20 to 25 min	6 to 8 min
Shrimp, headless	2 lbs	350°F	20 to 25 min	8 to 10 min
Spiny lobster tails	2 lbs	350°F	20 to 25 min	10 to 15 min

• Frozen fillets and steaks may be cooked without thawing if additional cooking time is allowed. Fillets or steaks to be breaded or stuffed should be thawed.

How To Cook Fish

Fish are delicious if cooked properly. We cook fish to develop their flavor, to soften the small amount of connective tissue present, and to make the protein easier to digest. Cooking fish at too high a temperature or for too long a time toughens them, dries them out, and destroys their fine flavor.

Raw fish have a watery, translucent look. During the cooking process the watery juices become milky colored, giving the flesh an opaque, whitish tint. This color change is unmistakable. When the flesh has taken on this opaque whitish tint to the center of the thickest part, fish are completely cooked. At this point the flesh will easily separate into flakes, and if there are bones present, the flesh will come away from them readily.

Most cooked fish tend to break up easily, so handle fish as little and as gently as possible during and after cooking to preserve their appearance.

Baking

Baking is a form of dry heat cooking and one of the easiest ways to cook fish. Bake in moderate oven at 350°F (175°C) on a well-greased baking dish to maintain the delicate flavor in the fish and to keep the fish tender and palatable. Fish not baked in a sauce or with a topping are basted with melted fat or oil to keep the surface moist.

Fish may be baked in the frozen state provided the cooking time is increased to allow time for thawing during the baking process and provided the recipe does not call for special handling such as stuffing or rolling.

Broiling

Broiling is a dry heat method of cookery but in broiling the heat is direct, intense, and comes from only one source. Choose pan-dressed fish, fillets, or steaks that are at least one inch thick. Baste fish well with melted fat or oil or a basting sauce before placing them under the broiler. Baste again while broiling to keep the fish moist. The length of time it takes to broil fish depends upon the thickness and the distance they are placed from the heat. As a general guide have the surface of the fish about 3 to 4 inches from source of heat and place thicker cuts farther from the heat than thin ones.

Deep-Fat Frying

Deep-fat frying is a term applied to cooking in a deep layer of fat. Use only very small fish or fillets. Dip into seasoned milk or beaten egg and then into crumbs, cornmeal, or batter. Place a single layer in a wire frying basket. In a deep fryer, heat enough vegetable oil to float the fish but do not fill the fryer more than half full. Heat to 350°F (175°C). Lower basket with fish gently into fryer to prevent excess bubbling and fry fish until it is brown and tender. Drain on absorbent paper.

Pan-Frying

Pan-frying is a term applied to cooking in a small amount of fat in a fry pan. Of all the ways of cooking fish, pan-frying is probably the most frequently used—and most frequently abused—method. When well controlled, it is an excellent way of cooking pan-dressed fish, fillets, and steaks.

Dip the fish in a liquid and then coat them with a breading. Heat about ⅛ inch of fat in the bottom of a heavy fry pan. Place one layer of breaded fish in the hot fat, taking care not to overload the pan and thus cool the fat. Fry until brown on one side, then turn and brown the other side. Cooking time will vary with the thickness of the fish. In general, allow about 8 to 10 minutes.

Oven-Frying

Oven-frying is not actually a true frying method. It is a hot-oven method that simulates fried fish.

For oven-frying, the fish are cut into serving-size portions, dipped in salted milk, and coated with toasted, fine, dry crumbs. The fish are then placed on a shallow, well greased baking pan. A little melted fat or oil is poured over the fish, and they are baked in an extremely hot oven (500°F or 260°C). Nice features of oven-frying are that the fish don't require turning, basting, or careful watching, and the cooking time is short, usually 10 to 15 minutes. The crumb coating and the high temperature prevent the escape of flavorful juices and give an attractive brown crust.

Poaching

Poaching is a method of cooking in a simmering liquid. The fish are placed in a single layer in a shallow, wide pan, such as a large fry pan, and barely covered with liquid. The liquid used in poaching may be lightly salted water, water seasoned with spices and herbs, milk, or a mixture of white wine and water, to name just a few. Simmer the fish in the liquid in a covered pan just until the fish flakes easily, usually 5 to 10 minutes. The liquid is often reduced and thickened to make a sauce for the fish.

Steaming

Steaming is a method of cooking fish by means of the steam generated from boiling water. When cooked over moisture in a tightly covered pan, the fish retain their natural juices and flavors. A steam cooker is ideal, but any deep pan with a tight cover is satisfactory. If a steaming rack is not available, anything may be used that prevents the fish from touching the water. The water used for steaming may be plain, or seasoned with various spices, herbs, or wine. When the water boils rapidly, the fish are placed on the rack, the pan is covered tightly, and the fish are steamed for 5 to 10 minutes, or until they flake easily when tested with a fork. Steamed fish may be served the same as poached fish.

Charcoal Broiling

Charcoal broiling is a dry heat method of cooking over hot coals. Fish, because they cook so quickly, are a natural for this method of cookery.

Pan-dressed fish, fillets, and steaks are all suitable for charcoal broiling. If frozen, the fish should be thawed in advance. Because fish flake easily as their cooking nears completion, use of a well-greased, long-handled, hinged wire grill is recommended.

Since charcoal broiling is a dry heat cooking method, thicker cuts of fish are preferable as they tend to dry out less during the process than thin ones. Also, to ensure serving juicy and flavorful fish, use a sauce that contains some fat and baste them generously before and while cooking.

Fish are usually cooked about 4 inches from moderately hot coals for 10 to 20 minutes, depending on the thickness of the fish.

Inspection and Grading

Inspection and grading of fish and fishery products are voluntary services that the U.S. Department of Commerce makes available to the seafood industry on a fee-for-service basis. Labels of fishery products that meet federal standards then may carry U.S. grade and inspection marks with the grade of the product and a statement that the product was packed under federal inspection.

Quality grades include Grade A fishery products, which are top or best quality, uniform in size, practically free from blemishes or defects, and of good flavor; Grade B, which is good quality but not so uniform in size nor free from blemishes and defects as the top grade; and Grade C, which is fairly good quality, considered wholesome and nutritious, but may not be so attractive in appearance as the other grades.

The U.S. Department of Commerce has issued standards for many frozen precooked and raw breaded fishery products to establish minimum percentages of flesh content. The chart on the following page lists the minimum percent flesh for breaded fishery products bearing the USDC Grade A and inspection marks.

MINIMUM PERCENT FLESH FOR BREADED FISHERY PRODUCTS BEARING USDC INSPECTION MARKS

Products	USDC Grade Mark Min. Percent Flesh by Weight	USDC Inspection Mark Min. Percent Flesh by Weight
Fish Fillets		
Raw Breaded Fillets	—*	50%
Precooked Breaded Fillets	—	50%
Precooked Crispy/Crunchy Fillets	—	50%
Fish Portions		
Raw Breaded Fish Portions	75%	50%
Precooked Breaded Fish Portions	65%	50%
Precooked Battered Fish Portions	—	40%
Fish Sticks		
Raw Breaded Fish Sticks	72%	50%
Precooked Breaded Fish Sticks	60%	50%
Precooked Battered Fish Sticks	—	40%
Scallops		
Raw Breaded Scallops	50%	50%
Precooked Breaded Scallops	50%	50%
Precooked Crispy/Crunchy Scallops	—	50%
Precooked Battered Scallops	—	40%
Shrimp		
Lightly Breaded Shrimp**	65%	65%
Raw Breaded Shrimp**	50%	50%
Battered Shrimp	—	40%
Imitation Breaded Shrimp***	—	No min. Encouraged to put percent on label
Miscellaneous		
Fish & Seafood Cakes	—	35%

* Means no USDC grading standard currently exists.

** FDA standards of identity require that any product, USDC inspected or not, labeled breaded shrimp must contain a minimum of 50% shrimp flesh by weight and if labeled lightly breaded must contain not less than 65% shrimp flesh.

***FDA standard of identity requires that any breaded shrimp product containing less than 50% shrimp flesh by weight, USDC inspected or not, must be labeled imitation shrimp.

6

POULTRY AND EGGS

Poultry

Poultry is marketed in ready-to-cook or ready-to-eat form. This may be as whole birds or parts, either chilled or frozen, or as frozen boneless chicken and turkey rolls. Many prepared food products such as chicken chow mein or chicken noodle casserole include poultry meat as an ingredient and are available frozen or canned. Freeze-dried poultry also is available and its weight is slightly more than doubled upon rehydration.

Federal Poultry Programs

All slaughtered poultry moving in interstate commerce is inspected for wholesomeness. This requires an examination of the bird, inside and out, by an official inspector. Poultry may also be graded for quality through a voluntary program. Officially inspected and graded poultry is prepared in processing plants that meet U.S. Department of Agriculture sanitary requirements. The grade mark (a shield carrying the grade letter A, B, or C) and the inspection mark (a circle stating "Inspected for wholesomeness by the U.S. Department of Agriculture") appear separately on the package label.

Grades for chickens, turkeys, ducks, geese, guineas, and pigeons have been established by the U.S. Department of Agriculture.

For each of these kinds of poultry, there are classes based on age, sex, and weight. The following listing gives the approximate ready-to-cook weight for various types of fowl:

Chickens

Rock Cornish . . . . not over 2 lb
Broiler or Fryer . . . . . . ¾ to not over 3½ lb
Roaster . . . . 2½ to over 5 lb
Capon . . . . 4 to 8 lb
Stewing Chicken, Hen
or Fowl . . . . 2½ to over 5½ lb

Turkeys

Fryer or Roaster (very
young turkeys) . . . . 4 to 8 lb
Young Turkey . . . . 8 to over 24 lb
Mature or old Turkey . . . . . . 8 to over 24 lb

Ducks

Broiler or Fryer
Duckling . . . . 3 to over 5 lb
Roaster Duckling . . . . 3 to over 5 lb
Mature or old Duck . . . . 3 to over 5 lb

Geese

Young Goose . . . . 4 to over 14 lb
Mature or old Goose . . . . 4 to over 14 lb

Guineas

Young Guinea . . . . ¾ to over 1½ lb
Mature or old Guinea . . . . . ¾ to over 1½ lb

Pigeons

Squab (young) . . . . 8 oz to over 14 oz
Pigeon (mature) . . . . 8 oz to over 14 oz

Cooking Methods

Poultry, whole birds or parts, may be roasted, fried, braised, or stewed.

Roasting

Allow about ½ cup stuffing per pound of ready-to-cook poultry. Stuff poultry lightly, just before roasting. If stuffing and bird are prepared the day before, refrigerate separately.

Roast stuffed poultry in uncovered shallow pan, without water at 325°F (165°C) (slow oven). The roasting timetable for chilled poultry gives approximate total time according to ready-to-cook weight. Differences among individual birds may necessitate some adjustment of the time given.

To test doneness, move poultry leg. Fowl is done if leg joint moves easily. The softness of the flesh on drumstick and thigh are further signs of doneness. A thermometer inserted so that the bulb is in the center of the inner thigh muscle should register 180° to 185°F (82° to 85°C) when the bird is done. The center of the stuffing should register not less than 165°F (75°C). Plan to finish cooking 20 to 30 minutes before serving time so that the meat can "rest" and then be carved more easily.

Broiling

To broil young chicken or Cornish game hen, cut into halves, quarters, or meat pieces. Season and brush with oil or melted fat. Broil 20 to 30 minutes or until brown; turn. Brush again with fat or oil and broil 15 to 25 minutes longer or until done. Allow 60 to 75 minutes broiling time for pieces of small turkeys and ducklings. Baste turkey pieces occasionally; ducks do not need basting.

ROASTING GUIDE FOR POULTRY

Kind of Poultry	Ready-to-Cook Weight	Approximate Total Roasting Time at 325° F
Chicken		
broilers or fryers	1-1/2 to 2-1/2 lb	1 to 2 hr
roasters, stuffed	2-1/2 to 4-1/2 lb	2 to 3-1/2 hr*
capons, stuffed	5 to 8 lb	2-1/2 to 3-1/2 hr*
Duck	4 to 6 lb	2 to 3 hr
Goose	6 to 8 lb	3 to 3-1/2 hr
	8 to 12 lb	3-1/2 to 4-1/2 hr
Turkey		
fryers or roasters (very young birds)	6 to 8 lb	3 to 3-1/2 hr*
roasters (fully grown young birds)		
stuffed	8 to 12 lb	3-1/2 to 4-1/2 hr*
	12 to 16 lb	4-1/2 to 5-1/2 hr
	16 to 20 lb	5-1/2 to 6-1/2 hr
	20 to 24 lb	6-1/2 to 7 hr
halves, quarters, and half breasts	3 to 8 lb	2 to 3 hr
	8 to 12 lb	3 to 4 hr
boneless turkey roasts†	2 to 10 lb	2 to 4 hr

*Poultry without stuffing may take less time.

†Internal temperature of boneless roasts when done is 170° F to 175° F.

Pan-Frying

Dredge pieces in seasoned flour or crumbs, if desired, or leave uncoated. Melt fat in a heavy skillet. Brown poultry over medium heat, turn, and brown other side. Continue to cook chicken slowly, uncovered, until tender (30 to 45 minutes total cooking time). For turkey and duckling, cook slowly, covered, 45 to 60 minutes, turning occasionally until tender.

Oven-Frying

Preheat oven to 350°F (175°C). Pan-fried poultry may also be cooked in a 350°F (175°C) (moderate) oven. Coat poultry pieces with seasoned flour and then dip in melted fat to coat both sides. Place in a greased baking dish, skin side down. Cook for 30 minutes, turn, and cook 20 to 30 minutes longer or until tender.

Deep-Frying

Coat poultry pieces with a thin batter, flour, or crumbs. Use a deep kettle and enough melted fat to cover chicken pieces. Heat fat to 365°F (185°C). Check temperature with a deep-fat thermometer. Fry a few pieces at a time for 10 to 15 minutes. Drain on paper towels to remove excess fat.

Braising

Preheat oven to 325°F or 165°C (or to 450°F or 235°C for young poultry). Brush ready-to-cook poultry with melted fat; season. Place on a rack in roaster or heavy pan and cover tightly. Roast until leg joints can be moved easily and flesh on leg is soft and pliable. During last 30 minutes, cook uncovered to allow poultry to brown.

To braise poultry pieces, dredge them in seasoned flour and brown in hot fat in heavy skillet. Add one cup water or clear chicken broth, cover, and cook in oven at 325°F (165°C).

Poultry may also be braised on top of the range. Use a heavy skillet and follow directions for oven method. Cook slowly over low to medium heat. Cooking time is 1½ to 2½ hours.

Stewing

Season poultry as desired. Place in deep kettle and add just enough water to cover. Bring to a boil, reduce heat, cover kettle, and simmer (do not boil) until meat is tender—2 to 3 hours.

Cooking Frozen Poultry

To cook commercially frozen stuffed poultry, follow directions on wrapper. For safe handling, frozen stuffed poultry must be cooked from the frozen state. Thaw unstuffed poultry until the poultry flesh is pliable; then cook according to directions for poultry that has not been frozen.

Storage and Use

- To refrigerate poultry, remove giblets and wrap separately. Wrap poultry loosely to permit air circulation. Store in refrigerator at 38°F (4°C) and use within 1 to 2 days.

- To refrigerate leftover stuffed poultry, remove stuffing, cool quickly, and store in a separate container. Wrap the cooked poultry loosely and store in the coldest part of the refrigerator. Cooked poultry, stuffing, and broth should be used within 1 or 2 days.

- To store either raw or cooked poultry in freezer, wrap in moisture-vaporproof material and keep in freezer at 0°F (−18°C) or below. Use giblets within 3 months; cooked poultry dishes, raw duck, and raw goose within 6 months; and chicken and turkey within a year.

- Never stuff poultry with a dressing before freezing or refrigerating.

- To thaw poultry that has been bought fresh and then frozen, use one of the following methods: (1) Keep poultry in its freezer wrapper and thaw in the refrigerator 1 to 3 days, depending on the size of the bird. (2) Leave poultry well sealed in freezer wrapper and thaw in cold water for 2 to 6 hours. (3) Place wrapped bird in a double paper bag or wrap in 2 or 3 layers of newspaper, close tightly, and thaw at room temperature. Allow 1 hour of thawing time per pound of poultry.

- Do *not* thaw commercially frozen *stuffed* poultry. This should be cooked from the frozen state according to package directions.

Eggs

Shell Eggs

Extra large-, large-, and medium-sized eggs are those found on the retail market most frequently. Most state laws require that the grade and size be shown on the carton label. Eggs which are officially graded under federal or federal-state supervision bear a grade mark in the form of a shield which states the grade (or quality) and the size (based on weight per dozen).

The factors used to determine the quality are: cleanliness and soundness of the shell, the size of the air cell, and the interior quality of the egg, which is judged by candling. Eggs of high interior quality have a large proportion of thick white, standing high around a high, firm yolk. The three U.S. consumer grades for shell eggs are Grade AA (Fresh Fancy), Grade A, and Grade B.

The U.S. weight classes for consumer grades for shell eggs are based on *net minimum weights* expressed in *ounces per dozen*. These are:

Jumbo	30 oz per doz
Extra large	27
Large	24
Medium	21
Small	18
Peewee	15

As quality and weight are judged separately, the consumer may find a number of combinations of grade and size. In each quality grade, there may be two or more sizes of eggs in the store.

Frozen Eggs

The principal commercial frozen egg products are whole eggs, egg whites, plain yolks, sugared yolks, salted yolks, and blends of whole eggs or yolks with other ingredients. All inspected egg products are pasteurized.

Frozen whole eggs consist of yolks and whites in their natural proportions as broken out of the shell and made into a fairly homogeneous mass before freezing.

Frozen egg whites are the separated whites, frozen without any added ingredients. Before they are frozen, the egg whites may be passed through fine screens or cut by rapidly revolving blades to break down the thick white. This permits faster whipping of whites.

Frozen egg yolks contain not less than 43 percent total egg solids. Frozen sugared yolks are a blended frozen product usually consisting of 90 percent yolks and 10 percent sugar by weight.

Frozen salted yolks usually consist of 90 percent yolks and 10 percent salt by weight. Frozen yolks with sugar or salt added thaw out smoothly without lumpy particles.

Frozen blended whole eggs include various mixes of whole eggs with added yolks made uniform in viscosity by stabilizing syrups.

Dried Eggs (Egg Solids)

Whole eggs, whites, and yolks are also prepared in dried form. In addition, several mixtures of eggs with milk and eggs with shortening are prepared for specific commercial uses.

Duck Eggs

The term *eggs* as used in most discussions of food, refers to those from chickens. Duck eggs, however, are available in some markets. Ordinarily they are somewhat larger than chicken eggs, have a tougher membrane, a thicker shell, and a stronger flavor. When duck eggs are beaten, the volume is less than that of chicken eggs. For this reason, they should be used cautiously in baked products, although they should be satisfactory for most baking purposes.

Storage and Use

• Eggs should be stored in the refrigerator with large end up. When stored at room temperatures, eggs lose more quality in a day than in a week in the refrigerator.

• For best flavor and cooking quality, eggs should be used within a week.

• To store leftover yolks, cover with cold water and refrigerate in a tightly covered container. Pour off water when ready to use the yolks. These should be used within one to two days.

• To store egg whites, refrigerate in a tightly covered container. Use within a day or two. Or freeze egg whites for longer storage and use promptly after thawing.

• Use eggs with cracked or soiled shells only in foods that are to be well cooked, preferably in cakes or other baked goods that require long exposure to heat. For omelets, meringues, soft custards that take only relatively short cooking time and for egg recipes that require no cooking, use only eggs with clean, sound shells.

• As a safe rule, use dried or frozen eggs only in foods that are to be thoroughly cooked.

To Freeze Eggs

Yolks:	Add (per cup) either:
1 c = 12 yolks (extra large)	a) 1 Tbsp sugar or
1 c = 14 yolks (large)	corn syrup
1 c = 16 yolks (medium)	b) ½ tsp salt

Whole Eggs:	Add (per cup) either:
(extra large) 1 doz = 3c	a) ½ Tbsp corn
(large) 1 doz = 2-⅓ c	syrup or sugar
(medium) 1 doz = 2 c	b) ½ tsp salt

Whipping Properties

Egg Whites

The foam of beaten egg white is light and relatively open in texture and may mound softly or form stiff peaks depending on the amount of beating. The volume increase is greater than that of other food forms such as whipped cream, for example, but drainage is fairly rapid unless some stabilizing agent is used. Several factors may affect the volume and stability of egg white foam.

Among these are the following:

• Egg whites that have been allowed to stand until the whites are room temperature—64°F to 74°F (18°C to 25°C)—give the best volume.

• The addition of 1 teaspoon cream of tartar to each cup of egg whites increases the stability of the foam but also increases whipping time.

• Sugar beaten into egg white foam decreases the volume but increases the stability of the foam. Sugar retards foaming action and should therefore be added small amounts at a time.

• Fat inhibits the foaming action of egg white. For that reason egg yolk, because of the fat content, should be carefully separated from the egg white to be beaten.

Whole Egg

Well-beaten egg increases in volume four to six times the original amount and has a soft, moist foam. Drainage is fairly rapid. Eggs that have reached room temperature after removal from the refrigerator give the best volume.

7

FRUITS

Fresh Fruits

Many varieties of fresh fruits are available all year round in almost every part of the United States because of improved transportation and storage facilities.

Kinds of Fruits

Fruits may be classified as follows:

Berries. Those commonly marketed are black-berries, blueberries, boysenberries, cranberries, currants, gooseberries, grapes, raspberries, and strawberries.

Citrus. These are the grapefruits, kumquats, lemons, limes, oranges, tangerines, and tangelos.

Drupes. This is the botanical name given to apricots, cherries, nectarines, peaches, plums, and prunes; also known as stonefruits.

Melons. These vine-grown fruits include cantaloupe, casaba, honeydew, Persian, and watermelon.

Pomes. Two fruits—apples and pears—comprise this group.

Tropical fruits. There are many species of tropical fruits but those that are marketed commonly throughout the United States are avocados, bananas, dates, figs, guavas, mangoes, papayas, persimmons, pineapples, and pomegranates.

Grades

Grades of fresh fruits are used primarily in wholesale channels of distribution. They have been widely used by growers, shippers, and car lot receivers for domestic and foreign shipment but have not been so extensively used in the retail trade as those for canned products which are packed in consumer-size containers. However, homemakers have made considerable use of U.S. grades in the purchase of such commodities as apples, grapefruit, oranges, and peaches.

In the U.S. standards for fresh fruits, the principal factors affecting the grade of the commodity are maturity; decay, if any; shipping quality; appearance; and waste caused by various defects. The U.S. No. 1 grade is designed to include a fairly good proportion of the commercial crop. Standards for some commodities provide a Fancy or Extra No. 1 grade for use of packers of superior fruits for which a premium is obtained. Apples, for example, may be graded U.S. Extra Fancy, U.S. Fancy, U.S. No. 1, or combinations of these grades. There are also lower U.S. grades for fresh fruits such as No. 2, No. 1 Cookers, and Combination.

Sizes

Fruits sold in quantity are usually sold by weight or count rather than size although count may depend on size. Medium sizes tend to be more desirable than very large, which often lack quality, or very small, which have little edible portion compared to wasted parts. At retail, many fruits that used to be sold by number may now be sold by weight.

A Few Reminders

● Apple varieties for eating out of hand or in salads or fruit cups include Delicious, McIntosh, Stayman, Golden Delicious, Jonathan, and Winesap. The tart and slightly acid apples— Gravenstein, Grimes Golden, Jonathan, and Newton—are excellent for pies and sauces. Firm-fleshed apples that hold shape well in baking include Rome Beauty, Northern Spy, Rhode Island Greening, Winesap, and York Imperial.

● Cherries may be of the sweet variety or they may be tart, sometimes called sour cherries, that are used in cooking and baking. These are lighter red in color than the sweet cherries and have a softer flesh. Most of the commercial crop of tart cherries goes to processors.

● Figs may be black, yellow, or green. For eating fresh, the black figs are popular.

● The European varieties of grapes include Thompson seedless (early green), Tokay (late red), Cardinal (early bright red), Emperor (late deep red), and Ribier (late black). The American varieties include Concord (blue-black), Delaware, Niagara, and Catawba.

● Grapefruit may be white- or pink-fleshed with or without seeds.

● Limes may be acid varieties grown in the U.S. (chiefly Persian and Bearss) or sweet varieties (Mexican and Tahitian).

● Of the melon family, the mature cantaloupe has no stem but a slight identation at the stem end and a yellow to light green netting. Casaba melon is pumpkin shaped and has no netting but does have shallow, irregular, lengthwise furrows. Honeydew melon is large, bluntly oval, and smooth. Persian melon resembles cantaloupe but is more nearly round, has a finer netting, and is similar in size to the honeydew.

● Orange varieties include Washington Navel from California and Arizona; Valencia from California, Arizona, Florida, and Texas; Parson Brown, Hamlin, and a variety called Pineapple from Florida and Texas; and Temple oranges from Florida. Murcott is a cross between a sweet orange and a mandarin.

● Peach varieties divide into freestone and clingstone. As the names imply, the flesh of the freestone peach separates readily from the pit whereas the reverse is true of the clingstone. In general, freestones are preferred for eating fresh and for freezing. Both kinds may be canned, but the clingstone maintains the firmer shape.

● Bartlett pears are summer and early fall pears that are eaten fresh and are also used in canning. Fall and winter pear varieties include Anjou, Bosc, Winter Nellis, and Comice. These keep well in cold storage.

● Plums may be red, green, or yellow. Prunes are freestone plums that are purplish-black and smaller and more oval than the other types.

Storage and Use

● Store citrus fruits—except tangerines—in the refrigerator uncovered. Place tangerines in a plastic bag for refrigerator storage.

● Store ripe stonefruits in refrigerator uncovered and plan to use within 3 to 5 days.

● To store ripe melons, first place them in a plastic bag to protect other foods from the pungent melon odor and store in refrigerator for use within a week.

● Let bananas ripen at room temperatures; then refrigerate. Cold temperatures may darken the skins but will not affect palatability.

● To ripen firm avocados, let them stand 3 to 5 days until softened; then refrigerate.

● To avoid the discoloration of pared apples, peaches, and avocado that occurs when the pared fruit is exposed to air, sprinkle cut fruit with lemon juice or ascorbic acid.

● To ripen cantaloupe, let stand at room temperature 2 to 4 days. Chill a few hours in refrigerator before serving.

Processed Fruits (Frozen, Canned, Dried)

Many fruits are available in frozen, canned, dried, and dehydrated forms. The number and kinds of processed foods available at the retail market are constantly increasing as new procedures and equipment are developed for processing foods of improved quality. Their convenience and availability all year round have added variety to menus particularly in winter.

Frozen and Canned Fruits

Fruits are frozen or canned according to kind of fruit, or in fruit combinations. They may be processed as whole fruits, in halves, in slices, or as sauce or juice. Both unsweetened and sweetened packs of many fruits are available.

Frozen fruits are most widely available in waxed or polycoated paperboard containers, or, in the case of some sweetened fruits, in cans. Many fruits are available in envelopes or bags of polyethylene, foil, or laminates. Frozen fruits resemble fresh fruit in flavor, but during freezing, texture changes often occur.

Canned fruit containers include cans and glass jars of various sizes and shapes.

Standards of identity for most canned fruits as well as minimum standards of quality for many of the principal ones have been established by the U.S. Food and Drug Administration. Grade standards which also reflect factors of quality for many frozen and canned fruits have been developed by the U.S. Department of Agriculture. Canners, freezers, and distributors often voluntarily use the grade designations on their labels. Grades reflect mainly differences in appearance. The factors most important in evaluating the quality of processed fruits are flavor, color, texture, uniformity of size and shape, ripeness, and absence of defects. The permissive grades established by industry for most processed fruits are A (Fancy), B (Choice), or C (Standard). The terms in parentheses are those in common commercial usage for designating the quality of processed products.

Dried Fruits

Apples, apricots, peaches, figs, prunes, and raisins are either sun-dried or mechanically dehydrated. The moisture content of the dried fruits ranges from 15 to 25 percent.

Quality levels or grades for most dried fruits are the same as for other fruits. The sizes of dried fruit—small, medium, large, extra large, and jumbo—appear on retail packages.

Prunes are size-graded according to the number per pound. Size grades vary somewhat with type. The numbers used indicate the count per pound for a given type and vary with size.

For example, 30's to 40's could mean a large French prune or a medium sized Italian or Imperial prune. Following are the ranges in size per pound for the various types of prunes:

French	Italian	Imperials and/or Sugars
30 to 40 per lb	25 to 35 per lb	15 to 20 per lb
40 to 50	35 to 45	18 to 24
50 to 60	30 to 40	20 to 30
60 to 70	40 to 50	30 to 40
70 to 80	50 to 60	40 to 50
80 to 90	60 to 70	50 to 60
90 to 100	70 to 80	60 to 70
100 to 120	80 to 90	
120 and up	90 to 100	

When "sulfur dioxide" appears on the label of dried apples, apricots, and peaches, the fruit has been treated with sulfur dioxide fumes to prevent darkening of color. The chemical is harmless and disappears in the steam when the fruit is cooked.

Quality Guide for Fruits[1]

Apples

What to look for: Firm, well-colored fruit. Apples must be mature when picked to have good flavor, crisp texture, and storing ability.

What to avoid: Immature apples that lack color for the particular variety; also, fruit with shriveled skin; overripe apples (indicated by a yielding to slight pressure on the skin and soft, mealy flesh); and apples affected by freeze (indicated by internal breakdown and bruised areas). Scald on apples (irregularly shaped tan or brown areas) may not seriously affect the eating quality of the apple.

Apricots

What to look for: Apricots that are plump and juicy looking and have a uniform, golden-orange color. Ripe apricots will yield to gentle pressure on the skin.

What to avoid: Dull-looking, soft, or mushy

---

[1] Based on *How to Buy Fresh Fruits,* Home and Garden Bulletin No. 141, U.S. Department of Agriculture, 1967.

fruit, and very firm, pale yellow, or greenish-yellow fruit. These are indications of overmaturity or immaturity, respectively.

Avocados

What to look for: For immediate use, slightly soft avocados which yield to a gentle pressure on the skin.

For use in a few days, firm fruits that do not yield to the squeeze test. Leave them at room temperature to ripen.

Irregular light brown markings are sometimes found on the outside skin. These markings have no effect on the flesh of the avocado.

What to avoid: Avocados with dark sunken spots in irregular patches or cracked or broken surfaces. These are signs of decay.

Bananas

What to look for: Bananas which are firm, bright in appearance, and free from bruises or other injury. The stage of ripeness is indicated by the skin color; best eating quality has been reached when the solid yellow color is specked with brown. At this stage, the flesh is mellow and the flavor is fully developed. Bananas with green tips or with practically no yellow color have not developed their full flavor potential.

What to avoid: Bruised fruit (which means rapid deterioration and waste); discolored skins (a sign of decay); a dull, grayish, aged appearance (showing that the bananas have been exposed to cold and will not ripen properly).

Occasionally, the skin may be entirely brown and yet the flesh will still be in prime condition. Flavor will be fully developed.

Blueberries

What to look for: A dark blue color with a silvery bloom which is a natural, protective waxy coating; blueberries that are plump, firm, uniform, dry, and free from stems or leaves.

Cantaloupes (Muskmelons) and Persian Melons

What to look for: The three major signs of full maturity: (1) The stem should be gone, leaving a smooth, symmetrical, shallow basin called a "full slip." If all or part of the stem base remains

or if the stem scar is jagged or torn, the melon is probably not fully matured. (2) The netting, or veining, should be thick, coarse, and corky—and should stand out in bold relief over some part of the surface. (3) The skin color (ground color) between the netting should have changed from green to a yellowish buff, yellowish gray, or pale yellow.

But also look for signs of ripeness, for a cantaloupe might be mature, but not ripe. A ripe cantaloupe will have a yellowish cast to the rind, have a pleasant cantaloupe odor when held to the nose, and will yield slightly to light thumb pressure on the blossom end of the melon.

What to avoid: Overripeness, shown by a pronounced yellow rind color, a softening over the entire rind, and soft, watery, and insipid flesh. Small bruises normally will not hurt the fruit, but large bruised areas should be avoided since they generally cause soft, water-soaked areas underneath the rind. Mold growth on the cantaloupe—particularly in the stem scar with wet tissue under the mold—indicates decay.

Casaba

What to look for: Ripe melons with a gold yellow rind color and a slight softening at the blossom end. Casabas have no odor or aroma.

What to avoid: Decayed melons, shown by dark, sunken water-soaked spots.

Cherries

What to look for: A very dark color, the most important indication of good flavor and maturity in sweet cherries. Bing, Black Tartarian, Schmidt, Chapman, and Republican varieties should range from deep maroon or mahogany red to black, for richest flavor. Lambert cherries should be dark red. Good cherries have bright, glossy, plump-looking surfaces and fresh-looking stems.

What to avoid: Overmature cherries lacking in flavor, indicated by shriveling, dried stems, and a generally dull appearance. Decay is fairly common at times on sweet cherries, but because of the normal dark color, decayed areas are often inconspicuous. Soft, leaking flesh, brown discoloration, and mold growth are indications of decay.

Cranberries

What to look for: Plump, firm berries with a lustrous color for the best quality. Duller varieties should at least have some red color. Occasional soft, spongy, or leaky berries should be sorted out before cooking, because they may produce an off-flavor.

Crenshaw

What to look for: A deep golden yellow rind, sometimes with small areas of a lighter shade of yellow; a surface that yields slightly to moderate pressure of the thumb, particularly at the blossom end; a pleasant aroma.

What to avoid: Slightly sunken, water-soaked areas on the rind (a sign of decay, which spreads quickly through the melon).

Grapefruit

What to look for: Firm, well-shaped fruits—heavy for their size, which are usually the best eating. Thin-skinned fruits have more juice than coarse-skinned ones. If a grapefruit is pointed at the stem end, it is likely to be thick-skinned. Rough, ridged, or wrinkled skin can also be an indication of thick skin and lack of juice.

Grapefruit often has skin defects—such as scale, scars, thorn scratches, or discoloration—which usually do not affect the eating quality.

What to avoid: Soft, discolored areas on the peel at the stem end; water-soaked areas; loss of bright color; and soft and tender peel that breaks easily with finger pressure. These are all symptoms of decay—which has an objectionable effect on flavor.

Grapes

What to look for: Well-colored, plump grapes that are firmly attached to the stem. White or green grapes are sweetest when the color has a yellowish cast or straw color, with a tinge of amber. Red varieties are better when a good red predominates on all or most of the berries. Bunches are more likely to hold together if the stems are green and pliable.

What to avoid: Soft or wrinkled grapes (showing effects of freezing or drying), grapes with bleached areas around the stem end (indicating injury and poor quality), and leaking berries (a sign of decay).

Honeyball and Honeydew

What to look for: Maturity, shown by a soft, velvety feel, and for ripeness, shown by a slight softening at the blossom end, a faint pleasant fruit aroma, and a yellowish white to creamy rind color.

What to avoid: Melons with a dead-white or greenish-white color and hard, smooth feel (which are signs of immaturity), large, water-soaked bruised areas (signs of injury), and cuts or punctures through the rind (which usually lead to decay). Small, superficial, sunken spots do not damage the melon for immediate use, but large decayed spots will.

Lemons

What to look for: Lemons with a rich yellow color, reasonably smooth-textured skin with a slight gloss, and those which are firm and heavy. A pale or greenish yellow color means very fresh fruit with slightly higher acidity. Coarse or rough skin texture is a sign of thick skin and not much flesh.

What to avoid: Lemons with a darker yellow or dull color, or with hardening or shriveling of the skin (signs of age), and those with soft spots, mold on the surface, and punctures of the skin (signs of decay).

Limes

What to look for: Limes with glossy skin and heavy weight for the size.

What to avoid: Limes with dull, dry skin (a sign of aging and loss of acid flavor), and those showing evidence of decay (soft spots, mold, and skin punctures).

Purplish or brownish irregular mottling of the outer skin surface is a condition called "scald," which in its early stages does not damage the flesh of the lime itself.

Nectarines

What to look for: Rich color and plumpness and a slight softening along the "seam" of the nectarine. Most varieties have an orange-yellow color (ground color) between the red areas, but some varieties have a greenish ground color. Bright-looking fruits which are firm to moderately hard will probably ripen normally within 2 or 3 days at room temperature.

What to avoid: Hard, dull fruits or slightly shriveled fruits (which may be immature—picked too soon—and of poor eating quality), and soft or overripe fruits or those with cracked or punctured skin or other signs of decay.

Russeting or staining of the skin may affect the appearance but not detract from the internal quality of the nectarine.

Oranges

What to look for: Firm and heavy oranges with fresh, bright-looking skin which is reasonably smooth for the variety.

What to avoid: Lightweight oranges, which are likely to lack flesh content and juice. Very rough skin texture indicates abnormally thick skin and less flesh. Dull, dry skin and spongy texture indicate aging and deteriorated eating quality. Also avoid decay—shown by cuts or skin punctures, soft spots on the surface, and discolored, weakened areas of skin around the stem end or button.

Peaches

What to look for: Peaches which are fairly firm or becoming a trifle soft. The skin color between the red areas (ground color) should be yellow or at least creamy.

What to avoid: Very firm or hard peaches with a distinctly green ground color, which are probably immature and won't ripen properly. Also avoid very soft fruits, which are overripe. Don't buy peaches with large flattened bruises (they will have large areas of discolored flesh underneath) or peaches with any sign of decay. Decay starts as a pale tan spot which expands in a circle and gradually turns darker in color.

Pears

What to look for: Firm pears of all varieties. The color depends on variety. For Bartletts, look for a pale yellow to rich yellow color; Anjou or Comice—light green to yellowish green; Bosc—greenish yellow to brownish yellow (the

brown cast is caused by skin russeting, a characteristic of the Bosc pear); Winter Nellis—medium to light green.

Pears which are hard when purchased will probably ripen if kept at room temperature, but it is wise to select pears that have already begun to soften—to be reasonably sure that they will ripen satisfactorily.

What to avoid: Wilted or shriveled pears with dull-appearing skin and slight weakening of the flesh near the stem—which indicates immaturity. These pears will not ripen. Also avoid spots on the sides or blossom ends of the pear, which mean that corky tissue may be underneath.

Pineapples

What to look for: The proper color, the fragrant pineapple odor, a very slight separation of the eyes or pips, and the ease with which the "spike" or leaves can be pulled out from the top. Pineapples are usually dark green in mature hard stage. As the more popular varieties (such as Red Spanish and Smooth Cayenne) ripen, the green color fades and orange and yellow take its place. When fully ripe, the pineapples are golden yellow, orange yellow, or reddish brown—depending on the variety, although one seldom-seen pineapple (the Sugar Loaf) remains green even when ripe.

Also look for the maturity, shown by plump glossy eyes or pips, firmness, a lively color, and fruits which are heavy for their size.

What to avoid: Pineapples with sunken or slightly pointed pips, dull yellowish-green color, and dried appearance (all signs of immaturity). Also avoid bruised fruit—shown by discolored or soft spots—which are susceptible to decay. Other signs of decay (which spreads rapidly through the fruit) are: traces of mold, an unpleasant odor, and eyes which turn watery and darken in color.

Plums and Prunes

What to look for: Plums and prunes with a good color for the variety, in a fairly firm to slightly soft stage of ripeness.

What to avoid: Fruits with skin breaks, punctures, or brownish discoloration. Also avoid immature fruits (relatively hard, poorly colored, very tart, sometimes shriveled) and overmature fruits (excessively soft, possibly leaking or decaying).

Raspberries, Boysenberries, etc.

What to look for: A bright clean appearance and a uniform good color for the species. The individual small cells making up the berry should be plump and tender but not mushy. Look for berries that are fully ripened—with no attached stem caps.

What to avoid: Leaky and moldy berries. Also note wet or stained spots on wood or fiber containers; these are possible signs of poor quality or spoiled berries.

Strawberries

What to look for: Berries with a full red color and a bright luster, firm flesh, and the cap stem still attached. The berries should be dry and clean; usually medium to small strawberries have better eating qualities than do the larger berries.

What to avoid: Berries with large uncolored areas or with large seedy areas (poor in flavor and texture), a dull shrunken appearance or softness (signs of overripeness or decay), or those

with mold, which can spread rapidly from one berry to another.

Tangerines

What to look for: Deep yellow or orange color and a bright luster as your best sign of fresh, mature, good-flavored tangerines. Because of the typically loose nature of the tangerine skin, they will frequently not feel firm to the touch.

What to avoid: Very pale yellow or greenish fruits, likely to be lacking in flavor (although small green areas on otherwise high-colored fruit are not bad) and tangerines with cut or punctured skins or very soft spots (all signs of decay, which spreads rapidly).

Watermelons

What to look for: (In cut melons) firm, juicy flesh with good red color, free from white streaks; seeds which are dark brown or black.

(In whole melons) a relatively smooth surface neither shiny nor dull; ends that are rounded and filled out; creamy colored underside.

What to avoid: Melons with pale-colored flesh, and white streaks or ''white heart,'' whitish seeds (indicating immaturity). Dry mealy flesh or watery, stringy flesh are signs of overmaturity or aging after harvest.

8

VEGETABLES

Fresh Vegetables

Many kinds of fresh vegetables may be found on the market all year round due to modern transportation and storage facilities. Vegetables are classified as follows:

Bulbs: Garlic and onion

Flowers and Fruits: Artichoke, broccoli, cauliflower, corn, cucumber, eggplant, okra, pepper, pumpkin, squash, and tomato

Leaves and Stems: Asparagus, Brussels sprout, cabbage, celery, Chinese cabbage, lettuce, rhubarb, and spinach

Legumes: Bean, Lima bean, lentil, pea, and soybean

Roots: Beet, carrot, parsnip, radish, rutabaga, sweet potato, and turnip

Tubers: Potato

Grades for Fresh Vegetables

Grades for fresh vegetables are used primarily in wholesale channels of distribution. They have been widely used by growers, shippers, and car lot receivers for domestic and foreign shipment but have not been so extensively used in the retail trade as those for canned products which are packed in consumer-size containers. However, considerable use has been made of U.S. grades by homemakers in the purchase of onions, potatoes, and carrots. In recent years consumer standards have been issued for beet greens, broccoli, Brussels sprouts, carrots, celery stalks, corn-on-the-cob, kale, parsnips, potatoes, spinach leaves, tomatoes, and turnips. These standards may be used to identify different qualities of these commodities packed in consumer-size packages.

In the U.S. standards for fresh vegetables, the principal factors affecting the grade of the commodity are maturity, decay, shipping quality, appearance, and waste caused by various defects. The U.S. No. 1 grade is designed to include a fairly good proportion of the commercial crop. Standards for some commodities provide a Fancy grade for use by packers of superior vegetables for which a premium is obtained. U.S. No. 1 is the highest grade for most vegetables. Other grades for fresh vegetables (No. 2 or Combination) are not likely to appear in retail stores.

A Few Reminders About Fresh Vegetables

• Asparagus (green) is sold fresh, frozen, or canned. White asparagus is available canned.

• Cabbage may be red; green with smooth leaves; or green with crinkly leaves—a variety known as *Savoy*.

• Most celery sold today is thick-branched green Pascal. Blanched golden-type celery and hearts of celery are also on the market.

• Greens for cooking include spinach, kale, collards, turnip greens, beet greens, chard, mustard, broccoli leaves, dandelion greens, and sorrel. Chicory, endive, and escarole are used as salad greens.

• Lettuce has many varieties. Perhaps the most commonly known is iceberg which has a large round solid head. Butterhead is slightly smaller and less compact and includes Big Boston and Bibb. Romaine or Cos lettuce plants are tall and cylindrical. Leaf lettuce, as the name implies, grows in loose-leafed heads.

• Onions range in flavor from mild to sharp. The most common are the globe onions which are round to oval in shape and used primarily as a cooking onion. Spanish onions resemble globe onions but are larger and milder. They are excellent for serving in raw slices as garnish or in salads. Granex-Grano onions are also a mild variety. Green onions are immature onions that have been harvested when very young. They have little or no bulb. Shallots are small onions that grow in clusters. Leeks are larger than shallots and have a slight bulb formation. Green onions, shallots, and leeks are sometimes called scallions.

• Parsley, which strictly speaking is an herb, is sold at vegetable counters. It may be curly-leafed or flat-leafed. Either kind serves as a garnish for about everything from soups to entrees to salads and vegetables. Because it ranks high in vitamin C, parsley can furnish added nutrition to the diet.

• Peppers may be mild-and-sweet or spicy-hot. Preference for one or the other depends somewhat on the section of the country. Vegetable stores in Italian-American districts carry small tender sweet peppers. The larger dark green peppers are marketed in various stages of maturity—those with streaks of red being the more mature.

• General-purpose potatoes form the bulk of the potatoes on the market except possibly for areas that specialize in potatoes suited particularly for baking. Of the baking potatoes, Russet Burbank is the variety most widely grown. *New potatoes* is a term used to describe the crop available in late winter and early spring and also to describe freshly dug potatoes.

• Rhubarb is unique in that it is sometimes classified as an herb and sometimes as a vegetable and is served as a fruit in sauces and pies.

• Squash of the summer variety are harvested when immature and include Crookneck (yellow), Straightneck, Patty Pan (green-white), Zucchini, and Italian Marrow (slender green). Fall and winter squash are marketed only when mature.

Varieties include Acorn, Butternut, Buttercup, Hubbard (green and blue), Delicious (green and gold), and Banana.

• Moist sweet potatoes with orange-colored flesh are known as yams or Puerto Rican sweet potatoes. Dry sweet potatoes have a pale yellow flesh and a low moisture content.

• Watercress—a member of the mustard family—is a favorite for tea sandwiches and a flavorful garnish for summer salads. Like parsley, watercress is high in vitamin C.

• Late winter storage rutabagas are sometimes coated with a thin layer of paraffin to prevent shriveling and loss of moisture. The paraffin comes off readily when the vegetable is peeled.

Frozen and Canned Vegetables

Vegetables may be frozen or canned in combination with other vegetables or separately according to kind. Different forms of many vegetables include whole, sliced, juice, and soup. Some vegetables and vegetable combinations such as peas and mushrooms are frozen in a butter or other sauce.

Frozen vegetables are most widely available in waxed or polycoated paperboard containers, and many are available in envelopes or bags of polyethylene, foil, or laminates. An increasing number of vegetable dishes which require only reheating before serving are appearing on the market.

Containers for canned vegetables include cans and glass jars in a number of shapes and forms.

Standards of Identity

Standards of identity for most canned vegetables as well as minimum standards of quality for many of the principal ones have been established by the U.S. Food and Drug Administration. Grade standards which also reflect factors of quality for many frozen and canned vegetables have been developed by the U.S. Department of Agriculture. Processors and distributors often voluntarily use the grade designations on their labels.

The quality factors used in determining the grades and the number of quality levels established differ with the product. In general, those factors most often influencing the quality of processed vegetables are flavor, color, tenderness and maturity, uniformity of size, clearness of liquid, and absence of defects.

The U.S. grades for most processed vegetables are A (Fancy), B (Extra Standard), C (Standard). The terms in parentheses are those in common commercial usage for designating the quality of processed products. Grade designations mainly reflect differences in appearance.

Dried Vegetables

Besides the familiar legumes (mature dry beans such as lentils, split peas, navy beans, etc.), additional vegetables in the dried form are becoming available on the market. These include mushrooms, onions, potato flakes and granules, sweet potatoes, parsley flakes, and chive flakes.

Quality Guide for Vegetables[1]

Artichokes

What to look for: Plump, globular artichokes that are heavy in relation to size, and compact with thick, green, fresh-looking scales. Size is not important in relation to quality.

What to avoid: Artichokes with large areas of brown on the scales and with spreading scales (a sign of age, indicating drying and toughening of the edible portions), grayish-black discoloration (caused by bruises), mold growth on the scales, and worm injury.

Asparagus

What to look for: Closed, compact tips, smooth, round spears, and a fresh appearance. A rich green color should cover most of the spear. Stalks should be tender almost as far down as the green extends.

What to avoid: Tips that are open and spread out, moldy or decayed tips, or ribbed spears (spears with up-and-down ridges, or spears that are not approximately round). These are all signs of aging, and mean tough asparagus and poor flavor. Also avoid excessively sandy asparagus, because sand grains can lodge beneath the scales and are difficult to wash out.

---

[1] Based on *How to Buy Fresh Vegetables,* Home and Garden Bulletin No. 143, U.S. Department of Agriculture, 1967.

Beans (Snap Beans)

What to look for: A fresh, bright appearance with good color for the variety. Get young, tender beans with pods in a firm, crisp condition.

What to avoid: Wilted or flabby bean pods, serious blemishes, and decay. Thick, tough, fibrous pods indicate overmaturity.

Beets

What to look for: Beets that are a rich, deep red color; firm, round, and smooth over most of the surface and have a slender tap root (the large main root). If beets are bunched, judge their freshness by the condition of the tops. Badly wilted or decayed tops indicate a lack of freshness, but the roots may be satisfactory if they are firm.

What to avoid: Elongated beets with round, scaly areas around the top surface; these will be tough, fibrous, and strong-flavored. Also avoid wilted, flabby beets—which have been exposed to the air too long.

Broccoli

What to look for: A firm, compact cluster of small flower buds, with none opened enough to show the bright yellow flower. Bud clusters should be dark green or sage green—or even green with a decidedly purplish cast. Stems should not be too thick or tough.

What to avoid: Broccoli with spread bud clusters, enlarged or open buds, yellowish green color, or wilted condition—signs of overmaturity and overlong display. Also avoid broccoli with soft, slippery, water-soaked spots on the bud cluster. These are signs of decay.

Brussels Sprouts

What to look for: A fresh, bright-green color, tight fitting outer leaves, firm body, and freedom from blemishes.

What to avoid: Brussels sprouts with yellow or yellowish-green leaves, or leaves which are loose, soft, or wilted. Small holes or ragged leaves may indicate worm injury.

Cabbage

What to look for: Firm or hard heads of cabbage that are heavy for their size. Outer leaves should be a good green or red color (depending on type), reasonably fresh, and free from serious blemishes. The outer leaves (called "wrapper" leaves) fit loosely on the head and are usually discarded, but too many loose wrapper leaves on a head cause extra waste.

Some early-crop cabbage may be soft or only fairly firm but is suitable for immediate use if the leaves are fresh and crisp. Cabbage out of storage is usually trimmed of all outer leaves and lacks color but is satisfactory if not wilted.

What to avoid: New cabbage with wilted or decayed outer leaves or with leaves turning decidedly yellow. Worm-eaten outer leaves often indicate that the worm injury penetrates into the head.

Storage cabbage with outer leaves badly discolored, dried, or decayed probably is overaged. Separation of the stems of leaves from the central stem at the base of the head also indicates overage.

Carrots

What to look for: Carrots which are well-formed, smooth, well-colored, and firm.

What to avoid: Roots with large green "sunburned" areas at the top (which must be trimmed) and roots which are flabby from wilting or show spots of soft decay.

Cauliflower

What to look for: White to creamy-white, compact, solid and clean curds. A slightly granular or "ricey" texture of the curd will not hurt the eating quality if the surface is compact. Ignore small green leaflets extending through the curd. If jacket leaves are attached, a good green color is a sign of freshness.

What to avoid: A spreading of the curd—a sign of aging or overmaturity. Also avoid severe wilting or many discolored spots on the curd. A smudgy or speckled appearance of the curd is a sign of insect injury, mold growth, or decay and should be avoided.

Celery

What to look for: Freshness and crispness in celery. The stalk should have a solid, rigid feel, and leaflets should be fresh or only slightly wilted. Also look for a glossy surface, stalks of

light green or medium green, and mostly green leaflets.

What to avoid: Wilted celery and celery with flabby upper branches or leaf stems; celery with pithy, hollow, or discolored centers in the branches. Celery with internal discoloration will show some gray or brown on the inside surface of the larger branches near the base of the stock.

Avoid also celery with "blackheart," a brown or black discoloration of the small center branches; insect injury in the center branches or the insides of outer branches; long, thick seedstem in place of the usually small, tender heart branches.

Chard *(See Greens)*

Chicory, Endive, Escarole

What to look for: Freshness, crispness, and tenderness. Look also for a good green color of the outer leaves except for Witloof or Belgian endive. This is a compact, cigar-shaped plant which is creamy white from blanching. The small shoots are kept from becoming green by being grown in complete darkness.

What to avoid: Plants with leaves which have brownish or yellowish discoloration or which have insect injury.

Chinese Cabbage

What to look for: Fresh, crisp, green plants that are free from blemishes or decay.

What to avoid: Wilted or yellowed plants.

Collards *(See Greens)*

Corn

What to look for: Fresh, succulent husks with good green color, silk ends that are free from decay or worm injury, and stem ends (opposite from the silk) that are not too discolored or dried. Select ears that are well covered with plump, not-too-mature kernels.

What to avoid: Ears with underdeveloped kernels which lack yellow color (in yellow corn), old ears with very large kernels, and ears with dark yellow kernels with depressed areas on the outer surface. Also avoid ears of corn with yellowed, wilted, or dried husks, or discolored and dried-out stem ends.

Cucumbers

What to look for: Cucumbers with good green color which are firm over their entire length. They should be well-shaped and well developed, but should not be too large in diameter. Good cucumbers typically have many small lumps on their surfaces. They may also have some white or greenish-white color and still be of top quality.

What to avoid: Overgrown cucumbers which are large in diameter and have a dull color, turning yellowish. Also avoid cucumbers with withered or shriveled ends—signs of toughness and bitter flavor.

Eggplant

What to look for: Firm, heavy, smooth, and uniformly dark purple eggplants.

What to avoid: Those which are poorly colored, soft, shriveled, cut, or which show decay in the form of irregular dark brown spots.

Endive, Escarole *(See Chicory)*

Greens

What to look for: Leaves that are fresh, young, tender, free from blemishes, and which have a good, healthy green color. Beet tops and ruby chard show reddish color.

What to avoid: Leaves with coarse, fibrous stems, yellowish-green color, softness (a sign of decay), or a wilted condition. Also avoid greens with evidence of insects—especially aphids—which are sometimes hard to see and equally hard to wash away.

Kale *(See Greens)*

Lettuce

What to look for: Signs of freshness in lettuce. For iceberg lettuce and Romaine, the leaves should be crisp. Other lettuce types will have a softer texture, but leaves should not be wilted. Look for a good, bright color—in most varieties, medium to light green.

What to avoid: Heads of iceberg type which are very hard and which lack green color (signs of overmaturity). Such heads sometimes develop discoloration in the center of the leaves (the "mid-ribs"), and may have a less attractive fla-

vor. Also avoid heads with irregular shapes and hard bumps on top, which indicate the presence of overgrown central stems.

Check the lettuce for tipburn, a tan or brown area (dead tissue) around the margins of the leaves. Look for tipburn on the edges of the head leaves. Slight discoloration of the outer or wrapper leaves will usually not hurt the quality of the lettuce, but serious discoloration or soft decay definitely should be avoided.

Mushrooms

What to look for: Young mushrooms that are small to medium in size. Caps should be either closed around the stem or moderately open with pink or light tan gills. The surface of the cap should be white or creamy—or, from some producing areas, light brown.

What to avoid: Overripe mushrooms (shown by wide-open caps and dark, discolored gills underneath) and those with pitted or seriously discolored caps.

Okra

What to look for: Tender pods (the tips will bend with very slight pressure) under 4½ inches long. They should have a bright green color and be free from blemishes.

What to avoid: Tough, fibrous pods, indicated by tips which are stiff and resist bending, or by a very hard body of the pod, or by pale, faded green color.

Onions

What to look for: Hard or firm onions which are dry and have small necks. They should be covered with papery outer scales and reasonably free from green sunburn spots and other blemishes.

What to avoid: Onions with wet or very soft necks, which usually are immature or affected by decay. Also avoid onions with thick, hollow, woody centers in the neck or with fresh sprouts.

Onions (Green), Shallots, Leeks

What to look for: Bunches with fresh, crisp, green tops. They should have well-blanched (white) portions extending two or three inches up from the root end.

What to avoid: Yellowing, wilted, discolored, or decayed tops (indicating flabby, tough, or fibrous condition of the edible portions). Bruised tops will not affect the eating quality of the bulbs if the tops are removed.

Parsnips

What to look for: Parsnips of small or medium width that are well formed, smooth, firm, and free from serious blemishes or decay.

What to avoid: Large, coarse roots (which probably have woody, fibrous, or pithy centers), and badly wilted and flabby roots (which will be tough when cooked).

Peppers (Sweet Green)

What to look for: Medium to dark green color, glossy sheen, relatively heavy weight, and firm walls or sides. Fully mature peppers of this type have a bright red color.

What to avoid: Peppers with very thin walls (shown by light weight and flimsy sides), peppers that are wilted or flabby with cuts or punctures through the walls, and peppers with soft watery spots on the sides (evidence of decay).

Potatoes

What to look for: (In new potatoes) well-shaped, firm potatoes that are free from blemishes and sunburn (a green discoloration under the skin). Some amount of skinned surface is normal, but potatoes with large skinned and discolored areas are undesirable.

(In general purpose and baking potatoes) reasonably smooth, well-shaped, firm potatoes free from blemishes, sunburn, and decay. These potatoes should be free from skinned surfaces.

What to avoid: Potatoes with large cuts or bruises (they will mean waste in peeling), those with a green color (probably caused by sunburn or exposure to light in the store), and potatoes showing any signs of decay. Also avoid sprouted or shriveled potatoes.

Radishes

What to look for: Medium-size radishes (¾ to 1⅛ inches in diameter) that are plump, round, firm, and of a good red color.

What to avoid: Very large or flabby radishes (likely to have pithy centers). Also avoid radishes with yellow or decayed tops.

Rhubarb

What to look for: Fresh, firm rhubarb stems with a bright, glossy appearance. Stems should have a large amount of pink or red color, although many good-quality stems will be predominantly light green. Be sure the stem is tender and not fibrous.

What to avoid: Either very slender or extremely thick stems, which are likely to be tough; also avoid wilted or flabby rhubarb.

Rutabagas *(See Turnips)*

Spinach *(See Greens)*

Squash (Summer)

What to look for: Squash that are tender and well developed, firm, fresh-appearing, and well formed. The skin of a tender squash is glossy instead of dull, and it is neither hard nor tough.

What to avoid: Stale or overmature squash, which will have a dull appearance and a hard, tough surface. Such squash usually have enlarged seeds and dry, stringy flesh.

Squash (Fall and Winter)

What to look for: Full maturity, indicated by a hard, tough rind. Also look for squash that is heavy for its size (meaning a thick wall and more edible flesh). Slight variations in skin color do not affect flavor.

What to avoid: Squash with cuts, punctures, sunken spots, or moldy spots on the rind—all indications of decay. A tender rind indicates immaturity which is a sign of poor-eating quality in winter squash varieties.

Sweet Potatoes

What to look for: Well-shaped, firm sweet potatoes with smooth, bright, uniformly colored skins, free from signs of decay. Because they are more perishable than Irish potatoes, extra care should be used in selecting sweet potatoes.

What to avoid: Sweet potatoes with worm holes, cuts, grub injury, or any other defects which penetrate the skin; this causes waste and can readily lead to decay. Even if you cut away the decayed portion, the remainder of the potato flesh which looks normal may have a bad taste.

Decay is the worst problem with sweet potatoes and is of three types: wet, soft decay; dry firm decay which begins at the end of the potato, making it discolored and shriveled; and dry rot in the form of sunken, discolored areas on the sides of the potato.

Tomatoes

What to look for: Tomatoes which are well formed, smooth, well-ripened, and reasonably free from blemishes.

For fully ripe fruit, look for an overall rich red color and a slight softness. Softness is easily detected by gentle handling.

For tomatoes slightly less than fully ripe, look for firm texture and color ranging from pink to light red.

What to avoid: Overripe and bruised tomatoes (they are both soft and watery) and tomatoes with sunburn (green or yellow areas near the stem scar) and growth cracks (deep cracks around the stem scar). Also avoid decayed tomatoes which will have soft, water-soaked spots, depressed areas, or surface mold.

Turnips (including Rutabagas)

What to look for: (In turnips) small or medium size, smooth, fairly round, and firm vegetables. If sold in bunches, the tops should be fresh and should have a good green color.

What to avoid: Large turnips with too many leaf scars around the top and with obvious fibrous roots.

What to look for: (In rutabagas) heavy weight for their size, generally smooth, round or moderately elongated shape. Good quality rutabagas should also be firm to the touch.

What to avoid: Rutabagas with skin punctures, deep cuts, or decay.

Watercress

What to look for: Watercress that is fresh, crisp, and rich green.

What to avoid: Bunches with yellow, wilted, or decayed leaves.

Cooking Methods

Fresh Vegetables

Vegetables are usually cooked by boiling, and less frequently, by baking, steaming, or steaming under pressure. The length of time required for a given vegetable to cook by any method cannot be stated exactly, because cooking time differs with the variety and maturity of each vegetable, the period and the temperature at which the vegetable was held after it was harvested, and the size of the pieces into which it was cut. Each vegetable should be cooked for the shortest time necessary to give a palatable product. *(See Timetable for Cooking Fresh Vegetables, page 90.)*

Frozen Vegetables

The length of time required for cooking (boiling) frozen vegetables is usually less than that required for fresh vegetables. This is because the blanching and freezing of vegetables tenderize them to some degree. Frozen vegetables should be brought quickly to a boil, then boiled gently until just tender. Because cooking time varies with different vegetables, package directions are the best guide for proper cooking of frozen vegetables.

Use of Pressure Saucepan

Manufacturer's directions for use of a pressure saucepan are the best guides since they are based on the manufacturer's particular make. The accompanying table suggests approximate cooking times at 15 pounds pressure. *One note of caution:* At the end of the cooking time, the pressure saucepan should be placed in cold water or under running cold water to reduce the pressure quickly and stop the cooking.

Storage and Use

• Store the following vegetables in refrigerator crisper or in a plastic bag in refrigerator: asparagus, broccoli, Brussels sprouts, beet greens, cabbage, cauliflower, cucumber, lettuce, collard greens, chard, green onions, mustard greens, peppers, spinach, turnip greens.

• Store sweet corn in husks, uncovered, in refrigerator.

• Store ripe tomatoes, uncovered, in the

refrigerator. Keep unripe tomatoes at room temperature but away from direct sunlight until they ripen.

• Store dry onions in loosely woven or open-mesh containers at room temperature or slightly cooler temperatures.

• Store potatoes in a dark, dry, well-ventilated place at temperatures between 45° and 50°F (7° and 10°C). Potatoes stored at room temperatures should be used within a week to prevent greening or sprouting and shriveling.

• Store these vegetables at 60°F (15°C): hard-rind squashes, eggplant, rutabagas, and sweet potatoes. Do not refrigerate; temperatures below 50°F (10°C) may cause chilling injury. If these vegetables must be kept at room temperature, plan to use them within a week.

• Use these vegetables within 1 or 2 days: asparagus, broccoli, Brussels sprouts, green peas and lima beans, lettuce and other salad greens, green onions, spinach, kale, collard greens, chard, beet greens, turnip greens, mustard greens, and sweet corn.

• Use these vegetables within 3 to 5 days: cauliflower, peppers, and cucumbers.

• Use these vegetables within 1 or 2 weeks: cabbage, carrots, beets, and radishes.

• If crisper is not kept two-thirds full, put vegetables in plastic bags before storing them in the crisper.

TIMETABLE FOR COOKING FRESH VEGETABLES

Vegetable	Boiling*	Steaming*	Pressure Saucepan (15 pounds pressure)*	Baking
Artichokes				
French or globe, whole	35 to 45 min		10 to 12 min	
Jerusalem, whole	25 to 35 min	35 min	4 to 10 min	30 to 60 min
Asparagus, whole or butts	10 to 20 min	12 to 30 min	1/2 to 2 min	
tips	5 to 15 min	7 to 15 min	1/2 to 1-1/2 min	
Beans				
Lima				
green	25 to 30 min	25 to 35 min	1 to 2 min	
Beans, Soy, green	20 to 30 min	25 to 35 min	2 to 3 min	
Beans, green, whole, or 1-inch pieces	15 to 30 min	20 to 35 min	1-1/2 to 3 min	
Frenched	10 to 20 min	15 to 25 min	1 to 2 min	
Beet greens	5 to 15 min			
Beets				
new, whole	30 to 45 min	40 to 60 min	5 to 10 min	40 to 60 min
old, whole	45 to 90 min	50 to 90 min	10 to 18 min	40 to 60 min
Broccoli				
heavy stalks, split	10 to 15 min	15 to 20 min	1-1/2 to 3 min	

Brussels sprouts				
whole	10 to 20 min	15 to 20 min	1 to 2 min	
Cabbage				
green				
quartered	10 to 15 min	15 min	2 to 3 min	
shredded	3 to 10 min	8 to 12 min	1/2 to 1-1/2 min	
red				
shredded	8 to 12 min	10 to 15 min	1/2 to 1-1/2 min	
Carrots				
young				
whole	15 to 20 min	20 to 30 min	3 to 5 min	35 to 45 min
sliced	10 to 20 min	15 to 25 min	1-1/2 to 3 min	30 to 40 min
mature				
whole	20 to 30 min	40 to 50 min	10 to 15 min	60 min
sliced	15 to 25 min	25 to 30 min	3 min	
Cauliflower				
whole	15 to 25 min	25 to 30 min	10 min	
flowerets	8 to 15 min	10 to 20 min	1-1/2 to 3 min	
Celery				
diced	15 to 18 min	25 to 30 min	2 to 3 min	
Chard				
Swiss	10 to 20 min	15 to 25 min	1-1/2 to 3 min	
Collards	10 to 20 min			
Corn				
on cob	6 to 12 min	10 to 15 min	1/2 to 1-1/2 min	
Eggplant				
sliced	10 to 20 min	15 to 20 min		
Kale	10 to 15 min			

(continued on next page)

TIMETABLE FOR COOKING FRESH VEGETABLES (Continued)

Vegetable	Boiling*	Steaming*	Pressure Saucepan (15 pounds pressure)*	Baking
Kohlrabi				
sliced	20 to 25 min	30 min		
Okra				
sliced	10 to 15 min	20 min	3 to 4 min	
Onions				
small				
whole	15 to 30 min	25 to 35 min	3 to 4 min	
large				
whole	20 to 40 min	35 to 40 min	5 to 8 min	50 to 60 min
Parsnips				
whole	20 to 40 min	30 to 45 min	9 to 10 min	30 to 45 min
quartered	8 to 15 min	30 to 40 min	4 to 8 min	
Peas				
green	12 to 16 min	10 to 20 min	0 to 1 min	
Potatoes				
white				
medium, whole	25 to 40 min	30 to 45 min	8 to 11 min	45 to 60 min
quartered	20 to 25 min	20 to 30 min	3 to 5 min	
Rutabaga				
diced	20 to 30 min	35 to 40 min	5 to 8 min	
Spinach	3 to 10 min	5 to 12 min	0 to 1-1/2 min	

Squash

Hubbard				
2-inch pieces	15 to 20 min	25 to 40 min	6 to 12 min	40 to 60 min
summer				
sliced	8 to 15 min	15 to 20 min	1-1/2 to 3 min	30 min

Sweet potatoes

whole	35 to 55 min	30 to 35 min	5 to 8 min	30 to 45 min
quartered	15 to 25 min	25 to 30 min	6 min	

Tomatoes	7 to 15 min		1/2 to 1 min	15 to 30 min

Turnips

whole	20 to 30 min	20 to 25 min	8 to 12 min	
sliced	15 to 20 min		1-1/2 min	

*For altitude cookery, increase cooking time 1 minute for each 1,000 feet above sea level if the time is 20 minutes or less and 2 minutes per 1,000 feet if time is more than 20 minutes.

At high altitudes, pressure and time will have to be adjusted. See chart, page 5.

GUIDE TO HERB-VEGETABLE COOKERY*

Vegetable	Appropriate Spice or Herb
Asparagus.	Mustard seed, sesame seed, or tarragon.
Lima beans.	Marjoram, oregano, sage, savory, tarragon, or thyme.
Snap beans	Basil, dill, marjoram, mint, mustard seed, oregano, savory, tarragon, or thyme.
Beets	Allspice, bay leaves, caraway seed, cloves, dill, ginger, mustard seed, savory, or thyme.
Broccoli	Caraway seed, dill, mustard seed, or tarragon.
Brussels sprouts.	Basil, caraway seed, dill, mustard seed, sage, or thyme.
Cabbage	Caraway seed, celery seed, dill, mint, mustard seed, nutmeg, savory, or tarragon.
Carrots.	Allspice, bay leaves, caraway seed, dill, fennel, ginger, mace, marjoram, mint, nutmeg, or thyme.
Cauliflower.	Caraway seed, celery salt, dill, mace, or tarragon.
Cucumbers	Basil, dill, mint, or tarragon.
Eggplant	Marjoram or oregano.
Onions	Caraway seed, mustard seed, nutmeg, oregano, sage, or thyme.
Peas.	Basil, dill, marjoram, mint, oregano, poppy seed, rosemary, sage, or savory.
Potatoes.	Basil, bay leaves, caraway seed, celery seed, dill, chives, mustard seed, oregano, poppy seed, or thyme.
Spinach	Basil, mace, marjoram, nutmeg, or oregano.
Squash.	Allspice, basil, cinnamon, cloves, fennel, ginger, mustard seed, nutmeg, or rosemary.
Sweet potatoes	Allspice, cardamom, cinnamon, cloves, or nutmeg.
Tomatoes	Basil, bay leaves, celery seed, oregano, sage, sesame seed, tarragon, or thyme.
Green salads	Basil, chives, dill, or tarragon.

NOTE: Pepper and parsley may be used with any of the above vegetables. Curry powder adds piquancy to creamed vegetables.

*Based on Spices and Herbs, *Vegetables in Family Meals,* Home and Garden Bulletin No. 105, U.S. Department of Agriculture, 1965.

9

GRAIN PRODUCTS

Cereal grains are the dry fruits of grasses—barley, corn, oats, rice, and wheat. The kernels of the various grains are similar in structure but differ in size and shape. The three structural parts of the kernel are *bran* which is the outer protective covering of the kernel; *endosperm* which comprises about 85 percent of the kernel and contains the food supply of the plant; and *germ* which contains elements necessary for new plant life.

Barley Products

Barley although low in protein and fat is high in mineral content. In the United States, this grain is sold mainly as *pearl barley* which is the whole grain with hulls and bran removed. It is used principally as a soup ingredient. The grain may also be made into a flour by a process similar to that for making wheat flour. *Barley flour* is used in this country chiefly in baby foods and breakfast cereals.

Corn Products

Corn meal is made by grinding cleaned white or yellow corn to a fineness specified by federal standards. Corn meal contains small amounts of fat and crude fiber and not more than 15 percent moisture.

Bolted white or yellow corn meal is ground finer than the above type but otherwise is similar.

Enriched corn meal contains added vitamins and

minerals per pound of corn meal. Following are the minimum and maximum amounts:

Thiamine	2.0 mg	3.0 mg
Riboflavin	1.2 mg	1.8 mg
Niacin	16.0 mg	24.0 mg
Iron	13.0 mg	26.0 mg

Enriched corn meal may also contain the following added nutrients per pound of meal:

Calcium	500 mg	750 mg
Vitamin D	250 IU	1000 IU

Corn flour may be a by-product in the preparation of corn meal or may be prepared especially by milling and sifting yellow or white corn.

Corn grits, grits, or hominy grits are made from white or yellow corn from which the bran and germ have been removed. Grits are more coarsely ground than corn meal.

Hominy is corn with the hull and germ removed, left whole, or broken into particles. Pearl hominy is whole grain hominy with the hulls removed by machinery. Lye hominy is whole grain hominy that has been soaked in lye water to remove the hulls. Granulated hominy is a ground form of hominy. Hominy grits are broken grains.

Cornstarch is the refined starch obtained from the endosperm of corn.

Waxy cornstarch is prepared from waxy corn. It is composed almost completely of amylopectin with little or no amylose. This starch acts as a stabilizer for frozen sauces and pie fillings.

Flavored cornstarch mixes are blends of cornstarch, sugar, and flavorings for making puddings and pie fillings. They are usually packaged in amounts to make one pint of pudding.

Instant cornstarch puddings are blends of dehydrated gelatinized starch, sugar, and flavorings for making puddings and pie fillings.

Corn cereals are usually ready-to-eat flakes or puffs, made from corn grits that have been cooked and dried or toasted. Corn cereals may be flavored, sugar-coated, and enriched with thiamine, riboflavin, niacin, and iron or fortified with vitamins and minerals.

Rice Products

Rice is the white starchy endosperm of the rice grain. Brown rice, also called hulled rice, is the grain from which only the hull has been removed. This type of rice contains about 8 percent protein and 79 percent carbohydrates (chiefly starch) and very small amounts of fat. Rice grains are classifed as long grain, medium grain, and short grain, according to varieties, and by size according to harvest, as follows:

head rice, whole grains and some ¾ grains
second head, ⅓ and ¾ grains
screenings, ¼ to ⅓ grains
brewers, small fragments of grains

Enriched rice is prepared by including a percentage of kernels which have been enriched with B vitamins and iron.

Precooked rice is packaged long-grain rice, cooked, rinsed, and dried by a patented process. This rice needs little preparation.

Parboiled rice has been steeped in warm or hot water, drained, steamed (usually under pressure), and dried before it is hulled and milled. Parboiling gelatinizes the starch and thereby alters the cooking characteristics. The grains are translucent and light to very light brown. Parboiling improves nutritive value in milled rice since the minerals and vitamins present in the outer coats migrate to the interior of the kernel during the process. Parboiling also improves keeping quality.

Converted rice is parboiled rice made by a specific patented process.

Rice bran consists of bran and germ with varying quantities of hulls. It is a smooth brownish powder with a faintly sweet taste.

Rice polish consists of inner bran layers and some endosperm. It is a smooth yellowish powder with a sweetish taste.

Wild rice is the long brownish grain of a reed-like water plant. It is hulled but not milled.

Rice flour is a white starchy flour milled from white rice.

Waxy rice flour is made from waxy rice. It is composed almost completely of amylopectin with little or no amylose. It acts as a stabilizer in sauces and gravies and is especially useful in preventing separation in these products when they are frozen.

Wheat Products

Cereals

Consumers often think of cereals as primarily breakfast foods, but there are also wheat products that serve well as meat or main-dish accompaniments.

Bulgur wheat, sometimes called parboiled wheat, is whole wheat that has been cooked, dried, partly debranned, and cracked into coarse, angular fragments. Rehydration requires simmering for 15 to 25 minutes. It may be used as an alternate for rice in many recipes, and resembels whole wheat in nutritive properties. This ancient all-wheat food originated in the Near East.

Cracked wheat is prepared by cracking or cutting cleaned wheat, other than durum, into angular fragments.

Farina is made from wheat other than durum with the bran and most of the germ removed. It is prepared by grinding and sifting the wheat to a granular form. Enriched farina contains the following minimum and maximum milligrams per pound:

Thiamine	2.0 mg per lb	2.5 mg per lb
Riboflavin	1.2 mg per lb	1.5 mg per lb
Niacin or		
niacinamide	16.0 mg per lb	20.0 mg per lb
Iron	13.0 mg per lb	

Calcium and vitamin D may also be added in

such quantity that each pound of farina contains not less than 500 milligrams of calcium and 250 IUs of vitamin D.

Other wheat cereals, prepared from whole wheat or parts of the grain, include ready-to-eat cereals and finely ground wheat meal. These products are precooked, flavored with malt and sugar, then dried in various forms, such as flakes or puffs. They are often enriched with thiamine, riboflavin, niacin, and iron or fortified with vitamins and minerals. They may be sugarcoated. *(See also Breakfast Cereals, page 98.)*

Wheat germ is the fat-containing portion of the wheat kernel. The germ is flattened and then sifted out as a yellowish oily flake.

Wurld wheat is similar to bulgur but is much lighter in color as a result of chemical peeling of the bran. The wheat is treated with sodium hydroxide and steam to remove some of the highly pigmented outer layers of kernel, is then scoured, neutralized with acid, rinsed, and dried. Wurld wheat is higher in cost and less nutritious than bulgur.

Flours

The term *flour* when used in recipes is understood to mean wheat flour unless otherwise designated as, for example, bread flour, cake flour, self-rising flour. When unqualified as to purpose or type, the flour is known as all-purpose or general-purpose flour. The following describes in more detail the various types of flour available in most markets:

Enriched flour is white flour which contains added vitamins and minerals. Following are the base amounts added per pound of flour:

Thiamine	2.9 mg
Riboflavin	1.8 mg
Niacin	24.0 mg
Iron	13.0 to 16.5 mg
Calcium (optional)	960.0 mg

Gluten flour is a mixture of wheat flour and gluten with a protein content of 41 percent. Gluten is the protein fraction of selected wheat flour. A gentle washing of a flour-water dough separates the protein from the starch. The protein is then dried under mild conditions to form a powder.

Self-rising flour is flour to which leavening ingredients and salt have been added in proper proportion for household baking. The leavening ingredients most commonly used, with soda, are monocalcium phosphate, sodium acid pyrophosphate, and sodium aluminum phosphate.

White flour, flour, wheat flour, plain flour are synonymous terms. Each refers to the flour that results from the milling and sifting of clean wheat. This type of flour consists essentially of endosperm and may be bleached or unbleached, which is creamy in color. Unbleached flour does not give the same quality product as the bleached flour.

Whole-wheat flour, graham flour, entire wheat flour are synonymous terms. Each is defined as the food prepared by so milling cleaned wheat other than durum wheat and red durum wheat that the proportions of the natural constituents of wheat remain unaltered.

Flours Classified by Use

All-purpose, general-purpose, or family flours are of such composition that they may be used satisfactorily for most household cookery purposes. They are usually blends of wheat which are lower in protein content than bread flours, but which contain enough protein to make good yeast bread in the home, yet not too much for good quick breads. Blends are prepared to conform to the baking demands of different areas; for example, a softer blend is marketed in the South for making quick breads, whereas a harder blend is marketed in the North for making yeast rolls and bread. All-purpose flour is also used in making pastries, cookies, and cakes.

Bread flours are milled from blends of hard spring and winter wheats or from either of these types alone. They are fairly high in protein and slightly granular to the touch. They may be bleached or unbleached. Bread flours are milled chiefly for bakers.

Cake flours are milled from soft wheats. They are short patents, representing the most highly refined flour streams of the mill. The protein content is low, and the granulation so uniform and fine that the flour feels soft and satiny. It is used primarily for baked products.

Cake flour is mixed with other ingredients, such as shortening, leavening agent, sugar, and dry milk, to make packaged cake mixes which require only the addition of liquid and sometimes eggs to prepare a batter.

Instant, instantized, instant-blending or quick-mixing flour is a grunular all-purpose flour. Regular all-purpose flour is exposed to hot water or steam to combine individual particles into agglomerates. Flour treated in such a manner blends more readily with liquid than does regular flour. Changes in formulas and preparation procedures are needed to assure good quality in the final baked products.

Pastry flours are made either of hard or soft wheats but usually of the latter. They are fairly low in protein and are finely milled, though not so fine as cake flour. They are designed for making pastries and specialty products and are used chiefly by bakers and biscuit manufacturers.

Classes of Wheat

Durum wheats (amber types) are used for making semolina, which in turn is made into macaroni, spaghetti, and other pasta.

Hard wheats include hard winter wheats and hard spring wheats. These are used for making bakery flours, bread flours, and all-purpose flours.

Soft wheats are used for making pastry flours, cake flours, all-purpose flours, and biscuit flours.

Other Flours and Cereals

Buckwheat flour is the finely ground product obtained by sifting buckwheat meal.

Oatmeal, or rolled oats, also called *oats,* is made by rolling the groats (oats with hull removed) to form flakes. Regular oats and quick-cooking oats differ only in thinness of flakes. For quick-cooking oats the finished groats (edible portion of the kernel) are cut into tiny particles which are then rolled into thin, small flakes. Although oatmeal is usually considered a breakfast cereal, many recipes call for its use in cooking and baking.

Potato flour is prepared from cooked potatoes that have been dried and ground.

Rye flour is the finely ground product obtained

by sifting rye meal. It is available in three grades: white, medium, and dark. Rye and wheat flours are the only flours containing gluten-forming proteins. Rye flour produces gluten of low elasticity.

Soy flour is highly flavored. It is combined with wheat flour in baked products because it lacks gluten-forming proteins needed for bread making. The amount of liquid in a recipe must be increased when soy flour is substituted for part of the wheat flour. *Full-fat soy flour* is made by grinding soybeans that have only the hull removed. *Low-fat soy flour* is made from the press cake after all or nearly all of the oil is taken out of the soybeans. The soybeans may be heat treated or conditioned with steam prior to oil extraction.

Soy grits are made from coarsely ground soy press cake and are a low-fat product.

Breakfast Cereals

Whole-grain cereals retain the natural proportions of bran, germ, and endosperm, and the specific nutrients that are normally contained in the whole unprocessed grain.

Enriched cereals contain added amounts of thiamine, riboflavin, niacin, and iron. The levels of nutrient enrichment are established by enrichment standards.

Fortified cereals contain added amounts of selected nutrients that may or may not have been present in the grain before processing.

Restored cereals contain added amounts of selected nutrients to supply the same approximate levels of these nutrients in the finished products as were present in the whole grain before processing.

Kinds of hot or ready-to-eat cereals include flaked, granulated, puffed, rolled, and shredded. To-be-cooked cereals include regular, quick-cooking, and instant varieties. Instant to-be-cooked cereals are prepared from precooked dried grains. Disodium phosphate is added, or the kernels are modified with a small amount of an enzyme preparation to permit quick entry of the water into the kernel. Some ready-to-eat cereals may be presweetened.

Pasta

Pasta includes macaroni, noodles, and spaghetti in one of 150 shapes. Pasta dough is made from semolina, salt, and water. Low-grade products occasionally include some farina. Pasta in the form of noodles has eggs added.

Storage and Use

• Store flours and cereals in tightly covered containers to keep out dust, moisture, and insects. Store in a dry place at room temperature.

• Cereals may be stored satisfactorily for 2 to 3 months; cornmeal and hominy grits for 4 to 6 months; bulgur and brown or wild rice for 6 months; and other rice for 1 year.

• To measure sifted or unsifted white flour, spoon tablespoons of the flour lightly into measuring cup until the flour overflows the cup. Or dip the measuring cup into the flour. Do *not* pack the flour by shaking the cup or hitting with a spoon. Level the flour with the straight edge of a spatula or knife.

• To measure whole-grain flours, instant flour, and meals, stir lightly with a fork or spoon but do not sift. Then measure according to directions for white flour given above.

• Store egg noodles or pasta tightly covered or well wrapped. These products store satisfactorily for a year.

10

LEAVENING AGENTS, SWEETENING AGENTS, FATS AND OILS

Leavening Agents

A leavening agent is a gas incorporated or formed in a batter or dough to make it rise, increase in volume or bulk, and become light and porous during preparation and subsequent heating. The amount of leavening gas in a mixture and the rate at which it is formed are of importance in establishing texture and other characteristics of leavened products.

There are three principal leavening gases:

Air

Air contributes to some of the volume of leavened products. Air is beaten or folded into mixtures or introduced into ingredients by beating, creaming, and sifting. It leavens by expansion during heating.

Water Vapor

Water vapor or steam is formed in any batter or dough as it is heated. It is the principal leavening agent in products such as popovers and cream puffs.

Carbon Dioxide

Carbon dioxide is a leavening agent produced in a batter or dough by chemical or biological reactions. Currently it is produced in breads and cakes from baking soda (sodium bicarbonate), baking powder, or sugar.

From Sodium Bicarbonate

Baking soda (sodium bicarbonate) plus an acid ingredient form carbon dioxide gas, water, and a salt of the acid ingredient. Common sources of acids for leavening are sour or acidified milk, molasses, and the dry acids and acid salts used in baking powders. The acidity of sour milk varies with its age and degree of sourness; the acidity of molasses also varies. The acidity of corn syrup, honey, and chocolate is too low for them to be used as the only source of acid. When sour milk or molasses is used, the baking soda should be mixed with the dry ingredients, since the reaction between baking soda and acid is immediate in a liquid medium. For proportions of baking soda and acid to use in place of baking powder see **Substitution of Ingredients**, page 18.

From Baking Powders

Baking powders are mixtures of dry acid or acid salts and baking soda with starch or flour added to standardize and help stabilize the mixtures. For use in low-sodium diets, baking powder with potassium bicarbonate, rather than sodium bicarbonate (baking soda), is available. According to the advisory standard used by the trade and regulatory officials,[1] baking powders must liberate at least 12 percent of carbon dioxide. Baking powders are classified according to their acid components as follows:

---

[1] Service Regulatory Announcement S.D. No. 2, Revision 4, issued August 1933, USDA, page 20.

Tartrate powders, in which the acid ingredients are potassium acid tartrate (cream of tartar) and tartaric acid. These are the quick-acting baking powders that form gas bubbles as soon as the batter is mixed.

Phosphate powders, in which the acid ingredient is either calcium acid phosphate or sodium acid pyrophosphate or a combination of these. Phosphate powders may be double-acting.

SAS-phosphate powders, in which the acid ingredients are sodium aluminum sulfate and calcium acid phosphate. This type is often referred to as combination or double-acting powder and may be so considered from the point of view that the acid phosphate reacts with the baking soda while the mixture is cold, whereas heat is necessary before the sulfate reacts.

All baking powders liberate some carbon dioxide in the cold batter or dough and some during the heating process. Tartrate powders release the largest amount of carbon dioxide while the mixture is cold and SAS-phosphate powders the least; phosphate powders are intermediate.

Because of different amounts of carbon dioxide lost during mixing and because of different weights per unit volume of the three types of baking powder, under experimental conditions optimum results are obtained with use of slightly different measures for different baking powders. In writing recipes for home use, the type of baking powder should be mentioned as well as the recommended amount. The directions given by the manufacturer may be used as a guide to specific amounts.

From Sugar

Carbon dioxide is formed by the action of yeast or certain bacteria with sugar. These reactions require a fermentation period prior to the baking period in order to produce the leavening gas.

Yeast—a microscopic, unicellular plant—under suitable conditions of temperature, nutrients, and moisture produces carbon dioxide from simple sugars formed from starch and/or granulated sugar. Yeast is marketed in two forms:

Compressed yeast is a moist mixture of yeast and starch. The yeast is in an active state. Presence of moisture makes the product perishable.

Active dry yeast is similar to compressed yeast except that the yeast-and-filler mixture has been dried and is then packaged in granular form.

Bacteria of certain species, under suitable conditions of temperature and moisture, grow rapidly and produce gases from sugar. Salt-rising bread is made from dough leavened in this manner.

Storage and Use

• Store baking powder, baking soda, and cream of tartar tightly covered in a dry place.

• Check the label on yeast products for the date beyond which the product is no longer usable and plan to use it within that period.

• To measure baking powder, baking soda, and cream of tartar, first stir the product to lighten it and break up any lumps. For best results, use standard measuring spoons and be sure the spoon is dry when product is measured.

Sweetening Agents

Sugars

The term sugar, when unqualified as to source, refers to refined sucrose derived from sugar beets or sugar cane. These two sugars are the same, and are 99.5 percent pure sucrose. As used in recipes, sugar refers to beet or cane granulated sugar.

White Sugar

Granulated sugar is the standard product for general use, variously branded "granulated," "fine granulated," "extra fine granulated." The variation indicates preference in terminology of the manufacturer rather than any definite particle size. It is available in numerous sizes and types of packages, from 1-pound cartons to 100-pound bags.

Superfine granulated sugar,[1] a specially screened, uniformly fine-grained sugar, is designed for special use in cakes and in mixed drinks and other uses where quick creaming or

---

[1] See footnote on page 102.

rapid dissolving is desirable. It is available in 1-pound cartons.

Powdered or confectioner's sugar[1] is granulated sugar crushed and screened to a desired fineness. It is used in frostings and icings and for dusting pastries, doughnuts, and so forth. It usually contains a small amount of cornstarch to prevent caking.

Special Forms of Sugar

Cut tablets are made from sugar which is molded into slabs that are afterward cut or clipped. Cut tablets of various sizes and shapes are packed in 1- and 2-pound cartons.

Pressed tablets are made by compressing moist, white sugar into molds to form the tablets which are afterward oven-dried to produce hard, smooth tablets. Tablets of various sizes and shapes come in 1- and 2-pound cartons.

Cubes, like pressed tablets, are formed in molds. Sizes range from 200 to 80 pieces to a pound. Cubes are packed in 1- and 2-pound cartons.

Brown Sugar

Brown sugar is a product which contains varying quantities of molasses, nonsugars (ash) naturally present in molasses, and moisture. It may be produced from the syrup remaining after the removal of commercially extractable white sugar or by the addition of refined syrups to specially graded, uniformly minute white sugar crystals. It is variously designated as "yellow," "golden brown," "light brown," and "dark" or "old-fashioned brown," indicating the color characteristic. Intensity of molasses flavor increases with color. Brown sugar imparts flavor and color to candies, baked goods, and the like. It is packed in 1-pound cartons and 2-pound plastic bags. The new granulated (brownulated) form of brown sugar contains enough molasses to provide a flavor of an intensity between the light and dark brown sugars; its use in baking requires adjustments in amounts of ingredients.

[1]The terminology in the sugar industry is not uniform. Some brands use the term superfine to mean powdered; others add X's on confectioner's sugar packages. No standard terminology applies to all brands for these two types of sugar.

Other Sugars

Maple sugar is the solid product resulting from the evaporation of maple sap or maple syrup. It consists mostly of sucrose with some invert sugar and ash.

Corn sugar is crystallized dextrose (glucose) obtained by hydrolizing cornstarch with acid.

Raw sugar is processed from cane sugar and retains some of the cane sugar molasses. Raw sugar has a pleasant taste but may contain molds, fibers, waxes, and other contaminants.

Syrups

From Sugar Cane

Cane syrup is the concentrated sap of sugar cane. It is made by evaporation of the juice of sugar cane or by solution of sugar cane concrete (concentrate). The recommended maximum ash content of the unsulfured product is 4.5 percent; sulfured, 6 percent.

Molasses is the mother liquid from which raw cane sugar has crystallized. The following types are usually found:

Table molasses, which is light in color, contains a higher percentage of sugars and a smaller percentage of ash than are present in cooking molasses.

Cooking (blackstrap) molasses is dark in color. Barbados molasses, which is specially treated cooking molasses, resembles cane syrup more than molasses in composition.

Refiners' syrup is the residual product obtained in the process of refining raw cane or beet sugar which has been subjected to clarification and decolorization. It is a solution, or solution and suspension, of sucrose and partially inverted sucrose, containing not more than 28 percent moisture. It is used extensively for flavoring corn syrup.

From Sorghum Cane

Sorghum syrup is obtained by concentration of the juice of the sugar sorghum. It contains not more than 30 percent water nor more than 6.25 percent ash calculated on a dry basis.

From Corn

Corn syrup (unmixed) is obtained by partial

SOLUBILITY OF SUGARS

Sugar	Temperature		Percentage of Sugar Saturated Solution	Amount Dissolved by 100 Grams Water*	Dissolved by 1 Cup Water (Calculated on the assumption that 1 cup sugar weighs 200 grams)	
Common sugars (Approximately 20° C)						
Dextrose	20° C	68° F	49.7 %	83.1 g	0.4 lb	1.4 c
Lactose	25° C	77° F	17.8 %	21.7 g	0.1 lb	0.4 c
Levulose	20° C	68° F	78.9 %	375.0 g	2.0 lb	
Maltose	21° C	70° F	44.1 %	78.9 g	0.4 lb	1.7 c
Sucrose	20° C	68° F	67.1 %	203.9 g	1.1 lb	2.4 c
Sucrose (0 to 100° C)	0° C	32° F	64.2 %	179.2 g	0.9 lb	2.1 c
	20° C	68° F	67.1 %	203.9 g	1.1 lb	2.4 c
	40° C	104° F	70.4 %	238.1 g	1.2 lb	2.8 c
	60° C	140° F	74.2 %	287.3 g	1.5 lb	3.4 c
	80° C	176° F	78.4 %	362.1 g	1.9 lb	4.3 c
	90° C	194° F	80.6 %	415.7 g	2.2 lb	4.9 c
	100° C	212° F	83.0 %	487.2 g	2.5 lb	5.8 c

*The resulting solutions are saturated at the temperatures indicated.

hydrolysis of cornstarch by use of acid, alkaline, or enzymatic catalysts or a combination of these. The resulting liquid is neutralized, clarified, and concentrated to syrup consistency. The principal ingredients are dextrose, maltose, and dextrins. Two types are commonly marketed.

Light corn syrup is corn syrup that has had clarifying and decolorizing treatment.

Dark corn syrup is a mixture of corn syrup and refiners' syrup. It is used as a table syrup and also for the same purposes as light corn syrup in combinations that give a desirable darker color and distinctive flavor.

From Maple Trees

Maple syrup is made by evaporation of maple sap or by solution of maple sugar. It contains not more than 35 percent water and weighs not less than 11 pounds to the gallon.

From Bees

Honey is the nectar of plants, gathered, modified, stored, and concentrated by honey bees. The water content of honey is limited to about 20 percent. Its principal ingredients are levulose (fructose) and dextrose (glucose). The term honey in cookery refers to extracted honey. The different flavors of honey are classified according to the plant from which the nectar is derived.

By Special Processes

Blended syrups are mixtures of different, but somewhat similar, types of syrups which are sold for table purposes. The composition of blended syrups is stated on the label.

Spray-dried syrups consist essentially of the solids of syrup which have been converted to the form of dry powder by spray-drying.

Storage and Use

• To store honey and syrups, keep the unopened containers at room temperature. Once the containers have been opened, refrigerate honey and syrups to protect against mold. If crystals form, place the container in hot water.

• Store white granulated sugar, covered, in a dry place. If the sugar becomes lumpy, sift before measuring.

• Store brown sugar in a plastic bag in air-tight container. If sugar hardens, place a piece of foil or plastic wrap directly on the sugar and set a wad of dampened paper towel on the foil. Cover container tightly. The sugar will absorb the moisture and become soft. Remove paper when it has dried out.

• To soften brown sugar quickly, heat it in a slow oven (250° to 300°F *or* 120° to 150°C) and measure as soon as the sugar becomes soft; it will harden again upon cooling.

• When measuring brown sugar, pack it firmly enough into the measuring cup for the sugar to retain the shape of the cup when turned out.

• Store powdered sugar in an airtight container to keep out moisture. If sugar becomes lumpy, sift before measuring.

No-Calorie and Low-Calorie Sweeteners

A no-calorie sweetener is a sugar substitute composed of sodium and calcium salts of cyclamate, cyclamate-saccharin, or saccharin only, usually dissolved in water. A low-calorie sweetener is a granulated artificial sweetener in which the cyclamate, cyclamate-saccharin, or saccharin only are combined with dextrin, lactose, or other bulking materials. In either form, these chemicals when in contact with the taste buds of the mouth can create a sweetening sensation more powerful than that of sugar. Unlike sugar, however, these artificial sweeteners cause little change in viscosity or density properties of solutions and give little bulk. The Food and Drug Administration has allowed saccharin to be sold without restriction, but all combinations containing cyclamate must be labeled as drugs.

Fats and Oils

Fats and oils are those substances of plant and animal origin which consist predominantly of glyceryl esters of the fatty acids. Generally, fatty acids are organic acids having a straight hydrocarbon chain and an even number of carbon atoms, and they may be saturated or unsaturated depending on the number of double bonds in the hydrocarbon chain. Fats with short-chain saturated fatty acids are generally liquid or soft at

TEMPERATURES AND TESTS FOR SYRUP AND CANDIES

Product	Final Temperature of Syrup at Sea Level*	Test of Doneness	Description of Test
Jelly	220° F / 104.5° C	——	Syrup runs off a cool metal spoon in drops that merge to form a sheet.
Syrup	230° F to 234° F / 110° C to 112° C	Thread	Syrup spins a 2-inch thread when dropped from fork or spoon.
Fondant Fudge .... Panocha	234° F to 240° F / 112° C to 115° C	Soft ball	Syrup, when dropped into very cold water, forms a soft ball which flattens on removal from water.
Caramels	244° F to 248° F / 118° C to 120° C	Firm ball	Syrup, when dropped into very cold water, forms a firm ball which does not flatten on removal from water.
Divinity Marshmallows ...... Popcorn balls	250° F to 266° F / 121° C to 130° C	Hard ball	Syrup, when dropped into very cold water, forms a ball which is hard enough to hold its shape, yet plastic.
Butterscotch Taffies	270° F to 290° F / 132° C to 143° C	Soft crack	Syrup, when dropped into very cold water, separates into threads which are hard but not brittle.
Brittle Glacé	300° F to 310° F / 149° C to 154° C	Hard crack	Syrup, when dropped into very cold water, separates into threads which are hard and brittle.
Barley sugar	320° F / 160° C	Clear liquid	The sugar liquefies.
Caramel	338° F / 170° C	Brown liquid	The liquid becomes brown.

*For each increase of 500 feet in elevation, cook the syrup to a temperature 1° F *lower* than temperature called for at sea level. If readings are taken in Celsius (Centigrade), for each 900 feet of elevation, cook the syrup to a temperature 1° C *lower* than called for at sea level.

room temperature; the fats become harder as chain lengths increase. Unsaturated fatty acids (having at least one double bond) are liquid at room temperature. Polyunsaturated fats contain large proportions of unsaturated fatty acids having more than one double bond.

As the terms are commonly used, "fats" are those that are solid at room temperature, while "oils" are those that are liquid at room temperature. Oils are further subdivided into "salad oils" and "cooking oils." Salad oils have been especially processed to remove higher melting portions, and therefore stay clear at refrigerator temperatures. Cooking oils have not been treated this way and become turbid at low temperatures.

Fats

Hydrogenated All-Vegetable Shortenings

Essentially these are solidified vegetable oils. Cottonseed oil and soybean oil are used primarily, but varying amounts of other oils such as corn oil and peanut oil are sometimes used.

The vegetable oils are refined to remove free fatty acids, and then bleached with absorbent materials to remove coloring materials. The purified oils are then hydrogenated.

Hydrogenation is the process of adding hydrogen to the oil under carefully controlled conditions to change the oil from a liquid to a solid. The hydrogenated oil (it is now a "fat" since it is solid at room temperatures) is then deodorized by treating with steam under a high vacuum and at high temperatures. This produces a bland flavor.

The last step in manufacture is called plasticizing and consists of rapidly chilling the hot oil and incorporating air or inert gas into it. The purpose of plasticizing is to produce the characteristic soft, creamy physical appearance. The product is then ready for packaging.

Almost all of the hydrogenated all-vegetable shortenings on the market contain small amounts of mono- and di-glyceride fats which improve the over-all baking performance of the shortening.

Animal Fat Shortenings

Shortenings of this type are made from lard which has been refined and/or slightly hydrogenated or otherwise modified to improve its flavor, keeping quality, and consistency. Various amounts of hydrogenated vegetable oils are sometimes mixed with the lard. The product is deodorized, plasticized, and packaged in much the same way as the hydrogenated all-vegetable shortenings. The finished shortening usually contains mono- and di-glyceride fats to improve baking performance, as well as a small amount of added antioxidant.

Compound Shortenings

These are made by mixing hard vegetable fats (highly hydrogenated oils) or hard animal fats with unhydrogenated vegetable oils. Compound shortenings have become relatively unimportant in recent years.

Lard

Lard is fat rendered from the fatty tissue of pork. Lard may be smooth or slightly grainy, depending on manufacturing treatment. It may be light or dark in color and strong or bland in flavor, depending on production and processing factors.

Refined steam-rendered lard makes up most of the lard on the retail market. It is made from the fat stripped from the internal organs of swine at the time of slaughter and from trimmings from the various market cuts, rendered under steam pressure at a high temperature and then refined.

Leaf lard is made from the leaf fat and is kettle-rendered at a low temperature. It is produced in limited amounts.

Other lards marketed in limited amounts include neutral, kettle-rendered, dry-rendered, drip-rendered, and hydrogenated lards.

Butter (*See page 48.*)

Margarine

Margarines are made from refined vegetable oils or a combination of animal fats and vegetable oils emulsified with cultured milk, sweet milk, nonfat dry milk solids, water, or a mixture of these. The emulsion is then cooled and kneaded by machine to produce the desired consistency. Color and butter-flavoring materials or butter are added during manufacture. Salt is optional. Today almost all margarines are enriched with added vitamins to make the food value equal to or greater than that of butter. The law requires that margarine contain 80 percent fat unless the product is intended as a diet substitute in which case the package must be labeled *imitation* or *diet*. Package labels must also state the type of fat or fats used. Regular margarine is packaged in 1-pound or ¼-pound prints. Whipped margarine is packaged in 1-pound tubs or ¼-pound prints. Soft margarine is packaged in ½-pound tubs, usually 2 tubs to a package.

Poultry Fat

The fat from chicken, turkey, duck, or goose may be home-rendered. Poultry fat may also be commercially rendered, usually from the leaf fat taken from the body cavity of chickens or turkeys, sometimes from the fat obtained by skimming the vats in which poultry is cooked for canning. The rendered leaf fat is firm, light in color, clear, and bland.

Drippings

Drippings are fats usually rendered in the process of cooking fat meats. Drippings are sometimes home-rendered from meat scraps.

Oils

Most edible oils commonly used in the American home are of vegetable origin. Vegetable oils are pressed or squeezed from the seeds or fruits of the plant under heavy pressure (a method known as expelling), or the oils are dissolved out with an organic solvent which is later evaporated off (a method called solvent extraction). The raw oils are refined, bleached, and deodorized before being packaged. Oils to be used as salad oils are further treated by exposure to low temperatures for a period of time. The oils are then filtered to remove high-melting portions of the oil so that the remainder will stay clear at refrigerator temperatures.

Virgin olive oil is pressed from fully ripe black olives. Refined olive oil is derived from additional pressings of the fruit that are then filtered through layers of felt to remove impurities. Refined olive oil is not bleached or deodorized.

Other frequently used oils prepared from seeds, fruits, or beans are: corn, cottonseed, peanut, soybean, and safflower.

Storage and Use

- Store lards and home-rendered fats such as poultry fats in the refrigerator.

- Refrigerate vegetable shortenings intended for storage of several months or more. These fats, however, will keep well at room temperature for shorter periods of time.

- Keep oils well capped and store at room temperature. When refrigerated, olive oil becomes thick and cloudy. Many vegetable oils, however, have been treated to prevent solidifying or clouding at refrigerator temperatures.

- For easy measuring, let refrigerated fats stand at room temperature before measuring.

- For frying foods at high temperatures use vegetable or olive oil. These oils have a higher smoking point than some lards, butter, and margarines. A mixture of vegetable oil and butter for frying purposes has a higher smoking point than butter alone.

Ways To Measure Fats and Oils

Butter or margarine purchased in bar form need not be measured with measuring cups. Simply keep in mind that a ¼-pound bar equals ½ cup or 8 tablespoons. Two bars equal 1 cup, and a pound equals 2 cups.

For other fats (not in bar form) use standard measuring cups. Press fat firmly into the cup until it is full. Level with the straight edge of a spatula or knife.

To measure divisions of a cup use one of the following methods:

Use individual cups measuring ¼, ⅓, or ½ cup;

Measure in tablespoons; or

Use the water displacement method if the water that clings to the fat will not affect the product. Pour cold water into a cup up to the measure which will equal 1 cup when the desired amount of fat is added. For example, if ¼ cup fat is needed, pour ¾ cup water into the measure. Add enough fat to the water to make the water level rise to the mark for 1 cup, being sure that the fat is entirely covered with water. Drain off the water.

Use a 1-pound bar of butter or other fat as equivalent to about 2 cups. A ¼-pound bar is about ½ cup, or 8 tablespoons.

For oils or melted fats, use standard glass measuring cup and pour the oil or melted fat to desired mark.

Smoke Points of Fats and Oils

Lards .... 183°-205°C (361°-401°F)

Vegetable oil .... 227°-232°C (441°-450°F)

Vegetable shortenings with
emulsifier .... 180°-188°C (356°-370°F)

Vegetable and animal shortenings
with emulsifier ..... 177°-184°C (351°-363°F)
without emulsifier .... 231°C (448°F)

11

MISCELLANEOUS FOODS

Definitions

Bread Crumbs

Dry bread crumbs are those that can be rolled fine. They are used for stuffings, for buttered crumbs, and for coating foods for frying. Packaged bread crumbs are of this type.

Soft bread crumbs are those prepared by crumbling 2- to 4-day-old bread. These are used for bread puddings, fondues, timbales, stuffings, and buttered crumbs.

Catsup

Catsup, catchup, or ketchup is prepared from concentrated tomato pulp and liquid, seasoned with onions and/or garlic, salt, vinegar, spices, and/or flavorings, and sweetened with sugar, dextrose, or corn syrup.

Chili Sauce

Chili sauce is similar to catsup but contains pieces of the whole peeled tomato with seeds and more sugar and onion than does catsup.

Chocolate

Chocolate is the product resulting from the grinding of cocoa nibs (cocoa, or cacao, beans that have been roasted and shelled).

Sweet chocolate (sweet chocolate coating) is chocolate mixed with sugar and may also contain added cocoa butter and flavorings. It is used for dipping confections.

Semisweet chocolate pieces or squares are formed from slightly sweetened chocolate. They are usually used whole in baking.

Unsweetened chocolate is the original baking or cooking chocolate with no sweeteners or flavorings added.

White chocolate is milk chocolate that contains mild flavor cocoa butter (the fat of the cocoa bean) but no additional cocoa solids. White chocolate keeps for a shorter time than the more familiar chocolates.

Cocoa

Cocoa is powdered chocolate from which a portion of the cocoa butter has been removed.

Breakfast cocoa is a high-fat cocoa which must contain at least 22 percent cocoa fat.

Cocoa has a medium fat content which can vary from 10 to 21 percent cocoa fat.

Dutch process cocoa can be either "breakfast cocoa" or "cocoa" which is processed with one or more alkaline materials as permitted under government regulations.

Instant cocoa is a mixture of cocoa, sugar, and an emulsifier. It can be prepared for use without cooking by adding hot liquid.

Coconut

Flaked or grated coconut is coconut meat cut into uniform shreds or flakes.

Coffee

Coffee is prepared by blending, roasting, and usually grinding green coffee beans. Flavor of the brewed beverage depends on the degree of roasting. In some parts of the country—notably Louisiana—coffee blended with chicory is favored.

Instant coffee is prepared by freeze-drying or by various extraction, evaporation, and drying processes.

Decaffeinated coffee is prepared by steaming and soaking green coffee with a chlorinated organic solvent to remove most of the caffeine.

Fruit Pectin

Fruit pectin is a water-soluble substance found in fruit. In the right proportion with sugar and acid, pectin forms a jelly. Liquid or bottled pectin is refined from citrus or apple pectin. Powdered pectin is made from the liquid pectin which is dried and powdered.

Gelatin

The term *gelatin* usually means the granulated, unflavored, unacidulated product. Gelatin is obtained by hydrolysis from collagen in bones and good-grade skin stock. In processing, gelatin may be alkaline- or acid-extracted. The form used in cooking in the United States is granulated.

Fruit-flavored gelatin is a mixture of plain gelatin, sugar, fruit acids, flavors, and coloring. It is sold in packages standardized to gel 1 pint or 1 quart of liquid. For industrial use, this product is packaged in 1-pound or larger containers.

Imitation Dairy Products

Some imitation dairy products resemble ice cream or ice milk, depending on the fat content. The products differ from the dairy products in that a fat such as hydrogenated vegetable oil replaces the butter fat used in ice cream or ice milk. Only a few states permit sale of these products.

Imitation milk and the cream substitutes known as nondairy creamers are combinations of nondairy ingredients made to resemble milk or cream. The ingredients include a vegetable fat, protein such as sodium caseinate or soya solids, corn syrup solids, flavoring agents, stabilizers, emulsifiers, and water. Nondairy substitutes for cream are also marketed in powdered form.

Filled milk is a combination of skim milk and vegetable fat or nonfat dry milk, water, and vegetable fat. Nutrient standards have not been established for filled milk.

Infant Foods

A wide variety of strained and junior or chopped foods is available. These include small containers, usually glass, of cooked cereals, strained fruits, strained vegetables, egg yolk, homogenized meat, and combinations or mixtures of these foods.

Mayonnaise and Salad Dressings

Mayonnaise is a permanent emulsion of oil droplets in water, stabilized with egg yolk. It is prepared from vegetable oil, vinegar or lime or lemon juice, eggs or egg yolks, and spices. Commercial mayonnaise must contain a minimum of 65 percent vegetable oil.

Salad dressing has substantially the same ingredients as those in mayonnaise, but a portion of the egg is replaced with a cooked starch paste, and the amount of oil is less than in mayonnaise. Salad dressing has 30 percent vegetable oil.

Some French dressings are temporary emulsions without egg. Other commercial French dressings are mulsified with small amounts of vegetable gums or pectins. These dressings contain also tomato paste or purée and a minimum of 35 percent vegetable oil.

Low-calorie dressings have a fruit or vegetable base and very little oil. They may also be artificially sweetened.

Mustard

A pungent condiment consisting of black and/or yellow mustard seed that is pulverized and made into a paste with water and/or vinegar. The paste may then be mixed with spices, sugar, and/or salt.

Nuts

Nuts are dry fruits which generally consist of a single kernel inside a woody shell. True nuts include filberts and hazelnuts. Almonds and pecans may have hard, soft, or paper-thin shells. Brazil nuts grow in segments encased in a single shell or husk. Peanuts are the pods of a vine of the pea family and are therefore classified as a legume.

Nuts are available either in the shell or shelled. Shelled nuts may be chopped, ground, blanched, halved, slivered, plain, toasted, or salted.

Peanut butter is a spread prepared from finely ground nuts which may be blanched or unblanched. Commercially prepared peanut butter may contain seasoning and stabilizing agents. These are listed on the label.

Olives and Olive Oil

The edible fruit of the olive tree is available in cans or jars as ripe olives, green fermented or green brined olives, or as oil.

Both green and ripe olives are treated to remove the characteristic bitterness of the nut. Ripe olives are packed in salt with or without spices and are available pitted, unpitted, whole, sliced, or chopped.

Green olives are fermented, and packed in brine, either whole, pitted, or pitted and stuffed with pimiento, almonds, capers, onions, or celery.

Dried or salt-cured olives are also known as Greek or Italian olives.

The U.S. grades for ripe or green olives are: Grade A (Fancy), Grade B (Choice), Grade C (Standard), and Substandard. Green olives are available in the following sizes. Ripe olives have a similar size range:

No. 1 (small) .... 128 to 140 per lb
No. 2 (medium) .... 106 to 127 per lb
No. 3 (large) .... 91 to 105 per lb
No. 4 (extra large) .... 76 to 90 per lb
No. 5 (mammoth) .... 65 to 75 per lb
No. 6 (giant) .... 53 to 64 per lb
No. 7 (jumbo) .... 46 to 52 per lb
No. 8 (colossal) .... 33 to 45 per lb
No. 9 (super colossal) .... 32 maximum

Pickles

Pickles are cucumbers, other vegetables, or fruits, prepared by fermentation or in vinegar, usually with salt, sugar, and spices added. There are three general groups: (1) fermented (salt and dill) pickles; (2) unfermented (fresh pasteurized); and (3) sweet, sour, and mixed pickles and relishes of various mixtures.

Salt

Salt is sodium chloride unless otherwise identified as, for example, potassium chloride. Salt (sodium chloride) is used to season and preserve foods. Sometimes spices and/or herbs or other seasonings are added as in onion, garlic, or celery salt. Salt may also be iodized.

Salt is made "free flowing" by the addition of a substance that prevents absorption of moisture from the air.

Pickling salt differs from common salt in that pickling salt does not contain additives that would cloud the pickle liquid. Pickling salt may be granulated or flaked. One cup of the granulated salt is equal to 1½ cups of flake salt.

Salt substitutes contain calcium, potassium, or ammonium in place of sodium.

Soups

Soups may be clear or thick and may be served hot or cold. Bouillon or broth is a thin soup prepared by simmering meat, fish, or vegetables in water to extract their flavor. Consommé is a clarified broth. Bisque is a rich cream soup. Chowder is a heavy thick soup prepared from meat, poultry, fish, and/or vegetables.

Spices and Herbs

Spices and herbs include a number of plant products that have aromatic odors and pungent flavors and are used to season foods. Most spices grow in tropical climates and herbs in temperate climates. They include:

Aril (a lacy layer of the nutmeg seed)—mace

Bark—cinnamon, cassia

Berry—allspice, juniper, pepper

Flower stigma—saffron

Flower buds or young berries—caper, clove

Fruit—cayenne pepper, paprika

Kernels or seeds—anise, caraway, cardamom, celery, dill, poppy, mustard, sesame, fennel, nutmeg, cumin

Leaves and stems—basil, bay, chervil, celery, chives, marjoram, dillweed, mint, parsley, oregano, rosemary, sage, savory, tarragon, thyme

Roots—ginger, turmeric, horseradish

Tapioca

Tapioca is made from flour obtained from the cassava root and is marketed in two forms:

Pearl tapioca consists of small pellets that thicken and become translucent in cooking. Pearl tapioca is made by mixing the tapioca flour with water and cooking it on heated metal surfaces just enough to form a shell on the pellets.

Quick-cooking tapioca consists of very fine pellets. It is made by grinding a cooked dough prepared from tapioca flour or by crushing pearl or native flake tapioca.

Flavored tapioca mixes are blends of quick-cooking tapioca, cornstarch, sugar, and flavorings.

Tea

Tea is prepared from the leaves of an evergreen tree or shrub (*thea sinensis*). The treatment of the leaves after they are picked produces the wide variety of teas. *Black tea* is prepared by allowing dried and rolled tea leaves to ferment before they are fired. *Green tea* is steamed, rolled, dried, and fired without fermentation. *Oolong tea* has partially fermented leaves. For *special teas*, the leaves are mixed with jasmine, gardenia, mint, orange, or spices.

Textured Vegetable Proteins

Textured vegetable protein products are made from edible protein sources. These products have a structure and texture that withstand hydration in food preparation.

Extruded products are colored and flavored to resemble a food such as ground beef and are most often used as extenders.

Spun soy products are also colored and flavored and shaped to resemble products such as ham, chicken cubes, beef or bacon pieces. Also available are frozen, canned, and dehydrated spun soy products.

Vinegars

The acidity of vinegars ranges between 4 and 6 percent (40 to 60 grain).

Vinegar or cider vinegar is the product made by the alcoholic and subsequent acetous fermentations of the juice of apples.

Malt vinegar is the product made by the alcoholic and subsequent acetous fermentations of an infusion of barley malt or cereals whose starch has been converted by malt.

Wine vinegar is the product made by the alcoholic and subsequent acetous fermentations of the juice of grapes.

Spirit, distilled, or grain vinegar is made by the acetous fermentation of dilute distilled alcohol.

Storage and Use

• Store nuts tightly covered in a cool, dry, dark place or in the freezer. Exposure to air, light, warmth, and moisture can cause rancidity.

• Store spices in a tightly closed container in a cool place.

• Keep mayonnaise and salad dressings made with eggs in the refrigerator once the jar has been opened.

• Keep gelatin in unopened package until ready for use and store in a dry place.

• To substitute fresh herbs for dried, use 2 teaspoons minced fresh herbs for each ¼ teaspoon of the dried product.

• Melt chocolate for cooking purposes in small container over hot water unless recipe states otherwise. Chocolate burns easily when exposed to direct heat.

12

FOOD BUYING GUIDES

BUYING GUIDE FOR POULTRY

Food Item and Form	Market Unit	Approximate Volume or Number of Servings per Market Unit*	Approximate Weight per Cup	
Chicken, ready-to-cook				
broiler-fryer	1-1/2 to 3-1/2 lb	2 to 4 servings		
roaster	1 lb	2-1/4 servings		
Rock Cornish hen	less than 2 lb	1 to 2 servings		
stewing	1 lb			
cooked, boned		2-1/2 servings		
diced		1-1/2 c	136 g	4.8 oz
ground			113 g	4.0 oz
canned, boned	5 to 6 oz	1-1/2 to 2 servings		
Duck, ready-to-cook	1 lb	2 to 2-1/2 servings		
Goose, ready-to-cook	1 lb	2 to 2-2/3 servings		
Turkey, ready-to-cook	1 lb			
cooked, boned, diced		1 to 2 servings	133 g	4.7 oz
canned, boned	5 oz	1-1/2 servings		

*Amounts are based on three ounces of cooked poultry meat without bone per serving.

BUYING GUIDE FOR DAIRY PRODUCTS

Food Item and Form	Market Unit	Approximate Volume per Market Unit	Approximate Weight per Cup	
Butter	1 lb	2 c	224 g	7.9 oz
whipped	1 lb	3 c	152 g	5.4 oz
Cheese				
Cheddar (natural or processed)	1 lb			
grated or chopped		4 c	113 g	4.0 oz
Cheddar or Swiss, sliced	1 lb	8 slices		
cottage	12 oz	1-1/2 c	236 g	8.3 oz
cream	8 oz	1 c	230 g	8.1 oz
spread	5 oz	1/2 c		
Parmesan, grated	3 oz	1 c	92 g	3.3 oz
Cream				
light (table)	1/2 pt	1 c	240 g	8.5 oz
heavy (whipping)	1/2 pt	1 c	236 g	8.3 oz
whipped		2 c		
sour	1/2 pt	1 c	241 g	8.5 oz
half and half (cream and milk), sweet	1 pt	2 c	242 g	8.5 oz
half and half, sour	1/2 pt	1 c	242 g	8.5 oz
Milk				
whole or skim	1 qt	4 c	242 g	8.5 oz
buttermilk	1 qt	4 c	242 g	8.5 oz
sweetened condensed	15 oz	1-1/3 c	306 g	10.8 oz
evaporated, whole or skim	14-1/2 oz	1-2/3 c	252 g	8.9 oz
reconstituted		3-1/3 c		
dry, whole	1 lb	3-2/3 c	131 g	4.6 oz
reconstituted		14 c		
dry, nonfat				
Instant	9-5/8 lb	4 c	75 g	2.6 oz
reconstituted		14 c	242 g	8.5 oz
Milk desserts				
ice cream	1 qt	4 c	142 g	5.0 oz
brick, sliced	1 qt	8 slices		
ice milk	1 qt	4 c	187 g	6.6 oz
sherbet	1 qt	4 c	193 g	6.8 oz
Yogurt	1/2 pt	1 c	246 g	8.7 oz

BUYING GUIDE FOR MEAT

Food Item and Form	Market Unit	Approximate Volume or Number of Servings per Market Unit*	Approximate Weight per Cup	
Meat, fresh or frozen				
boned or ground meat	1 lb		227 g	8.0 oz
cooked		3 to 4 servings		
diced		1-1/2 to 2 c	142 g	5.0 oz
meat with minimum amount of bone (steaks, roasts, chops, etc.)	1 lb			
cooked		2 to 3 servings		
meat with large amount of bone (shoulder cuts, short ribs, neck, etc.)	1 lb			
cooked		1 to 2 servings		
diced		1 c	142 g	5.0 oz
Cured and/or smoked				
ham, ground	1 lb		170 g	6.0 oz
cooked, ground		2-1/2 to 3 servings	109 g	3.8 oz
diced		1-1/2 to 2 c	147 g	5.2 oz
bacon	1 lb	24 slices		
frankfurters	1 lb	4 to 12 sausages		
luncheon meat, sliced	12 oz	8 slices		
diced			141 g	5.0 oz
Canned				
corned beef	12 oz	4 servings		
ham, smoked	1-1/2 lb	6 to 8 servings		
diced		3-3/4 to 4-1/2 c		
luncheon meat	12 oz	4 servings		
sausage, Vienna	4 oz	8 to 10 sausages		
Dried				
chipped beef	4 oz	1-2/3 servings		

*Three ounces of cooked meat is the usual amount for one serving.

BUYING GUIDE FOR FISH AND SHELLFISH

Food Item and Form	Market Unit	Approximate Servings per Market Unit*	Approximate Weight per Cup	
Fish, fresh or frozen				
whole	1 lb	1-1/2		
chunks	1 lb	3		
dressed	1 lb	2-1/3		
fillets	1 lb	3-1/3		
steaks	1 lb	3		
cakes, frozen	1 lb	5-1/3		
portions, unbreaded, frozen	1 lb	4		
portions, breaded, fried or raw, frozen	1 lb	5-1/3		
sticks, frozen	1 lb	5-1/3		
Fish, canned				
gefilte fish	1 lb	3	162 g	5.7 oz
mackerel	15 oz	4-1/4	182 g	6.4 oz
Maine sardines	12 oz	3-3/4	160 g	5.6 oz
salmon	1 lb	4-1/4	168 g	5.9 oz
tuna	7 oz	2	170 g	6.0 oz
Fish, cured				
lox	1 lb	5-1/3		
salt fish	1 lb	5-1/3		
smoked fish	1 lb	3-1/2		
Shellfish				
Clams, fresh or frozen				
in shell (hard)	1 doz	2		
in shell (soft)	1 doz	1		
shucked	1 lb	2-1/2		
frozen, breaded, raw	1 lb	4-1/2		
clams, canned, minced	7-1/2 oz	2-1/2	158 g	5.6 oz
Crabs, fresh or frozen				
in shell (Blue)	1 lb	3/4		
in shell (Dungeness)	1 lb	1-1/4		
crab meat	1 lb	5	163 g	5.7 oz
crab cakes, frozen	1 lb	5		
crab legs and sections, frozen	1 lb	2-1/2		
deviled, frozen	1 lb	5-1/3		
Crab meat, canned	6-1/2 oz	1-3/4		
Lobsters, fresh or frozen				
in shell	1 lb	1-1/4		
meat	1 lb	4-3/4	154 g	5.4 oz
spiny tails, frozen	1 lb	2-2/3		
Oysters, fresh or frozen				
in shell	1 doz	2		

Food Item and Form	Market Unit	Approximate Serving per Market Unit*	Approximate Weight per Cup	
Oysters, fresh or frozen (continued)				
shucked	1 lb	2	235 g	8.3 oz
breaded, frozen	1 lb	4-2/3		
Oysters, canned, whole	5 oz	1-2/3	156 g	5.5 oz
Scallops, fresh or frozen				
shucked	1 lb	3-1/3		
breaded, frozen	1 lb	4		
Shrimp, fresh or frozen				
in shell	1 lb	2-2/3		
raw, peeled	1 lb	3-1/3		
cooked, peeled, cleaned	1 lb	5-1/3		
breaded, frozen	1 lb	4-1/2		
Shrimp, canned	13-1/4 oz	4-1/3	129 g	4.6 oz

*One serving equals three ounces of cooked boneless fish or shellfish.

BUYING GUIDE FOR LEAVENING AGENTS

Food Item and Form	Market Unit	Approximate Volume per Market Unit	Approximate Weight in Grams per Teaspoon	Approximate Weight in Grams per Tablespoon
Baking powder				
Phosphate	12 oz	1-2/3 c	4.1 g	12.7 g
SAS-Phosphate	14 oz	2-1/2 c	3.2 g	10.2 g
Tartrate	6 oz	1-1/4 c	2.9 g	9.2 g
Baking soda	1 lb	2-1/3 c	4.0 g	12.2 g
Cream of tartar	1-3/4 oz	5-1/4 Tbsp	3.1 g	9.4 g
Yeast				
Active dry	0.28 oz	1 Tbsp	2.5 g	7.5 g
Compressed	0.60 oz	4 tsp	4.2 g	12.8 g

BUYING GUIDE FOR EGGS

Food Item and Form	Market Unit	Approximate Volume or Number per Market Unit	Approximate Weight per Cup	
Eggs, whole				
fresh	1 doz	12 eggs	248 g	8.8 oz
extra large	1 doz	3 c		
large	1 doz	2-1/3 c		
medium (44 g)	1 doz	2 c		
small	1 doz	1-3/4 c		
frozen	1 lb	1-7/8 c	248 g	8.8 oz
dried, sifted	1 lb	5-1/4 c	86 g	3.0 oz
Whites				
fresh	1 doz	12 whites	246 g	8.7 oz
extra large	1 doz	1-3/4 c		
large	1 doz	1-1/2 c		
medium (29 g)	1 doz	1-1/3 c		
small	1 doz	1-1/4 c		
frozen	1 lb	1-7/8 c	246 g	8.7 oz
dried, sifted	1 lb	5 c	89 g	3.1 oz
Yolks				
fresh	1 doz	12 yolks	233 g	8.2 oz
extra large	1 doz	1 c		
large	1 doz	7/8 c		
medium (15 g)	1 doz	3/4 c		
small	1 doz	2/3 c		
frozen	1 lb	2-1/4 c	233 g	8.2 oz
dried, sifted	1 lb	5-1/2 c	80 g	2.8 oz

BUYING GUIDE FOR FRUITS

Food Item and Form	Market Unit	Approximate Volume or Pieces per Market Unit	Approximate Weight per Cup*	
Apples				
fresh, whole	1 lb	3 medium		
pared and sliced		2-3/4 c	122 g	4.3 oz
sauce, sweetened (not canned)		1-3/4 c	252 g	8.9 oz
frozen, sliced, sweetened	20 oz	2-1/2 c	205 g	7.2 oz
canned, sliced	20 oz	2-1/2 c	204 g	7.5 oz
juice	46 fl oz	5-3/4 c	249 g	8.8 oz
sauce	1 lb	1-3/4 c	259 g	9.1 oz
dried	1 lb	4-1/3 c	104 g	3.7 oz
cooked		8 c	244 g	8.6 oz
Apricots				
fresh, whole	1 lb	8 to 12	115 g	4.1 oz
sliced or halved		2-1/2 c	156 g	5.5 oz
canned, whole (medium)	1 lb	8 to 12	225 g	7.9 oz
halved (medium)	1 lb	12 to 20 halves	217 g	7.7 oz
dried	11 oz	2-1/4 c	150 g	5.3 oz
cooked, fruit and liquid		4-1/3 c	285 g	10.0 oz
Avocado				
fresh	1 lb			
sliced, diced, wedges		2-1/2 c	142 g	5.0 oz
Bananas				
fresh, whole	1 lb	3 to 4		
sliced		2 c	142 g	5.0 oz
mashed		1-1/3 c	232 g	8.2 oz
dried	1 lb	4-1/2 c	100 g	3.5 oz
Blueberries				
fresh	1 lb	2 c	146 g	5.2 oz
frozen	10 oz	1-1/2 c	161 g	5.7 oz
canned	14 oz	1-1/2 c	170 g	6.0 oz
Cherries				
fresh, red, pitted	1 lb	2-1/3 c	154 g	5.4 oz
frozen, red, tart, pitted	20 oz	2 c	242 g	8.5 oz
canned, red, tart, pitted	1 lb	1-1/2 c	177 g	6.2 oz
sweet, unpitted	1 lb	1-3/4 c	177 g	6.2 oz
Cranberries				
fresh, uncooked	1 lb	4 c	151 g	5.3 oz
sauce		4 c	215 g	7.6 oz
canned, sauce	1 lb	1-2/3 c	278 g	9.8 oz
juice	1 qt	4 c	250 g	8.8 oz

(continued on next page)

BUYING GUIDE FOR FRUITS (Continued)

Food Item and Form	Market Unit	Approximate Volume or Pieces per Market Unit	Approximate Weight per Cup*	
Currants				
dried	1 lb	3-1/4 c	140 g	4.9 oz
Dates				
dried, whole	1 lb	60 dates		
pitted, cut	1 lb	2-1/2 c	178 g	6.3 oz
Figs				
fresh	1 lb	12 medium		
canned	1 lb	12 to 16 figs	230 g	8.1 oz
dried, whole	1 lb	44 figs		
cut fine		2-2/3 c	168 g	5.9 oz
Fruit juice				
frozen	6 fl oz	3/4 c		
canned	46 fl oz	5-3/4 c	247 g	8.7 oz
Fruits				
mixed, frozen	12 oz	1-1/3 c		
canned, cocktail or salad	17 oz	2 c	229 g	8.1 oz
Grapefruit				
fresh	1 lb	1 medium		
sections		1 c	194 g	6.8 oz
frozen, sections	13-1/2 oz	1-1/2 c	219 g	7.7 oz
canned, sections	16 oz	2 c	241 g	8.5 oz
Grapes, fresh				
seeded	1 lb	2 c	184 g	6.5 oz
seedless	1 lb	2-1/2 c	169 g	6.0 oz
Lemons				
fresh	3 lb	1 doz		
juice		2 c	247 g	8.7 oz
frozen, juice	6 fl oz	3/4 c	283 g	10.0 oz
canned, juice	8 fl oz	1 c	245 g	8.6 oz
Melon				
frozen, balls	12 oz	1-1/2 c	231 g	8.2 oz
Oranges				
fresh	6 lb	1 doz		
diced or sectioned		12 c	214 g	7.5 oz
juice		4 c	247 g	8.7 oz
frozen, juice, reconstituted	6 fl oz	3 c	268 g	9.5 oz
canned, juice	46 fl oz	5-3/4 c	247 g	8.7 oz
canned, mandarin, fruit and juice	11 oz	1-1/4 c	250 g	8.8 oz

Food Item and Form	Market Unit	Approximate Volume or Pieces per Market Unit	Approximate Weight per Cup*	
Peaches				
fresh	1 lb	4 medium		
sliced		2 c	177 g	6.2 oz
frozen, slices and juice	10 oz	1-1/8 c	251 g	8.8 oz
canned, halves	1 lb	6 to 10 halves	224 g	7.9 oz
slices	1 lb	2 c	218 g	7.7 oz
dried	1 lb	3 c	160 g	5.6 oz
cooked		6 c	244 g	8.6 oz
Pears				
fresh	1 lb	4 medium		
sliced		2-1/8 c	213 g	7.5 oz
canned, halves	1 lb	6 to 10 halves	227 g	8.0 oz
Pineapple				
fresh	2 lb	1 medium		
cubed		3 c	146 g	5.2 oz
frozen, chunks	13-1/2 oz	1-1/2 c	204 g	7.2 oz
canned, chunks, tidbits	29 oz	3-3/4 c	198 g	7.0 oz
crushed	29 oz	3-3/4 c	260 g	9.2 oz
sliced	20 oz	10 slices	208 g	7.3 oz
juice	46 fl oz	5-3/4 c		
Plums				
fresh	1 lb	8 to 20 plums		
halved		2 c	185 g	6.5 oz
canned, whole	1 lb	10 to 14 plums	223 g	7.9 oz
Prunes				
canned	1 lb	10 to 14 prunes	196 g	6.9 oz
dried, whole	1 lb	2-1/2 c	176 g	6.2 oz
cooked		4 to 4-1/2 c	229 g	8.1 oz
pitted	1 lb	2-1/4 c	162 g	5.7 oz
cooked		4 to 4-1/2 c	210 g	7.4 oz
Raisins				
seeded, whole	1 lb	3-1/4 c	142 g	5.0 oz
chopped		2-1/2 c	182 g	6.4 oz
seedless, whole	1 lb	2-3/4 c	146 g	5.2 oz
cooked		2-3/4 c	183 g	6.5 oz
chopped		2 c	189 g	6.7 oz
Rhubarb				
fresh	1 lb	4 to 8 pieces		
cut			122 g	4.3 oz
cooked		2 c	242 g	8.5 oz

(continued on next page)

BUYING GUIDE FOR FRUITS (Continued)

Food Item and Form	Market Unit	Approximate Volume or Pieces per Market Unit	Approximate Weight per Cup*	
Rhubarb (continued)				
frozen, sliced	12 oz	1-1/2 c	168 g	5.9 oz
Strawberries				
fresh, whole	1-1/2 lb	4 c	144 g	5.1 oz
sliced		4 c	148 g	5.2 oz
frozen, whole	1 lb	1-1/3 c	204 g	7.2 oz
sliced or halved	10 oz	1 c	235 g	8.3 oz

*Weight per cup is that of food alone without liquid, unless otherwise noted.

COMMONLY AVAILABLE PACKAGING FOR FRUITS OR JUICES

Item	Frozen	Canned		Dried
Fruit	10 oz pkg	8-1/2 to 8-3/4 oz	1 c	8 oz
	13-1/2 oz can	16 to 17 oz.	1-3/4 to 2 c	11 oz
	16 oz pkg	20 oz	2-1/4 to 2-1/2 c	16 oz
	20 oz pkg or can	29 oz	3-1/4 to 3-1/2 c	32 oz (prunes)
		6 lb 2 oz to 6 lb 12 oz . .	12 to 13 c	
Juice	6 fl oz (concentrate)	6 to 8 fl oz	3/4 to 1 c	
	12 fl oz (concentrate)	12 fl oz	1-1/2 c	
		16 fl oz	2 c (1 pt)	
		18 fl oz	2-1/4 to 2-1/2 c	
		32 fl oz	4 c (1 qt)	
		46 fl oz	5-3/4 c	
		3 qt.	12 c	

BUYING GUIDE FOR VEGETABLES

Food Item and Form	Market Unit	Approximate Volume or Pieces per Market Unit	Approximate Weight per Cup*	
Asparagus, spears				
fresh	1 lb	16 to 20		
cooked		2 c	181 g	6.4 oz
canned	14-1/2 to 16 oz	12 to 18	195 g	6.9 oz
Frozen spears, cuts, and tips	10 oz	2 c	181 g	6.4 oz
Beans, green				
fresh	1 lb	3 c	114 g	4.0 oz
cooked		2-1/2 c	125 g	4.4 oz
frozen	9 oz	1-1/2 c	161 g	5.7 oz
canned	15-1/2 oz	1-3/4 c	135 g	4.8 oz
Beans, kidney, canned	16 to 17 oz	2 c	187 g	6.6 oz
dried	1 lb	2-1/2 c	184 g	6.5 oz
cooked		5-1/2 c	185 g	6.5 oz
Beans, Lima, shelled				
fresh	1 lb	2 c	155 g	5.5 oz
cooked		1-2/3 to 2 c	166 g	5.9 oz
frozen	10 oz	1-3/4 c	173 g	6.1 oz
canned	16 oz	2 c	170 g	6.0 oz
dried	1 lb	2-1/2 c	180 g	6.3 oz
cooked		5-1/2 c	186 g	6.6 oz
Beans, navy, dried	1 lb	2-1/3 c	190 g	6.7 oz
cooked		5-1/2 c	191 g	6.7 oz
Beans, soybeans, dried	1 lb	2 c	210 g	7.4 oz
Beets, without tops				
fresh	1 lb	2 c	145 g	5.1 oz
cooked		2 c	180 g	6.3 oz
canned	16 to 17 oz	2 c	167 g	5.9 oz
Broccoli, fresh, cooked	1 lb	2 c	164 g	5.8 oz
Broccoli, spears, chopped, frozen	10 oz	1-1/2 c	188 g	6.6 oz
Brussels sprouts				
fresh	1 lb	4 c	102 g	3.6 oz
cooked		2-1/2 c	180 g	6.4 oz
frozen	10 oz	18 to 24 sprouts		
Cabbage				
fresh	1 lb			
shredded		3-1/2 to 4-1/2 c	80 g	2.8 oz
cooked		2 c	146 g	5.2 oz

(continued on next page)

BUYING GUIDE FOR VEGETABLES (Continued)

Food Item and Form	Market Unit	Approximate Volume or Pieces per Market Unit	Approximate Weight per Cup*	
Carrots, without tops				
fresh	1 lb	3 c	130 g	4.6 oz
shredded		2-1/2 c	112 g	4.0 oz
diced			137 g	4.8 oz
cooked		2 to 2-1/2 c	160 g	5.6 oz
frozen	1 lb			
cooked		2-1/2 c	165 g	5.8 oz
canned	16 oz	2 c	159 g	5.6 oz
Cauliflower, fresh	1 lb	1-1/2 c	104 g	3.7 oz
cooked		1-1/2 c	125 g	4.4 oz
frozen	10 oz	2 c	152 g	5.4 oz
cooked		1-1/2 c	179 g	6.3 oz
Celery, fresh	1 lb	2 bunches	121 g	4.3 oz
cooked		2 to 2-1/2 c	153 g	5.4 oz
Corn, fresh ears	1 doz			
cooked		5-6 c	165 g	5.8 oz
frozen, cut	10 oz	1-3/4 c	135 g	4.8 oz
cooked		1-1/2 to 2 c	182 g	6.4 oz
canned, cream style	16 to 17 oz	2 c	249 g	8.8 oz
whole kernel	12 oz	1-1/2 c	169 g	6.0 oz
Eggplant, fresh	1 lb			
diced		2-1/2 c	99 g	3.5 oz
cooked		2-1/2 c	213 g	7.5 oz
Greens, fresh	1 lb		77 g	2.7 oz
cooked		3 c	190 g	6.7 oz
frozen	10 oz	1-1/2 to 2 c	187 g	6.6 oz
Lentils, dried	1 lb	2-1/4 c	191 g	6.7 oz
cooked		5 c	202 g	7.1 oz
Lettuce, head	1 lb (about)	6-1/4 c		
leaf	1 lb	6-1/4 c		
Romaine	1 lb	6 c		
endive	1 lb (about)	4-1/4 c		
Mixed vegetables, frozen	10 oz	2 c	182 g	6.4 oz
canned	16 to 17 oz	2 c	179 g	6.3 oz
Mushrooms, fresh, sliced	1 lb	2 to 3 c	68 g	2.4 oz
canned	4 oz	2/3 c	161 g	5.7 oz

Food Item and Form	Market Unit	Approximate Volume or Pieces per Market Unit	Approximate Weight per Cup*	
Okra, fresh, cooked	1 lb	2-1/4 c	177 g	6.2 oz
frozen	10 oz	1-1/4 c	209 g	7.4 oz
canned	15-1/2 oz	1-3/4 c	171 g	6.0 oz
Onions, fresh	1 lb	3 large		
chopped		2 to 2-1/2 c	135 g	4.8 oz
cooked			197 g	6.9 oz
frozen, chopped	12 oz	3 c		
canned	16 to 17 oz	2 c		
dried			64 g	2.3 oz
Parsnips, fresh	1 lb	4 medium		
cooked		2 c	211 g	7.4 oz
Peas, green, fresh, in pod	1 lb			
shelled		1 c	138 g	4.9 oz
cooked		1 c	163 g	5.7 oz
frozen	10 oz	2 c	156 g	5.5 oz
cooked		2 c	167 g	5.9 oz
canned	1 lb	2 c	168 g	5.9 oz
dried, split	1 lb	2-1/4 c	200 g	7.1 oz
cooked		5 c	194 g	6.8 oz
Peas, black-eyed, fresh	1 lb		144 g	5.1 oz
cooked		2-1/3 c	162 g	5.7 oz
frozen, cooked	10 oz	1-1/2 c	171 g	6.0 oz
canned	16 to 17 oz	2 c	205 g	7.2 oz
dried, split	1 lb		200 g	7.1 oz
cooked			248 g	8.7 oz
Potatoes, white, fresh	1 lb	3 medium	164 g	5.8 oz
cooked, diced, or sliced		2-1/4 c	163 g	5.7 oz
mashed		1-3/4 c	207 g	7.3 oz
frozen, French fried or puffs	9 oz	3 to 4		
canned, whole	16 to 17 oz	8 to 12	179 g	6.3 oz
dried flakes	6 to 7 oz	4-1/2 c	36 g	1.3 oz
reconstituted		10-3/4 c	212 g	7.5 oz
dried granules	1 lb	2-1/4 c	201 g	7.1 oz
reconstituted		10-1/2 c	212 g	7.5 oz
Pumpkin, fresh, cooked, mashed	1 lb	1 c	247 g	8.7 oz
canned	16 to 17 oz	2 c	244 g	8.6 oz
Radishes, sliced	6 oz	1-1/4 c		

(continued on next page)

BUYING GUIDE FOR VEGETABLES (Continued)

Food Item and Form	Market Unit	Approximate Volume or Pieces per Market Unit	Approximate Weight per Cup*	
Rutabaga, fresh, cubed	1 lb	2-1/2 c	139 g	4.9 oz
cooked		2 c	163 g	5.7 oz
Sauerkraut, canned	15 to 16 oz	3 c	188 g	6.6 oz
Spinach, fresh	1 lb	3 c	54 g	1.9 oz
cooked		1 c	200 g	7.1 oz
frozen	10 oz	1-1/2 c	190 g	6.7 oz
canned	15 oz	2 c	221 g	7.8 oz
Squash, winter, fresh	1 lb			
cooked, mashed		1 c	244 g	8.6 oz
frozen	12 oz	1-1/2 c	242 g	8.5 oz
canned	15 to 16 oz	1-3/4 to 2 c		
Squash, summer, fresh	1 lb		136 g	4.8 oz
cooked, mashed		1-2/3 c	238 g	8.4 oz
frozen, sliced	10 oz	1-1/2 c	211 g	7.4 oz
canned	1 lb			
Sweet potatoes, fresh	1 lb	3 medium		
cooked, sliced			232 g	8.2 oz
frozen	12 oz	3 to 4	200 g	7.1 oz
canned	16 to 17 oz	1-3/4 to 2 c	220 g	7.8 oz
dried, flakes	1 lb		115 g	4.1 oz
reconstituted			255 g	9.0 oz
Tomatoes, fresh	1 lb	3 to 4 small	162 g	5.7 oz
cooked		1-1/2 c		
canned, whole	16 oz	2 c	238 g	8.4 oz
sauce	8 oz	1 c	258 g	9.1 oz
Turnips, fresh	1 lb	3 medium	134 g	4.7 oz
cooked		2 c	196 g	6.9 oz

*Weight per cup is that of food alone without liquid.

BUYING GUIDE FOR CEREALS AND FLOURS

Food Item and Form	Market Unit	Approximate Volume or Pieces per Market Unit	Approximate Weight per Cup	
Cereals				
bulgur	1 lb	2-3/4 c	162 g	5.7 oz
cooked		8 c	230 g	8.1 oz
cornmeal				
white	1 lb	3-1/2 c	129 g	4.6 oz
yellow	1 lb	3 c	152 g	5.4 oz
cooked		16-2/3 c	238 g	8.4 oz
farina	1 lb	3 c		
cooked		16-2/3 c	238 g	8.4 oz
hominy, whole	1 lb	2-1/2 c	182 g	6.4 oz
cooked		16-2/3 c		
grits	1 lb	3 c	154 g	5.4 oz
cooked		10 c	236 g	8.3 oz
oats, rolled	1 lb	6-1/4 c	72 g	2.5 oz
cooked		8 c	240 g	8.5 oz
ready-to-eat				
flaked			32 g	1.1 oz
granulated			87 g	3.1 oz
puffed			23 g	0.8 oz
shredded			37 g	1.3 oz
rice, white, polished				
long grain	1 lb	2-1/2 c	182 g	6.4 oz
medium grain	1 lb	2-1/3 c	193 g	6.8 oz
short grain	1 lb	2-1/4 c	200 g	7.1 oz
cooked		8 c	169 g	6.0 oz
precooked	8 oz		185 g	6.5 oz
prepared		2 c	164 g	5.8 oz
brown	1 lb		185 g	6.5 oz
parboiled	14 oz	2 c	198 g	7.0 oz
soy grits, stirred, low-fat	1 lb	3 c	149 g	5.3 oz
wheat germ	12 oz	3 c	113 g	4.0 oz
whole	2 lb	4-1/2 c	198 g	7.0 oz
Flours				
corn	2 lb	8 c	116 g	4.1 oz
gluten	2 lb	6-1/2 c		
sifted			142 g	5.0 oz
rice	2 lb			
sifted		7 c	126 g	4.4 oz
stirred, spooned		5-3/4 c	158 g	5.6 oz

(continued on next page)

BUYING GUIDE FOR CEREALS AND FLOURS (Continued)

Food Item and Form	Market Unit	Approximate Volume or Pieces per Market Unit	Approximate Weight per Cup	
Flours (continued)				
rye	2 lb			
light, sifted		10 c	88 g	3.1 oz
dark, sifted		7 c	127 g	4.5 oz
soy	2 lb			
full-fat, sifted		15 c	60 g	2.1 oz
low-fat		11 c	83 g	2.9 oz
wheat				
all-purpose, sifted	2 lb	8 c	115 g	4.1 oz
unsifted, spooned		7 c	125 g	4.4 oz
instant		7-1/4 c	129 g	4.6 oz
bread, sifted	2 lb	8 c	112 g	4.0 oz
cake, sifted	2 lb	9-1/4 c	96 g	3.4 oz
spooned		8-1/4 c	111 g	3.9 oz
pastry, sifted	2 lb	9 c	100 g	3.5 oz
self-rising, sifted	2 lb	8 c	106 g	3.7 oz
whole-wheat, stirred	2 lb	6-2/3 c	132 g	4.7 oz
Pasta				
macaroni, 1-inch pieces	1 lb	3-3/4 c	123 g	4.3 oz
cooked		9 c	140 g	4.9 oz
macaroni, shell	1 lb	4 to 5 c	115 g	4.1 oz
cooked		9 c		
noodles, 1-inch pieces	1 lb	6 to 8 c	73 g	2.6 oz
cooked		8 c		
spaghetti, 2-inch pieces	1 lb	4 to 5 c	94 g	3.3 oz
cooked		9 c	160 g	5.6 oz
Starch				
corn, stirred	1 lb	3-1/2 c	128 g	4.5 oz
potato, stirred	1 lb	3-1/4 c	142 g	5.0 oz

BUYING GUIDE FOR SWEETENING AGENTS

Food Item and Form	Market Unit	Approximate Volume per Market Unit	Approximate Weight per Cup	
Sugar				
brown (packed)				
light	1 lb	2-1/4 c	200 g	7.1 oz
dark	1 lb	2-1/4 c	200 g	7.1 oz
granulated	1 lb	3 c	152 g	5.4 oz
cane or beet, granulated	5 lb	11-1/4 c	200 g	7.1 oz
superfine	2 lb	4-2/3 c	196 g	6.9 oz
confectioner's, unsifted	1 lb	3 to 4 c	123 g	4.3 oz
confectioner's, sifted		4-1/2 c	95 g	3.4 oz
Corn syrup, light and dark	16 fl oz	2 c	328 g	11.6 oz
Honey	1 lb	1-1/3 c	332 g	11.7 oz
Maple syrup	12 fl oz	1-1/2 c	312 g	11.0 oz
Molasses, cane	12 fl oz	1-1/2 c	309 g	10.9 oz
Sorghum	1 lb	1-1/3 c	330 g	11.6 oz

BUYING GUIDE FOR FATS AND OILS

Food Item and Form	Market Unit	Approximate Volume per Market Unit	Approximate Weight per Cup	
Butter (see Dairy Products)				
Oils: corn, cottonseed, olive, peanut, and safflower	1 qt	4 c	210 g	7.4 oz
Margarine	1 lb	2 c	224 g	7.9 oz
whipped	1 lb	3 c	149 g	5.3 oz
Hydrogenated fat	1 lb	2-1/3 c	188 g	6.6 oz
Lard and rendered fat	1 lb	2 c	220 g	7.8 oz
Suet, chopped medium fine	1 lb	3-3/4 c	120 g	4.2 oz

BUYING GUIDE FOR MISCELLANEOUS FOODS

Food Item and Form	Market Unit	Approximate Volume per Market Unit	Approximate Weight per Cup	
Bread, sliced	1 lb	12 to 16 slices		
crumbs, soft		10 c	46 g	1.6 oz
dry	10 oz	2-3/4 c	113 g	3.6 oz
Catsup, tomato	14 oz	1-1/2 c	273 g	9.6 oz
Chocolate, bitter or semisweet	8 oz	1 c	225 g	7.9 oz
prepared drink		30 c		
Cocoa	8 oz	2 c	112 g	4.0 oz
prepared drink		50 c		
instant	8 oz	1-2/3 c	139 g	4.9 oz
prepared drink		28 c		
Coconut, long thread	1 lb	5-2/3 c	80 g	2.8 oz
canned, moist	1 lb	5 c	85 g	3.0 oz
Coffee	1 lb	5 c	85 g	3.0 oz
brewed		40 to 50 c		
instant	2 oz	1-1/4 to 1-1/2 c	38 g	1.4 oz
brewed		60 c		
Crackers				
graham	1 lb	66		
crumbs		4-1/3 c	86 g	3.0 oz
soda	1 lb	82		
crumbs		7 c		
soda, crumbs, fine	10 oz	4 c	70 g	2.5 oz
saltines	1 lb	130 to 140		
Gelatin, unflavored, granulated	1 oz	1/4 c	150 g	5.3 oz
flavored	3 oz	7 Tbsp	179 g	6.3 oz
prepared		2 c	271 g	9.5 oz
Infant foods				
strained and junior (chopped)	3-1/4 to 3-1/2 oz	6 Tbsp		
	4-1/4 to 4-3/4 oz	9 Tbsp		
	7-1/2 to 8 oz	15 Tbsp		
juice	4 fl oz	1/2 c		
Mayonnaise	1 pt		243 g	8.6 oz
Nuts, shelled				
almonds, blanched	1 lb	3 c	152 g	5.4 oz
filberts, whole	1 lb	3-1/2 c	134 g	4.7 oz
peanuts	1 lb	3 c	144 g	5.1 oz
pecans, halved	1 lb	4 c	108 g	3.8 oz
chopped	1 lb	3-1/2 to 4 c	118 g	4.2 oz

Food Item and Form	Market Unit	Approximate Volume per Market Unit	Approximate Weight per Cup	
Nuts (continued)				
pistachio	1 lb	3-1/4 to 4 c	125 g	4.4 oz
walnuts, Persian, English				
halves	1 lb	3-1/2 c	100 g	3.5 oz
chopped	1 lb	3-1/2 c	119 g	4.2 oz
Pasta				
macaroni, 1-inch pieces	1 lb	4 to 5 c	123 g	4.3 oz
cooked		9 c	140 g	4.9 oz
macaroni, shell	1 lb	4 to 5 c	115 g	4.1 oz
cooked		9 c		
noodles, 1-inch pieces	1 lb	6 to 8 c	73 g	2.6 oz
cooked		8 c		
spaghetti, 2-inch pieces	1 lb	4 to 5 c	94 g	3.3 oz
cooked		9 c	160 g	5.6 oz
Peanut butter	18 oz	2 c	251 g	8.9 oz
Salad dressing, French	1 pt		248 g	8.8 oz
Salt, free-running	1 lb	1-1/2 c	288 g	10.2 oz
Soups, frozen condensed	10 to 10-1/2 oz	1 to 1-1/2 c		
ready-to-serve	15 oz	1-1/2 to 2 c		
canned, condensed	10-1/2 to 11-1/2 oz	1-1/4 c		
prepared		2-1/2 c		
ready-to-serve	8 oz	1 c	227 g	8.0 oz
dried	2-3/4 oz			
reconstituted		3 c	231 g	8.2 oz
Spices, ground	1-1/4 to 4 oz	4 Tbsp		
Tapioca, quick-cooking	8 oz	1-1/2 c	152 g	5.4 oz
Tea, leaves	1 lb	6-1/3 c	72 g	2.5 oz
brewed		300 c		
instant	1-1/2 oz	1-1/4 c	34 g	1.2 oz
brewed		64 c		
Water			237 g	8.4 oz

13

FOOD PRESERVATION

Drying

The U.S. Department of Agriculture and state Extension Services offer bulletins with instructions for drying foods and for constructing dehydrators, and there are also a few accurate, very complete commercial books on how to dry foods.[1] Following are facts to be considered before drying is begun:

• Stored in any jar with a tight-fitting lid, dried foods take little space, have a long shelf life, and require little special equipment for preparation or use.

• Dried foods are drastically reduced in volume, often one-quarter of the original volume. As a result they often are consumed in over-large amounts because they seem small and light-weight, with no attention given to their high caloric content.

• Drying temperatures must be high enough to prevent food poisoning, but not so high as to cause deterioration of the product. Generally, temperatures between 120°F (50°C) and 140°F (60°C) are used.

• Most fruits, some vegetables, meats, poultry, fish, herbs, nuts, and seeds dry well, but they must be of high quality and fresh to produce the maximum quality product.

• Most fruits and vegetables require pretreatment in order to retain color, stop enzyme action, or speed drying.

• Testing for dryness should be done when the food is at room temperature, as hot food will respond differently.

• Drying racks may be homemade or commercial, but they should not include such harmful metals as galvanized or cadmium-coated products, copper, or aluminum.

• Conditioning the food in a large glass jar for one week after drying will ensure evenness of drying and thoroughness and accuracy in drying.

• Dried foods should be stored in a cool, dry, dark place for maximum shelf life. Plastic bags do not protect from insect damage.

• If they are to be reconstituted, dried foods will be more tender if "plumped" in water before cooking.

• Since a dehydrator is a sizable investment, families should experiment with drying foods and using dried foods before purchasing one.

• Although some dehydrator demonstrators claim there is no nutrient loss when using this equipment, exposure to air and light and heat, peeling, liquid evaporation, and cutting the food mean some nutrients are lost.

• Microwave ovens are not recommended for

---

[1] Among these are *How to Dry Food for the Home,* Bulletin C166, Cooperative Extension, by S. O. Kennedy (Reno: University of Nevada, 1975); *Drying Foods at Home,* Leaflet 2785, Cooperative Extension, by M. W. Miller (Berkeley: University of California, 1975); *Modern Food Preservation,* by M. McWilliams and H. Paine (Redondo Beach, Calif: Plycon Press, 1977); and *Food Dehydration, Volume 2,* by W. B. Van Arsdel et al. (Westport, Conn.: Avi Publishing Co., 1973).

drying except for herbs and flowers. The food tends to burn or dry excessively in one spot while being moist in others.

Food for Drying

Most fruits dry well. Those which *do not* include: avocados and olives because of high fat content; berries (other than strawberries), guavas, and pomegranates because of high seed content; citrus fruits because of juice content and soft pulp; crabapples, quince, and muskmelon because of objectionable flavors when raw or dried. Berries may be combined with other fruits to make fruit leather, or sieved before pouring onto trays for fruit leather.

Select firm, ripe fruits. Bruised fruits can often be used in fruit leather but are not suitable for halves or slices.

Many vegetables are difficult to dry, store, or rehydrate satisfactorily. Some which dry well are inexpensive all year and therefore probably not good choices unless they are home grown or the dry form is convenient. Carrots, corn, mushrooms, onions, parsnips, peas, peppers, and potatoes dry well.

Select absolutely fresh, mature vegetables of high quality. They should be washed well just before drying.

Meat, poultry, or fish should be lean because fat turns rancid during storage. Meat must also be very fresh. Meats are dried as jerky, cooked meats, smoked meats, or meat leathers.

Herbs are collected for drying according to the part being dried. Leaves should be collected just before the plant flowers; flowers should be collected just after the blossoms have opened; seeds should be collected when mature and no longer green.

Select freshly picked herbs, gathered just after the dew is off. Herbs dry well in the microwave oven or at room temperatures if household dust is not a problem.

Nuts and seeds are naturals for drying. They are usually used in dried form for making desserts or salads or eaten as snacks.

Canning

Canning is an economical and practical method of preserving food at home. Among other things, it is a way to save food that might otherwise be wasted.

Organisms that cause food spoilage—molds, yeast, and bacteria—are always present in the air, water, and soil. Enzymes that may cause undesirable changes in flavor, color, and texture are present in raw foods. When food is canned, it must be processed at a high enough temperature and for a period that is long enough to destroy spoilage organisms. This heating process also stops the action of enzymes.

Pressure Canning

This processing method, utilizing a home pressure canner (not a saucepan or steamer), is used for low-acid foods. Every vegetable—except tomatoes and pickled vegetables—all meat, poultry, and seafood are processed at 10 pounds of pressure at sea level. Clostridium botulinum spores can survive boiling-water bath temperatures, but are killed by the high temperature reached in a pressure canner. The pressure canner dial gauge should be tested for accuracy each canning season.

Pressure canning of **vegetables** takes two forms:

Raw Pack. Pack cold, raw vegetables (except corn, lima beans, and peas) tightly into container and cover with boiling water.

Hot Pack. Preheat vegetables in water or steam. Cover with cooking liquid or boiling water.

Follow the manufacturer's directions for the canner you are using. Here are a few pointers on the use of pressure canner:

• Put two or three inches of boiling water in the bottom of the canner.

• Set filled jars on rack in pressure canner so that steam can flow around each container.

• Fasten pressure canner cover securely so that no steam can escape except through vent (petcock or weighted-gauge opening).

• Watch until steam pours steadily from vent. Let it escape for 10 minutes or more to drive all air from the canner. Close petcock.

• Let pressure rise to 10 pounds (240°F *or* 115°C). The moment this pressure is reached, start counting processing time. Keep pressure constant by regulating heat under the canner. Do

TIMETABLE FOR HOME CANNING VEGETABLES IN PRESSURE CANNER

Vegetable	Preheating*	Process in Pressure Canner at 10 Pounds Steam Pressure (240° F or 115.6° C)†			
		In glass jars		In tin cans	
		Pints	Quarts	No. 2 cans	No. 2½ cans
Preheated pack (hot pack)					
Asparagus, 1-inch pieces	Boil 3 minutes	25 min	30 min	20 min	20 min
Beans, fresh, Lima	Bring to boil	40 min	50 min	40 min	40 min
Beans, green, 1-inch pieces	Boil 5 minutes	20 min	25 min	25 min	30 min
Beets, small, whole; larger beets cut on 1/2-inch slices after preheating	Boil until skins slip easily	30 min	35 min	30 min	30 min
Carrots, sliced or diced	Bring to boil	25 min	30 min	20 min	25 min
Corn, cream style	Heat to boiling	1 hr, 25 min		1-3/4 hr	
Corn, whole kernel	Heat to boiling	55 min	1 hr, 25 min	1 hr	1 hr
Hominy	Cook until kernels are soft	1 hr	1 hr, 10 min	1 hr	1 hr, 10 min
Mushrooms, small, whole; large, halved, or quartered	Steam 4 minutes or heat 15 minutes in covered pan	30 min		30 min	
Okra, 1-inch lengths or whole	Cook 1 minute	25 min	40 min	25 min	35 min
Peas, black-eyed	Bring to boil	35 min	40 min	30 min	35 min
Peas, green	Bring to boil	40 min	40 min	30 min	35 min
Potatoes, whole, 1 to 2-1/2 inches in diameter	Cook 10 minutes	30 min	40 min	35 min	40 min
Potatoes, 1/2-inch cubes	Cook 2 minutes	35 min	40 min	35 min	40 min
Pumpkin, 1-inch cubes	Bring to boil	55 min	1-1/2 hr	50 min	1-1/4 hr
Pumpkin, strained	Simmer until heated through	1 hr, 5 min	1-1/3 hr	1-1/4 hr	1-1/2 hr

	Preparation				
Spinach	Steam 10 minutes or until well wilted	1 hr, 10 min	1-1/2 hr	1 hr, 5 min	1-1/4 hr
Squash, summer, 1/2-inch slices . . .	Bring to boil	30 min	40 min	20 min	20 min
Squash, winter, 1-inch cubes	Bring to boil	55 min	1-1/2 hr	50 min	1-1/4 hr
Squash, winter, strained	Simmer until heated through	1 hr, 5 min	1-1/3 hr	1-1/4 hr	1-1/2 hr
Sweet potatoes, dry pack, pieces . . .	Boil or steam 20 to 30 minutes	1 hr, 5 min	1 hr, 35 min	1-1/3 hr	1 hr, 35 min
Sweet potatoes, wet pack, cut in pieces	Boil or steam until skins slip easily	55 min	1-1/2 hr	1 hr, 10 min	1-1/2 hr

Raw pack (cold pack)

Asparagus		25 min	30 min	20 min	20 min
Beans, fresh, Lima		40 min	50 min	40 min	40 min
Beans, green, 1-inch pieces		20 min	25 min	25 min	30 min
Carrots, sliced or diced		25 min	30 min	25 min	30 min
Corn, cream style		1 hr, 35 min		1-3/4 hr	
Corn, whole kernel		55 min	1 hr, 25 min	1 hr	1 hr
Peas, black-eyed		35 min	40 min	35 min	40 min
Peas, fresh, green		40 min	40 min	30 min	35 min
Squash, summer, 1/2-inch slices . . .		25 min	30 min	20 min	20 min

*Preheat as directed in boiling water, steam, or own liquid. For flavor, add 1/2 teaspoon salt per pint jar, 1 teaspoon per quart jar. Cover with hot cooking liquid or boiling water if necessary, adjust lids and process for the length of time specified for each vegetable.

†Add 1/2 pound to the gauge pressure for each additional 1,000 feet in altitude. (See chart "Steam Pressures at Various Altitudes and Temperatures," page 5.)

not lower pressure by opening petcock. Keep drafts from blowing on canner.

• When processing time is up, remove canner from heat immediately. Let canner stand at room temperature until pressure is zero. Never try to rush the cooling. When pressure registers zero, wait two minutes, then slowly open petcock. Unfasten cover and tilt the far side up so steam escapes away from you. Take jars from canner.

For processing time for vegetables, follow the chart on pages 134 and 135.

With meat, poultry, and seafood, freshness and high quality must be considered when purchasing, and processing should take place within 24 hours. When processing home-grown meat or poultry, processing should occur within 24-48 hours after slaughter. The hot pack method of pressure canning is recommended.

Put large, cut-to-measure pieces of boned, defatted meat in a large shallow pan. Add just enough water to keep meat from sticking. Cover and cook slowly on top of the range or in a 350°F (175°C) oven until the meat is medium done, turning it occasionally so it precooks evenly.

Pack hot meat loosely, leaving 1 inch of headspace. Add 1 teaspoon salt per quart. Add boiling meat juice (extended with boiling water if necessary), leaving 1 inch of headspace. Wipe jar rims carefully to remove any fat. Adjust lids.

Pressure-process at 10 pounds for 90 minutes.

Water Bath

This processing method is used for all acid foods: fruits, tomatoes, and pickled vegetables. The water bath canner must be at least 4 inches higher than the tops of the jars. It needs a cover and a wire rack. A pressure canner may be used for a water bath, with the petcock left wide open to prevent pressure buildup.

For fruits and tomatoes, the water bath takes two forms:

Raw Pack. Put cold, raw fruits into container and cover with boiling hot syrup, juice, or water. Press tomatoes down in the containers so they are covered with their own juice; add no liquid.

Hot Pack. Heat fruits in syrup, in water or steam, or in extracted juice before packing. Juicy fruits and tomatoes may be preheated without added liquid and packed in the juice that cooks out.

Sugar syrup concentrations used in canning fruits are as follows:

Type	Sugar	Water	Yield
Thin syrup	30% 2 c	4 c	5 c
Medium syrup	40% 3 c	4 c	5½ c
Heavy syrup	50% 4¾ c	4 c	6½ c

Put filled glass jars into canner containing water. For raw pack in glass jars have water in canner hot but not boiling; for all other packs have water boiling.

Add boiling water if needed to bring water an inch or two over tops of containers; do not pour boiling water directly on glass jars. Put cover on canner.

When water in canner comes to a rolling boil, start to count processing time. Boil gently and steadily for time recommended for the food being canned. Add boiling water during processing if needed to keep containers covered. Remove containers from the canner immediately when processing time is up.

For processing time, follow chart on page 138. See also yield for fruit chart on page 139.

For all pickle and relish products, processing in the water bath is recommended. DO NOT USE OPEN KETTLE CANNING. Use vinegar with 5 percent to 6 percent acidity. Canning and pickling salt should be used for all brines.

• For brined or fermented pickles: use a reliable recipe and a curing process of 2 to 4 weeks.

• For fresh pack pickles: cure them in brine for several hours or overnight.

• For relishes prepared from fruits and vegetables: chop, season, and then cook.

• For fruit pickles: prepare them from whole fruits and simmer in a spicy, sweet-sour syrup.

Jellies and Jams

Jelly, jam, conserve, marmalade, preserves are all fruit products that add zest to meals. Most of them also provide a good way to use fruit not at its best for canning or freezing: the largest or smallest fruits and berries and those that are irregularly shaped. Basically these products are much alike; all of them are fruit preserved by means of sugar and usually all are jellied to some extent.

YIELD OF HOME CANNED AND HOME FROZEN VEGETABLES FROM RAW MATERIALS

Food Item	Purchasing Unit* with Net Weight	Approximate Range of Yield (Canned)	Approximate Range of Yield (Frozen)
Asparagus.............	40 lb (Bushel*)	9 to 16 qt	7 to 11 qt
	24 lb (Crate)	5 to 10 qt	6 to 8 qt
Beans, Lima, in pod	32 lb (Bushel*)	6 to 10 qt	
Beans, snap	30 lb (Bushel*)	12 to 22 qt	15 to 22 qt
Beets, without tops	52 lb (Bushel*)	14 to 24 qt	17 to 22 qt
bunched	70 lb (Western crate)	19 to 32 qt	
Broccoli	25 lb (Crate)		12 qt
Brussels sprouts	(4-qt Boxes)		3 qt
	36 lb (Crate)		18 qt
Carrots, without tops	50 lb (Bushel*)	17 to 20 qt	16 to 20 qt
bunched	75 lb (Western Crate)	26 to 33 qt	
Cauliflower	20		7 to 12 qt
Corn, in husks	35 lb (Bushel*)	6 to 10 qt (kernels)	7 to 9 qt (kernels)
Greens	18 lb (Bushel*)	3 to 8 qt	6 to 9 qt
Okra	26 lb (Bushel*)	17 qt	
Peas, green, in pod	30 lb (Bushel*)	5 to 10 qt	6 to 8 qt
Squash, summer	40 lb (Bushel*)	10 to 20 qt	16 to 20 qt
winter	11 lb (Bushel*)		4 qt
Sweet potatoes	50 lb (Bushel*)	16 to 22 qt	
Tomatoes	53 lb (Bushel*)	14 to 22 qt	
	32 lb (Lug box)	8 to 13 qt	

* Legal weight of a bushel of vegetables varies in different states.

TIMETABLE FOR HOME CANNING FRUITS IN BOILING-WATER BATH

Fruit	Preheating*	Process in Boiling-Water Bath†			
		In glass jars		In tin cans	
		Pints	Quarts	No. 2	No. 2½
Preheated pack (hot pack)					
Apples, pieces	Boil 5 minutes	15 min	20 min	10 min	10 min
Applesauce	Heat through	10 min	10 min	10 min	10 min
Apricots, halved	Heat through	20 min	25 min	25 min	30 min
Berries, except strawberries (firm berries)	Heat to boiling	10 min	15 min	15 min	20 min
Cherries	Heat to boiling	10 min	15 min	15 min	20 min
Fruit juices	Heat to simmering	5 min	5 min	5 min	5 min
Fruit purees	Heat to simmering	10 min	10 min	10 min	10 min
Peaches, halved	Heat through	20 min	25 min	25 min	30 min
Pears, halved	Heat through	20 min	25 min	25 min	30 min
Plums, whole or halved	Heat to boiling	20 min	25 min	15 min	20 min
Rhubarb, 1/2-inch pieces	Heat to boiling	10 min	10 min	10 min	10 min
Strawberries	Heat to boiling	15 min	15 min	10 min	15 min
Tomatoes, quartered	Heat to boiling	10 min	10 min	10 min	10 min
Tomato juice	Heat to boiling	10 min	10 min	15 min	15 min
Raw pack (cold pack)					
Apricots, halved		25 min	30 min	30 min	35 min
Berries, except strawberries (soft berries)		10 min	15 min	15 min	20 min
Cherries		20 min	25 min	20 min	25 min
Peaches, halved		25 min	30 min	30 min	35 min
Pears, halved		25 min	30 min	30 min	35 min
Plums		20 min	25 min	15 min	20 min
Tomatoes, whole, halved, or quartered		35 min	45 min	45 min	55 min

*Preheat in sugar syrup, in fruit juice, or in water, except berries, rhubarb, and tomatoes which should be heated to boiling without added liquid. Allow about 2/3 to 3/4 cup syrup per pint jar or 1 to 1-1/2 cups syrup per quart jar.

†For altitude cooking, increase processing time 1 minute for each 1,000 feet above sea level, if the time is 20 minutes or less, and 2 minutes per 1,000 feet if processing is more than 20 minutes.

NOTE: Begin to count time when water in bath boils.

YIELD OF HOME CANNED AND HOME FROZEN FRUITS FROM RAW MATERIALS

Food Item	Purchasing Unit* (Net Weight)	Approximate Range of Yield (Canned)	Approximate Range of Yield (Frozen)
Apples	48 lb (Bushel)	16 to 25 qt	16 to 20 qt
	44 lb (Box)	14 to 23 qt	14 to 18 qt
Apricots	48 lb (Bushel)	12 to 24 qt	30 to 36 qt
	22 lb (Crate)	6 to 12 qt	14 to 17 qt
Berries (except strawberries)	36 lb (24-qt Crate)	11 to 24 qt	16 to 20 qt
Cherries, as picked	56 lb (Bushel)	22 to 32 qt (unpitted)	18 to 22 qt
Cranberries	25 qt (Box)		
Grapes	48 lb (Bushel)	12 to 20 qt	
	18 lb (12-qt Basket)	5 to 7 qt	
	28 lb (Lug box)	7 to 8 qt	
	20 lb (4-Basket Crate)	5 to 7 qt	
Peaches	48 lb (Bushel)	16 to 24 qt	16 to 24 qt
	20 lb (Lug box)	7 to 10 qt	6 to 10 qt
Pears	50 lb (Bushel)	17 to 25 qt	20 to 25 qt
	46 lb (Western box)	15 to 28 qt	18 to 23 qt
Pineapples	70 lb (Crate)	12 to 16 qt	28 to 35 qt
Plums	56 lb (Bushel)	22 to 36 qt	19 to 28 qt
	20 lb (Crate)	8 to 13 qt	6 to 10 qt
Rhubarb	10 lb	7 to 10 qt	5 to 8 qt
Strawberries	36 lb (24-qt Crate)	7 to 16 qt	19 to 30 qt

* Legal weight of a bushel of fruit varies in different states.

Jelly is made from fruit juice; the product is clear and firm enough to hold its shape when turned out of the container.

Jam is made from crushed or ground fruit. It tends to hold its shape but generally is less firm than jelly.

Conserves are jams made from mixture of fruits, usually including citrus fruits. Often raisins and nuts are added.

Marmalade is a tender jelly with small pieces of fruit distributed evenly throughout. A marmalade commonly contains citrus fruit.

Preserves are whole fruits or large pieces of fruit in a thick syrup, often slightly gelled.

Fruit butter is a smooth, less sweet preserve made from fruit pulp run through a sieve and cooked.

The four essential ingredients of jellies and jams are fruit or juice, pectin, acid, and sugar.

Fruit gives each product its characteristic flavor and furnishes at least a part of the pectin and acid required for successful gels. It also provides mineral salts, which add to the flavor. Flavorful varieties of fruits are best for jellied products because the fruit flavor is diluted by the large proportion of sugar necessary for proper consistency and good keeping quality.

Pectin is a binding agent and a carbohydrate possessing gelling power. Some kinds of fruit have enough natural pectin to make high-quality products. Others require added pectin, particularly when they are used for making jellies, which should be firm enough to hold their shape. All fruits have less pectin when they are fully ripe than when they are underripe.

Commercial fruit pectins, which are made from apples or citrus fruits, are on the market in both liquid and powdered form. Either form is satisfactory when used in a recipe developed especially for that form.

The advantages of using pectin are that fully ripe fruit can be used, cooking time is short, and the yield is greater. Fruit pectins should be stored in a cool, dry place to keep their gel strength. They should not be held over from one year to the next.

A **gel meter** is a good way to test the amount of pectin in juice intended for jelly. It is a graduated glass tube that measures the amount of pectin in fruit juices and indicates how much pectin to add to make the juice gel. The juice must be at room temperature.

Acid is needed for flavor and gel formation. The acid content varies in different fruits and is higher in underripe fruits. With fruits low in acid, lemon juice or citric acid is commonly added to make jellied products. Commercial fruit pectins contain some acid. To increase acid, add 1 tablespoon of lemon juice or vinegar to 1 cup of juice. (⅛ tablespoon of citric acid can be used instead of 1 tablespoon of lemon juice). The taste test for acidity is that it should be as sour as a tart apple.

The formula for sugar is ¾ : 1 using cane or beet sugar. It is best to add sugar at the beginning of the process. Sugar helps in gel formation, serves as a preserving agent, and contributes to the flavor. It also has a firming effect on fruit, a property that is useful in the making of preserves. Corn syrup or honey can replace part of the sugar.

Although not essential, a pinch of salt improves flavor.

Equipment needed to make jelly or jam includes:

- large kettle
- jelly bags or fruit press, used for extracting juice for jellies; jelly bags can be made from several thicknesses of closely woven cheesecloth, or firm unbleached muslin
- thermometer, which helps when making fruit products without pectin
- quart measure
- measuring cups and spoons
- paring knives
- bowl
- long-handled spoon
- ladle
- timer
- containers, jelly glasses or canning jars (to be filled to ⅛ of an inch from the top)
- lids
- paraffin, to be poured on finished product to a depth of ⅛ of an inch

There are two primary methods of jelly and jam preparation. One is the long boil, which gives a richer fruit flavor but results in a darker color. The second is the short boil, which results in a lighter color but requires the addition of liquid or powdered pectin.

To make small amounts of jelly (8 to 10 glasses) using the long-boil method, measure juice and sugar into a large kettle. Heat juice to boiling and add sugar. Stir only until dissolved. Boil rapidly to gelling point. Skim the foam as it accumulates using a spoon dipped in hot water.

Making jelly without pectin requires less sugar per cup of fruit juice, a longer boiling time, and the yield is less. Gelling tests for making jelly without pectin are:

Spoon or sheet test: Dip a cool metal spoon in boiling jelly, then carry it out of the steam and pour from the spoon. The liquid should pour in a sheet.

Freezer test: Pour a small amount of boiling jelly on a cold plate and place in freezer. When it is cooled, see if it gelled.

To make jelly with pectin using the short-boil method, mix powdered pectin with unheated fruit juice. If using liquid pectin, add it to the boiling juice and sugar mixture and boil for one minute at a full rolling boil.

Filling and sealing containers when jelly is done:

For jelly, fill to ⅛ inch from top and seal. Invert 1 minute. Use ⅛ inch of paraffin for short-term storage. Spin to seal, then fill hole in center. Do not process in hot-water bath.

For sweet spreads, let stand 5 minutes, stirring occasionally to keep fruit from floating. Then process in hot-water bath at 180°F (82°C) for 20 minutes for pint jars. When using boiling-water bath, process for 10 minutes at 212°F (100°C) for pint jars.

Freezing

Freezing preserves many foods with little change in flavor, color, texture, and nutrition value. One of the simplest methods of home food preservation, freezing does not sterilize the product; it simply retards the growth of harmful bacteria and molds. Therefore, good sanitation procedures are necessary for freezing. The wrapping or container for the food that is being frozen is also important. Boxes and bags especially made for freezing, as well as jars, are available. If a wrap is used, it should:

- be impermeable to oxygen
- be odorless
- possess high wet strength
- be greaseproof
- be nonadherent to the frozen product
- be puncture resistant
- be easy to mark
- not crack at low temperatures.

Types of freezer wrap vary in form and in storage ability. Waxed-one-side freezer paper will store food for up to two months. Various coated and laminated freezer papers and polyethylene films will store for up to four months. For storage over 90 days and up to one year, wraps impermeable to oxygen, such as aluminum foil, Saran-type film, polyester film, and films combining polyethylene and cellophane, should be used. To avoid freezer burn, foods should be tightly wrapped to remove any air, and headspace should be allowed for expansion.

Basic Steps in Freezing

- Use only quality fresh products
- Work under the most sanitary conditions
- Have everything that is needed organized to save time and energy
- Use appropriate packing materials
- Follow directions for the product you are freezing:

   Blanch or scald vegetables; cool quickly
   Use ascorbic acid for certain fruits to prevent discoloration
   Use dry sugar or syrup pack for fruits
   Keep meats cold while preparing for freezing

- Package, removing all air
- Label with date and name of product
- Promptly place in freezer in single layers
- Maintain 0°F (−18°C) in freezer
- Keep an inventory
- Use all products within recommended storage period.

How To Pack Fruits

Fruits should be slightly riper than for canning. Frozen fruit can be used in jelly- and jam-making later in the year. Fruits can be packed in syrup or dry sugar. Yields of frozen fruit from fresh fruits can be found on page 139.

• Syrup pack: Dissolve sugar in water (do not heat) until solution is clear. Use just enough syrup to cover the fruit in the container. Allow ½-inch headspace.

Type of Syrup	Sugar	Water	Amount of Syrup
30%	2 cups	4 cups	5 cups
40%	3 cups	4 cups	5½ cups
50%	4¾ cups	4 cups	6½ cups
60%	7 cups	4 cups	7¾ cups

• Sugar pack: Works well for soft fruits. Add sugar to clean, prepared fruits. Let stand 10 to 15 minutes. Stir to coat each piece. Pack fruit tightly in storage container.

• Dry pack: Pack fruit in containers without sugar or syrup. No headspace is necessary.

• Water pack: This can be used for apricots and peaches. Mix 1 teaspoon ascorbic acid with 1 quart water.

Ascorbic acid should be used with fruits that tend to darken quickly (peaches, apricots, figs, sweet cherries, pears, and apples) and manufacturers' directions followed as to method and amount.

Vegetables

Speed from garden to freezer is the important factor in vegetable freezing. Blanching is absolutely necessary to prevent loss of quality and to preserve nutrient content. If this is not done, frozen vegetables lose their quality in two months or less, off flavors develop, and color, nutrient content, and texture deteriorate. In the blanching process, cleaned, sorted, and cut vegetables are lowered into boiling water for a specific amount of time and then quickly cooled before packing to freeze. (See page 143 for blanching times and page 137 for yields of frozen vegetables from fresh produce.)

Meat

Freezing is the best method of meat storage. Starting with a wholesome, high quality product will ensure the best results. All meat should be wrapped in moisture-vapor-proof material that is impermeable to oxygen. (See chart on page 57 for the guide to length of storage time for meats.)

Thawing

The following chart gives approximate thawing times for some products. But the product should be watched for overthawing and loss of texture. Many items are cooked directly from the frozen state. If in doubt, refer to manufacturer's directions or a reliable manual.

Foods Not Suitable for Freezing

Some foods not suitable for freezing include raw cabbage, cake batters, raw celery, cream pie fillings, custards, egg whites (hard cooked), lettuce, mayonnaise, potato salad, salad dressing, and watermelon.

If Food Freezer Stops

If power fails or the food freezer stops operating normally, try to determine how long it will be before the freezer will be back in operation.

A fully loaded freezer usually will stay cold enough to keep foods frozen for two days if the cabinet is not opened. In a cabinet with less than half a load, food may not stay frozen more than one day. The food will be safe to refreeze if it still contains ice crystals or is refrigerator temperature of approximately 50°F (10°C). It will not be as good quality if refrozen, but it will be safe to eat.

If normal operation cannot be resumed before the food will start to thaw, use dry ice. If dry ice is placed in the freezer soon after the power is off, 25 pounds should keep the temperature below freezing for two or three days in a 10-cubic-foot cabinet with half a load, and three to four days in a loaded cabinet. Place the dry ice on cardboard or small boards on top of packages and do not open cabinet again except to put in more dry ice or to remove it when normal operation is resumed.

Another answer to the problem is to move the food to a locker plant, using insulated boxes or thick layers of paper to prevent thawing. The locker plant can refreeze the packaged food more quickly and thus refreeze food of better quality.

TIMETABLE FOR BLANCHING VEGETABLES PRIOR TO FREEZING

Vegetable*	Heated in Boiling Water	Vegetable*	Heated in Boiling Water
Asparagus, small stalks	2 min	Corn (cont.)	
Medium stalks	3 min	Large ears (over 1-1/2 inches in diameter)	11 min
Large stalks	4 min	Whole kernel and cream style	4 min†
Beans, Lima, small beans or pods	2 min	Greens, beet, chard, kale, mustard, spinach, turnip	2 min
Medium beans or pods	3 min	Collards	3 min
Large beans or pods	4 min	Kohlrabi, 1/2-inch cubes	1 min
Beans, green, or wax	3 min	Whole, small to medium in size	3 min
Beets, small	25 to 30 min	Okra, small pods	3 min
Medium	45 to 50 min	Large pods	4 min
Broccoli, flowerets 1-1/2 inches in diameter	3 min (in steam) 5 min	Parsnips, 1/2-inch cubes or slices	2 min
Brussels sprouts, small heads	3 min	Peas, black-eyed	2 min
Medium heads	4 min	Green	1-1/2 min
Large heads	5 min	Peppers, halves	3 min
Cabbage, coarse shreds or thin wedges	1-1/2 min	Slices	2 min
Carrots, whole carrots, small	5 min	Pumpkin	Until soft
Diced, sliced, strips	2 min	Rutabagas, 1/2-inch cubes	2 min
Cauliflower, 1-inch pieces	3 min	Squash, summer, 1/2-inch slices	3 min
Celery, 1-inch lengths	3 min	Winter	Until soft
Corn, sweet, on the cob		Sweet potatoes	Until almost tender
Small ears (1-1/4 inches or less in diameter)	7 min	Tomato juice (simmer tomatoes)	5 to 10 min
Medium ears (1-1/4 to 1-1/2 inches in diameter)	9 min	Turnips, 1/2-inch cubes	2 min

*For each pound of prepared vegetable use at least 1 gallon of boiling water. After heating the specified time, cool promptly in cold water and drain.

†Time given is for cooking the ears of corn before the kernels are cut off the cob.

APPROXIMATE THAWING TIME FOR FROZEN FOODS

Product	Hours at Room Temperature*	Hours in Household Refrigerator	Other Time Frame
Bread	3 - 4		20 - 25 mins. (325°F or 165°C oven)
Cake	1 - 2		20 - 25 mins. (250-300°F or 120-150°C oven)
Pie, baked			Allow baked fruit or vegetable pie to stand at room temperature for a short time. Then put it in 350°F (175°C) oven on lower shelf before it begins to thaw; heat until just warm, about 30 minutes.
Pie, unbaked			Thaw unbaked frozen pie on lower shelf of preheated 450°F (230°C) oven for 10-15 minutes; complete baking at 400°F (205°C).
Fruit, pint	3 - 4	5 - 6	1/2 - 3/4 hours (in cold running water)
Meat, per pound		5 - 8	
Chicken, less than 4 lb		12 - 16	
Ducks, 3 - 5 lbs		24 - 36	
Geese, 4 - 14 lbs		24 - 48	
Turkey, 4 - 11 lbs		24 - 36	
Turkey, 12 - 24 lbs		48 - 72	

*Food should not be thawed without special protection at room temperature for longer than 6 hours.

14

SOURCES OF INFORMATION

Additional information on food and food preparation may be obtained from the following:

AMERICAN ASSOCIATION OF CEREAL CHEMISTS
3340 Pilot Knob Road
St. Paul, MN 55121

AMERICAN CHEMICAL SOCIETY
1155 Sixteenth St., NW
Washington, DC 20036

AMERICAN DIETETIC ASSOCIATION
430 North Michigan Ave.
Chicago, IL 60611

AMERICAN DRY MILK INSTITUTE, INC.
150 North Franklin St.
Chicago, IL 60606

AMERICAN EGG BOARD
205 West Touhy Ave.
Park Ridge, IL 60068

AMERICAN HOME ECONOMICS ASSOCIATION
2010 Massachusetts Ave., NW
Washington, DC 20036

AMERICAN STANDARDS ASSOCIATION
10 East 40th St., New York, NY 10016
American Standard Dimensions, Tolerances, and Terminology for Home Cooking and Baking Utensils, Z61.1, 1963. $1.00 per copy

CEREAL INSTITUTE
135 South LaSalle St., Chicago, IL 60603

EVAPORATED MILK ASSOCIATION
Home Economics Educational Services
910 Seventeenth St., NW
Washington, DC 20006

FOOD AND NUTRITION INFORMATION AND
    EDUCATIONAL MATERIALS CENTER
Room 304, NAL Building
Beltsville, MD 20705

INSTITUTE OF FOOD TECHNOLOGISTS
221 N. LaSalle St., Suite 2120
Chicago, IL 60601

NATIONAL ASSOCIATION OF FROZEN FOOD
    PACKERS
919 Eighteenth St., NW
Washington, DC 20006

NATIONAL CANNERS ASSOCIATION
1133 Twentieth St., NW
Washington, DC 20036

NATIONAL DAIRY COUNCIL
111 North Canal St., Chicago, IL 60606

NATIONAL LIVE STOCK AND MEAT BOARD
36 South Wabash Ave., Chicago, IL 60603

POULTRY AND EGG NATIONAL BOARD
8 South Michigan Ave., Chicago, IL 60603

SOCIETY FOR NUTRITION EDUCATION
2140 Shattuck Ave., Suite 1110
Berkeley, CA 94704

WHEAT FLOUR INSTITUTE
14 East Jackson Blvd., Chicago, IL 60604

SUPERINTENDENT OF DOCUMENTS
U.S. Government Printing Office
Washington, DC 20402
Composition of Foods . . . Raw, Processed, Prepared, USDA Handbook No. 8, $1.50.

UNITED STATES DEPARTMENT OF AGRICULTURE
Washington, DC 20250

Office of Information

Beef and Veal in Family Meals, Home and Garden Bulletin No. 118

Cereals and Pasta in Family Meals, Home and Garden Bulletin No. 150

Cheese in Family Meals, Home and Garden Bulletin No. 112

Eggs in Family Meals, Home and Garden Bulletin No. 103

Freezing Meat and Fish in the Home, Home and Garden Bulletin No. 93

Fruits in Family Meals, Home and Garden Bulletin No. 125

Home Canning of Fruits and Vegetables, Home and Garden Bulletin No. 8

Home Canning of Meat and Poultry, Home and Garden Bulletin No. 106

Home Freezing of Fruits and Vegetables, Home and Garden Bulletin No. 10

Keeping Food Safe to Eat, Home and Garden Bulletin No. 162

How to Buy Beef Steaks, Home and Garden Bulletin No. 145

How to Buy Canned and Frozen Vegetables, Home and Garden Bulletin No. 167

How to Buy Cheddar Cheese, Home and Garden Bulletin No. 128

How to Buy Dry Beans, Peas, and Lentils, Home and Garden Bulletin No. 177

How to Buy Eggs, Home and Garden Bulletin No. 144

How to Buy Fresh Fruits, Home and Garden Bulletin No. 141

How to Buy Fresh Vegetables, Home and Garden Bulletin No. 143

How to Buy Instant Nonfat Dry Milk, Home and Garden Bulletin No. 140

How to Buy Meat for Your Freezer, Home and Garden Bulletin No. 166

How to Use USDA Grades in Buying Food, Dairy Products, Poultry, Fruits and Vegetables, Eggs, Meat, Home and Garden Bulletin No. 708

Lamb in Family Meals, Home and Garden Bulletin No. 124

Milk in Family Meals, Home and Garden Bulletin No. 127

Nutritive Value of Foods, Home and Garden Bulletin No. 72

Nuts in Family Meals, Home and Garden Bulletin No. 176

Pork in Family Meals, Home and Garden Bulletin No. 160

Poultry in Family Meals, Home and Garden Bulletin No. 110

Storing Perishable Foods in the Home, Home and Garden Bulletin No. 78

Vegetables in Family Meals, Home and Garden Bulletin No. 105

Agricultural Marketing Service

U.S. grade standards for foods are published in the *Federal Register* as they are developed or revised. Single copies of reprints are free from the following commodity divisions of the Agricultural Marketing Service: Dairy, Fruits and Vegetables, Grain, Live Stock, and Poultry.

Federal and State Standards for the Composition of Milk Products (and Certain Non-Milkfat Products) as of January 1, 1974, Agricultural Handbook No. 51

UNITED STATES DEPARTMENT OF HEALTH AND HUMAN SERVICES, Washington, DC 20204

Food and Drug Administration, Division of Public Information
Definitions and standards for foods, and amendments to the Federal Food, Drug, and Cosmetic Act are published in the *Federal Register* as they are revised. Single copies of reprints are free.

Public Health Service
Sanitary standards for milk as stated in the *Milk Ordinance and Code*.

UNITED STATES DEPARTMENT OF THE INTERIOR
Washington, DC 20240

Fish and Wildlife Service, Bureau of Commercial Fisheries

GUNDERSON, FRANK L. and others. *Food Standards and Definitions in the United States; A Guide*. New York: Academic Press, 1963, 269 pp., $10. This book lists standards of identity, grades, and definitions of foods. A convenient and reliable guide to existing standards.

INDEX